FASHION & STYLE

Fashion & Style

MIKE STARKEY

MONARCH
Crowborough

First British edition 1995

British Library Cataloguing in Publication Data
A catalogue record for this book is available
from the British Library.

ISBN: 1 85424 238 5

Produced by Bookprint Creative Services
P. O. Box 827, BN21 3YJ, England for
MONARCH PUBLICATIONS
Broadway House, The Broadway
Crowborough, East Sussex, TN6 1HQ.
Printed in England by Clays Ltd, St Ives plc

For Joel and Joy, who think dressing up is great: so does God.

CONTENTS

ACKNOWLEDGEMENTS

Most of Part One, *Fashioned in His Image*, was based on an MA dissertation I wrote at St John's College, Nottingham, with the impressively obscure title of, *When Clothing Becomes 'Style': A Study in Moral Boundaries as Cultural Paradigms.* That is what academia does to you. Thanks to Roy McCloughry who supervised the original dissertation and offered many helpful tips.

Special thanks go to three people who have been an inspiration to many of us thinking about Christian perspectives on modern culture: Lesslie Newbigin, Graham Cray and Elaine Storkey. It has been a privilege for me that all three have commended the book so warmly. Also thanks to the designer, Amanda King, who not only did the illustrations, but also offered comments on the text, and to the models Ashley Meaney, Liz Horne and Helen Starkey. Needless to say, none of them are responsible for any shortcomings in the book.

I have deliberately avoided footnotes and cross-references. This has been to keep the tone less academic and to help it flow better. However, one or two works deserve special mention. On the biblical side, Edgar Haulotte's 1966 work, *Symbolique du Vêtement Selon la Bible* (sadly, never translated into English) was crucial, as was Richard Mouw's analysis of Isaiah, *When the Kings Come Marching in.* For historical material, I owe a particular debt of gratitude to Aileen Ribeiro's *Dress and*

Morality, and Leland Ryken's exciting reassessment of the Puritans, *Worldly Saints*. From the mass of material I accumulated on fashion, the most consistently provocative and helpful was by Elizabeth Wilson. The World Development Movement was an invaluable resource on the global clothing industry. Some of the material in the book has already appeared as features in *Third Way* and *Woman Alive* magazines.

Just a brief word on the issue of inclusive language. In my examples I have deliberately avoided the awkward device of making all personal pronouns neuter ('they', rather than the gender-specific 'he' or 'she'). Instead, I have aimed at an even balance of male and female terms. Needless to say, if I use a female pronoun when referring to some hypothetical designer, this is not used exclusively – as if implying that all or most designers are female – any more than my use of male pronouns is similarly restrictive.

Lastly, thanks are due to Naomi, who not only allowed me to steal most of an article she wrote on modelling for my Chapter 7, checked the manuscript and made helpful suggestions, but also put up with an absentee husband – who was upstairs on the computer when he should have been downstairs doing the ironing.

FOREWORD

The Church is called to proclaim the Christian faith afresh in each generation. To fulfil this task Christians need to understand the culture of their day or they can neither answer its questions nor challenge its idolatries. Equally necessary is a biblically based understanding of the application of the gospel to each major sphere of life.

This book addresses an aspect of contemporary Western culture which is of increasing public significance and ongoing theological neglect – clothing and fashion. It challenges two delusions; one in culture and one in the Church.

Mike Starkey shows how many people in our culture believe that their personal identity is entirely a matter of their own creation. That they can only be who they make themselves to be, or rather what they display themselves to be. 'I am seen therefore I am', and I am what you see, no more and no less. He shows how the fashion industry colludes with this depthless vision and feeds off it. In a society where identity and truth are reduced to style, fashion reveals the nature of our contemporary dilemma and the shallowness of our convictions.

The world of fashion cries out for a full-blooded alternative vision rooted in the redemption which comes through Christ. But the Church has been unable to offer such an alternative because it has had such a negative view of the whole enterprise; considering it simultaneously too trivial for consideration and

11

too dangerous a temptation to vanity. The absence of genuinely Christian thinking about fashion in this culture literally means that many who create their sense of identity through what they wear cannot hear what we are saying because of the way we look!

Mike addresses the Church's delusion first, challenging from scripture some traditional unthinking assumptions and building in their place a positive view of clothing and style which he illustrates from church history. Then, armed with a redemptive alternative which restores fashion to its intended place in the created order, he addresses the relationship between identity and clothing.

This is a clear, pithily written book relating the gospel to a central dimension of everyday culture. A treatment like this is long overdue and I warmly commend it.

Graham Cray, Ridley Hall, Cambridge

PART ONE

Fashioned in His Image

CHAPTER I

DOWDINESS AND GODLINESS

> The others did not know what to think, but Lucy was so excited that they all went back with her into the room. She rushed ahead of them, flung open the door of the wardrobe and cried, 'Now! go in and see for yourselves.'
> (Lewis, C.S. *The Lion, the Witch and the Wardrobe*)

I Have a Dream . . .

The evening is warm; the air thick with the fragrance of trains, after-shave and the hot meals from the Buffet. Yves St Launderette, top fashion designer and winner of countless international style awards, watches the Inter-City 125 ease up alongside the platform.

He folds back the sleeve of his yellow linen jacket and glances at the blue paisley face of his watch. Finally, he looks up and down the train to find his guests. Ah, there's one, climbing from the front carriage. He runs towards the man in the black leather kilt with the dazzling white, slicked-back hair. 'Jean-Paul! Great to see you! And Vivienne, so glad you could make it!'

Vivienne Eastwood and Jean-Paul Gauloise have been looking forward to this quiet weekend with Yves St Launderette for weeks: just the three of them, at Yves' new place in the country – sharing new design concepts, discussing new fabrics, comparing notes on ethnic patterns and zip styles. Vivienne pulls her violent purple kimono round her more tightly, brushes back her mane of lavender-coloured hair, leans forward and kisses Yves on the cheek.

'We'll go to my place later', says Yves. 'First, to the Bible study!'

Vivienne grins delightedly. 'You kept that one a secret, Yves! I do so love going to church Bible studies. It's been so exciting for me to go to my local Brethren home-group and to learn what a strong biblical foundation there is for our line of work.'

'*Oui!*' agrees Jean-Paul, 'Ever since the Baptist Union put out its national statement, 'Style and Obedience: Fashionable Dress as a Response to Grace', I've never missed a Sunday morning service.' He flashes the enormous silver cross round his neck at his friends and winks.

Yves nods. 'You haven't seen anything yet. You just won't believe the fashion experimentation at our study group in St Helen's. I thought Milan and Paris were daring this season, but you wait till you see what the Mother's Union members manage to rustle up . . . by restyling items from the church bazaar and the local Oxfam shop – Unbelievable!'

Vivienne sighs. 'You know, the Superintendent of our Methodist Circuit sent back those ear-rings I styled for him. Said they were too conventional for a man in his position. Actually, I think he was right. And they *did* need to be bigger so they wouldn't be hidden by his hair.'

The Great Renunciation

But then we return to earth with a bump, to the real world in which the Christian wardrobe contains little more than Narnia. A real world where Christians only have one peg for stylish dress, the first half of a before-and-after conversion story. A real world in which fashion is used as an index of moral laxity, the more showy the garb, the deeper the slide into 'worldliness'.

The Church Fathers, especially Tertullian and Clement of Alexandria, raged against luxury in apparel. Medieval Christian moralists compared the elaborate 'horns' on the fashionable head-dresses of the day to those of the devil. John Wesley and George Fox (respectively, founders of Methodism and the Quakers) vigorously advocated plain, utilitarian dress. Fox even berated his contemporaries, the Puritans, for their 'ribbons and costly apparel'.

A person's dress has widely been deemed a reliable indicator of their state of grace. Most Christian literary paradises presuppose that the dress of the New Jerusalem will be spartan white linen, and Thomas More's *Utopia* of 1516 presents a society not only without fashion, but without tailors and dressmakers, since More holds them responsible for the evils of stylish dress.

Today, references to personal style appear in a range of Christian literature (popular and academic alike) but only to be dismissed with a sneer, contrasted unfavourably with whatever the writer is advocating: be it spirituality, environmental concern, compassion, or modesty. The recent revival of Christian interest in the arts, particularly in music, painting, sculpture and architecture, has still bypassed and disregarded clothing, even *haute couture*.

And yet the subject of clothing is inescapable. Not only do all of us spend most of our time living in it, many of us also spend much of our free time reading about it, browsing for it, dreaming of it and purchasing it. Image consultants estimate that around 65 per cent of the way others evaluate us is based on our dress. Our clothing can profoundly affect the way we feel about ourselves, our level of self-esteem, our moods, even the sort of person we feel we are. The clothes people wear largely determine whom we are likely to consider as a possible partner, especially in the early days of a romance. The costume gallery of London's Victoria and Albert Museum is by far the most popular area to visitors, and the V&A's winter 1994–1995 exhibition, *Street Style*, drew an astonishing 10,000 visitors a week. Clothing is the clearest expression of the mood of any particular era, its *zeitgeist*. In the words of *Independent* fashion writer Marion Hume (2nd December 1994), fashion is the most responsive of all the barometers of social change, 'You can react more speedily to the demands of the times with three-and-a-half metres of cloth than you can with, say, 5,000 tonnes of reinforced concrete.'

The ubiquity, popularity and importance of clothing make the almost total absence of constructive Christian comment on the subject shocking. Perhaps the churches' sartorial silence is due to a widespread assumption that – well – we all know what the Christian verdict on stylish dress should be. A big thumbs-down.

One way to look at the history of fashion in the West for around the past 200 years is as a battle between 'artificials' and 'authentics'. The former (at their extreme in dandies and punks) celebrate the very cultural, aesthetic aspects of clothing which the latter (in their different ways, groups as diverse as hippies, stockbrokers and the Amish of North America) claim to suspect. Historically, Christians have almost always sided with the 'authentics'. Even Christians who are in principle sympathetic to the notion of looking good frequently draw a line at the periodic shifting of styles which we call fashion.

The sartorial consequence of this is that among many Christian groups, dowdiness is next to godliness. The grey suit, the anorak, the sensible tweed skirt are not merely cultural preferences of a peculiarly conservative variety, they are conscious or unconscious theological statements. Flashy dress is sub-Christian. Plain is preferable. Conservative theology and conservative dress are close cousins, each supporting and slapping the back of the other. By and large, the more conservative the theology, the more conservative the dress. The height of your sole reflects the state of your soul; as one rises, the other falls.

Such a theology of personal adornment in a church necessarily means that a punk will have to cease being a punk after conversion. The goth will lose her gothiness, the metal-head will be alloyed into something more acceptable. The abnormal and deviant must be toned down if they are to find a home in a system locked in a grim embrace with ideals of the 'normal' and 'undeviant'. The modern-day followers of the young, long-haired Middle-Eastern traveller are to have a short-back-and-sides and sensible jerseys.

Today's church is a fashion black hole: a large object of

alarming density into which unwitting pilgrims are sucked. Our women are pulled irresistibly into Laura Ashley and Marks & Spencer dresses, while the men are instantly homogenised into some variation of today's mandatory uniform of the kingdom of God: for work, a grey suit of drab cut; for leisure, an anorak, sandals-with-socks, beige trousers with strikingly non-matching jacket, and (worst of all) rainbow braces for special occasions.

The issue is not simply whether Christians draw the line in the right place over specific fashion items, but whether the very ways Christians approach such cultural issues is increasingly alien to the majority of people in society. As we address moral dilemmas over clothing, messages are sent out to the surrounding culture. People hear not only the moral judgements we make on specific issues of dress, identity, sin and style, they also hear something of the ways we go about making those decisions. How do we as Christians go about deciding what is good or bad, helpful or unhelpful?

The messages being sent out by countless Christians today are redolent of a past age. These Christians show by their observations on contemporary dress that they are victims of a knee-jerk conservatism, with a framework for assessing dress which automatically condemns anything new and unfamiliar. They are sending out messages to a watching world that to become a Christian, in addition to accepting the creeds, one will also have to find a way of living in a culture that no longer exists for most people. Our moral judgements are part of our mission. We need to tread carefully; a furrowed brow aimed at a Doc Marten boot or nose-ring in a morning service will say far more about our understanding of the gospel than a hundred sermons on the free grace of God.

In this book I criticise the attitudes of many Christians towards clothing, both of the past and present, and of world-denying evangelicals in particular. But this is not done in any spirit of bitterness, superiority or mockery, as by a critical outsider looking in. Rather, it is a debate over a family meal table. It is written in a spirit of love and concern, from firmly within

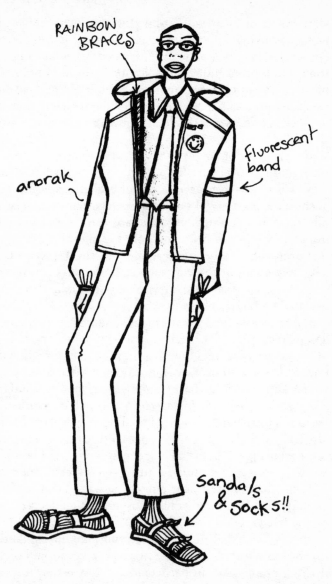

RAINBOW BRACES

anorak

fluorescent band

sandals & socks!!

'The mandatory uniform of the kingdom of God: anorak, sandals-with-socks, beige trousers with strikingly non-matching jacket, and – worst of all – rainbow braces for special occasions' (p 19)

the tradition of historic, biblical Christianity, with the single goal of glorifying God in our world. I pray it will achieve this in two ways: firstly, by helping Christians interact creatively but critically with our culture; and, secondly, by challenging those outside the church to understand that the gospel – far from being old-fashioned or irrelevant – has something dynamic and highly relevant to say to their culture and their own, everyday concerns.

Time to Reassess

I believe a fundamental reassessment of the boundaries which Christians draw over style is long overdue. In this book, I use the terms 'fashion' and 'style' more or less interchangeably to refer to aesthetic dress, which might change with the times. The message of the book is that neither beauty in dress nor changing styles are wrong *per se*. Quite the opposite. I argue that there is a strong case – and, importantly, a strong biblical case – to be made for the Christian as the one who dresses more brightly, more creatively, more experimentally than anybody else in our culture.

In Part One, *Fashioned in His Image*, I shall take a close look at each of the major arguments which have been used by Christians against fashion. I then suggest that all of these arguments, whilst claiming to be biblical, are in fact deeply rooted in attitudes uncritically absorbed from the surrounding culture. The three central arguments under consideration in Chapters Two to Five are:

1) Fashion is 'worldly'
2) Fashion is somehow 'unnatural'
3) A preoccupation with fashion is an indicator of pride.

Part One attempts to unpick each of these arguments, and demonstrate that theological conservatism need not logically imply cultural conservatism. Indeed, it ought to imply the reverse. The gospel itself carries a kind of cultural mandate which celebrates colour, vibrancy, style, creativity, radicalism. As I continue I shall build up a survey of the hundreds of biblical passages relating to clothing, and see what a clear pro-clothing pattern emerges. And on the way I shall launch a few broadsides at those down the ages and in the pulpits of today who have denounced adornment in the name of Christianity. I shall also give a thumbs-up to some unexpected allies from church history who enjoyed dressing up in style.

But does that mean that fashion (and more particularly, the worldwide fashion industry) is therefore immune from criticism? Or that our society has a healthy approach to what it wears, and where it buys? Far from it. In Part Two, *Dressed to Kill*, I shall firstly look at the misuse of clothing and body image at the individual level. By examining the snobbery of labels, the rise of the fashion shopaholic, the compulsive dieter and body-builder, modelling, and the role of modern consumerism in shaping our attitudes towards personal identity and image, I shall conclude that the abuses of fashion are no superficial issue, but symptoms of a malaise deep in the heart of our culture.

I will also take a long, hard look at the ethics (or lack of them) in the production and retailing of modern fashion. No matter how good fine clothing may be in itself, the contexts in which it is used can make it a vehicle of exploitation and injustice. This is the subject of the penultimate chapter. This overview of the ways clothing is misused in the modern western world then culminates in Chapter 10, which offers a Christian response to the modern identity crisis, using the biblical language of clothing as its basis.

But first comes Part One, a series of glimpses into why so many Christians have been so hostile to looking good.

CHAPTER 2

BODY AND SOUL

'The greatest provocations of lust are from our apparel'
Burton, R. 1621, *Anatomy of Melancholy*

Wearing Spectacles

Rose-tinted spectacles and dark sunglasses will each colour the world I see differently. Wearing lenses made of clear glass, lenses which are as distorting as bottle bases, or lenses which have been painted black, will significantly affect my vision.

But the most potent pair of spectacles any of us will ever use are worn not in front of the eyes, but behind them, inside our heads. For it is there that we carry our world view, our framework for making sense of the confusing mass of sense data which crowds in on us every waking moment. My world view is the pair of mental spectacles through which I view everything, it is the unifying vision which not only affects how I see the world; it even affects what I see there, highlighting some things and masking others, revealing some things as desirable, others to be avoided.

Christian in Bifocals

However, my world view spectacles are different from my sunglasses in one important respect. I can not only look through the sunglasses at the world, I can also take them off and look

23

at the sunglasses themselves. But most of us rarely examine our world views. They remain the lenses through which we look at the rest of the world, unconsciously worn, unexamined. Most people are even unaware that they are wearing world view spectacles at all, which is what makes them so fascinating – and so dangerous.

We all wear these spectacles-behind-the-eyes. We all have a world view, a 'big picture' within which all the small pieces of the puzzle find their place. My world view will be shaped by factors such as the culture into which I was born, my upbringing, my education and my chosen faith-commitments. It will help me see the answers to all the big questions of life: How should I think? How should I live? What matters most in life? Is there a meaning to it all? It is usually easier to spot other people's world view spectacles than our own, particularly when their opinions, beliefs and priorities suddenly clash with our own. Our own spectacles are so familiar, so comfortable, that we easily forget they are there at all.

The fact remains: we all wear a pair of world view spectacles (whether we know it or not) and none of us could operate without them.

Many Christians down the centuries have worn spectacles with bifocal lenses. They have (usually unconsciously) worn glasses which divide everything up into a series of polar opposites. For them, key aspects of life are seen as possessing two distinct aspects; one good, the other bad. To this bifocal way of looking, 'spirit' is good, 'flesh' is bad; 'heavenly' is positive, 'worldly', negative; 'high' art is better than 'low' art; the 'unchanging' is superior to the 'changing'; 'masculinity' is somehow superior to or more noble than 'femininity'; the 'inner world' of the person superior to the 'outer' world of material objects.

The bifocal world view has deep roots, not limited to any particular denomination: it has found its home in Protestant, Catholic and Orthodox settings alike. Such a world view is frequently known as 'dualism', since it is all about carving up experience into binary opposites. Some people wrongly assume that all Christianity is inherently dualistic, since this is the only version of it they have ever heard. From childhood, so many of us have been brought up to believe anything enjoyable is evil. Memories of earnest, black-clad preachers bearing down upon us from a great height, reviling 'worldliness', and urging us to set our minds on the hereafter, die hard.

Small surprise that there has been little place accorded to fashion in such a tradition. Few preachers are known for their empathetic response to street style. Between the pulpit and the catwalk lie a million miles of empty space. Jean-Paul Gaultier and John-Paul II inhabit different universes.

This is because fashion naturally finds its home on the 'negative' side of every single one of the dualisms which have historically held so much of the church in their grip. Fashion is intimately linked to human flesh. It is defiantly 'worldly'. It is a transient and outward form of 'low' art, indulged primarily by women!

Dualistic versions of Christianity will never be reconciled to style in dress unless the validity of their world view of polar opposites is fundamentally questioned. This book argues that our grim preacher needs to be pulled from his pulpit and packed off home, freeing the congregation to discover a God who is colourful, generous and loving. Many of the pulpit tirades to which we may have been subjected over the years will need to be reassessed. But before we start the reassessment, we shall look more closely at the case which has been made for a Christianity which looks at the world through bifocals.

Body and Soul

The bifocal tradition of Christianity looks down its nose in disgust at the physical body in general, and sex in particular. Some churches have handed down a legacy of shame surrounding the sensual, as if our five senses were instruments of the devil, rather than gifts of the Creator.

The recent public perception of Christian attitudes to the body has been profoundly coloured by the enormous success of novels such as Jeanette Winterson's *Oranges are Not the Only Fruit*, in which a young girl throws off the shackles of her sexually and emotionally repressed Protestant upbringing. This is combined with myriad books on Catholics and sex, where the only guideline for authors is that the word 'guilt' must be sprinkled liberally and at random. The neurotic, twitchy perspective which shudders in horror at the merest hint that humans have bodies is frequently taken to represent the entire Christian tradition.

It is beyond doubt that some Christians have had this attitude, especially at the lunatic fringe. However, the tradition which equates sex with sin and shame is only one strand among many Christian approaches to the physical. We shall explore others in due course, and argue that this tradition is less than faithful to the emphases of the Bible. But we must concede this much to the critics: that this negative perspective did command many of the leading figures of the early church.

Tertullian and Ambrose preferred the extinction of the human race to its propagation through 'sinful' acts, the former claiming that marriage and adultery are only different in their degree of illegitimacy. For Augustine of Hippo, the passion accompanying sex is always sinful, and for Aquinas the sexual act is questionable since it subordinates reason to passion. Origen, the 3rd century Egyptian, took Matthew 19:12 (on being a eunuch for the sake of the kingdom of God) so literally that he had himself castrated.

Jerome wrote that the only good in marriage was that it produces virgins, and Jovinian was excommunicated for suggesting that marriage is no worse in God's sight than virginity. Some early Christian ascetics showed how little they cared for the material body by refusing to wash – ever. The result was bodies covered in lice and beards which were permanently smelly and matted. The stronger the odour, the deeper the holiness. The negative verdict on the body and its sexuality has been particularly rife in Catholicism, with the Council of Trent in the mid-16th century teaching that virginity is morally superior to marriage.

However, this attitude is far from limited to Catholic circles. Many traditions in Protestantism share its suspicion of the body, such as New England Evangelicalism. The Massachusetts non-conformist minister Cotton Mather (1663–1728) wrote of the day when he was 'emptying the cistern of nature' up against a wall. At the same time, a passing dog performed the same action, prompting Mather to bewail: 'What mean and vile things are the children of men, in this mortal state! How much do our natural necessities abase us and place us in some regard, on the level with the very dogs!'

From that point on, he vowed that every time he went to the lavatory he should strain to turn his thoughts upwards, to less sordid, less material things. Otherwise, he said, he would be reduced to the level of the beasts.

Likewise, today's pews are still filled with many who believe that Christianity is somehow about the triumph of the 'spiritual' over the 'physical'. As we shall discover, such a bifocal vision is a travesty of biblical Christianity. But down the ages, it has exerted a strong influence, resulting not least in a condemnation of bodily adornment as sexually risqué.

The great 18th century preacher and philosopher Jonathan Edwards resolved to keep his body 'in continual mortification . . . never to expect or desire any worldly ease or pleasure'.

Modern objections to dress as excessively provocative were pre-empted in a late 14th century sermon by a preacher called Master Robert Rypon, 'All kinds of rayment are now rather for vainglory . . . and assuredly most of all to excite lust alike in men as in women.' And in his 1621 *Anatomy of Melancholy*, the English clergyman, scholar and writer Robert Burton observed that 'the greatest provocations of lust are from our apparel'.

At the heart of this tradition is a sense that we can wear clothes, but only as long as we are suitably miserable about it, since clothes act as a standing reminder of humanity's original nakedness, sin and guilt.

The dress-to-depress lobby frequently cite Adam and Eve's realisation of their nakedness (Gen 3:7), and God's subsequent clothing of the couple, 'The LORD made garments of skin for

Adam and his wife and clothed them.' (Gen 3:21). The context of God's clothing Adam and Eve, they argue, is the couple's banishment from Eden. Far from being a cause of celebration, the very origins of clothing are in a loss of bodily innocence. Dress thus becomes a result of the Fall, a reluctant second-best in which God himself appears unable to countenance sexual immodesty and shame at nakedness.

Worldly and Spiritual

In this bifocal, anti-body tradition, the 'world' is a term used to denote all that is evil in nature and human culture.

The Desert Fathers fled the cities of the 3rd century into the deserts of Egypt, Syria and Palestine. For them, the Christian life could only be attained by the mortification of all natural appetites. In this, the Desert Fathers were pioneers of the western monastic tradition, for which fashionable dress could only be viewed negatively. The Rule of St Benedict demanded renunciation of all ownership, and the holding of everything in common. Clothing had to be basic, functional and minimal.

The 11th century Cluniac order taught that the 'secular' world was irremediably sinful and the life of the ascetic monk the only sure way to salvation, and the Carthusians sought such complete isolation and solitude that they rarely ventured outside their cells. By the 12th century, poverty was seen as the definitive hallmark of the truly 'spiritual' life. Likewise, the full title of Thomas à Kempis's 15th century classic is, *On the Imitation of Christ and Contempt for the World*. It counsels its reader to 'give up this worthless world' and 'learn indifference to all that lies outside'. Christ is one who teaches us to 'spurn the things of the earth, and to loathe what is temporal.' Purification is seen as freedom from the corrupting influence of the material world and its cultures.

Despite the revolution in theology brought about by the 16th century Reformation, the new evangelical emphases failed to obliterate the asceticism of medieval Catholicism. The Anabaptists (a strong, radical tradition in Protestantism from the 16th century to the present day) had a stress on separation from the 'world', and holiness as withdrawal. Their descendants in the modern-day Amish (as portrayed in the Harrison Ford film, *Witness*) push this principle to its logical conclusion of severing most contact with all outside their community.

This world-denying emphasis remained strong in other branches of American evangelicalism. The great evangelist Dwight L. Moody stated in a sermon, 'I look upon this world as a wrecked vessel. God has given me a lifeboat and said to me, "Moody, save all you can".' The same basic approach is still heard among evangelicals today. The following statement, from a sermon by a Northern Irish Free Presbyterian, is typical: 'We live not for the things of time, but for the things of eternity. The child of this world may be fascinated by worldly things . . . he has very little else to live for.'

Biblical justification for an attitude which is suspicious of the physical body and the physical world is claimed from St Paul:

> Therefore, I urge you, brothers, in view of God's mercy, to offer your *bodies* as living sacrifices, holy and pleasing to God – which is your spiritual act of worship. *Do not conform any longer to the pattern of this world*, but be transformed by the renewing of your mind . . . (Rom 12:1,2 – *italics author's emphasis*)

Some claim the passage appears on the face of it to encourage mortification of the physical and a shunning of human culture. This, at least, is how it is frequently used by a range of Christian traditions. And this interpretation merely confirms the worst fears of a watching world already convinced that believers are rabid anti-body and anti-sex campaigners, whose most burning zeal is to stamp out fun wherever it may be found.

However, there can be no doubt that Paul would be horrified if he heard the sorts of stances his letters were being used to support today. This narrow, anti-body understanding of the passage certainly cannot be what Paul intended, as we shall see later in this chapter.

Inner and Outer

The same tradition of Christianity has placed a premium on the inner world rather than the outer. It has fostered that inner world known alternately as piety, devotion, contemplation, spirituality and meditation, but has tended to shun the outer world of action, speech, dynamism, and the visible.

The 19th century hymn writer Isaac Williams expresses the distinction in a verse of his popular hymn, *Be Thou my Guardian and my Guide*:

> And if I tempted am to sin,
> And *outward* things are strong
> Do thou, O Lord, keep watch *within*,
> And save my *soul* from wrong. *(Emphasis mine)*

The same distinction has remained fundamentally unaltered for centuries, up to the present day. The American author James Houston, in his 1989 guide to prayer, *The Transforming Friendship*, summarises what he feels to be the heart of the modern dilemma: 'We scramble to achieve an enviable image to display to others. We become "outward" people, obsessed with how we appear, rather than "inward" people, reflecting on the meaning of our lives.' (p17).

The same conclusions have been drawn time after time by a fundamentally bifocal Christianity: looking inward is good, looking outward is bad. Truth is more likely to be found 'in here', not 'out there'. 'Inner depths' are prized more highly than 'outer' activities or adornments.

Male and Female

Negative attitudes to the body have been widespread in the Christian tradition. However, women have been singled out as somehow more 'bodily' than men. In bifocal Christianity, if men have been defined by their mind and reason, women have been seen as closer to 'nature'. Masculinity has been associated with a particular conception of reason as logic and cool-headedness, those qualities which rise above the 'merely' physical, whilst femininity has been associated with physicality. And the central human act which reminds us of the earthy, flesh-and-blood character of our bodies is exclusively female, that of childbirth. Christian theologians have not been alone in saying this; it has been rife in many cultures, not least in the modern, 'scientific' West since the 18th century.

The frequent misogyny of the Church Fathers is explained in large part by this association between the female and 'the flesh'. Augustine reacts against crude gender stereotyping, but still ends up linking femaleness more with bodily functions. For Augustine, there are two uses of human reason: a higher, contemplative form and a lower, practical function. Women's subordination to men is, he says, *symbolic* of the subordination of the mind's practical reason to higher contemplation. The higher contemplates the eternal, while the lower reason controls the merely temporal and manages the affairs of life.

But Augustine is a model of enlightenment and civility compared to the 11th century monk, Petrus Damiani, who saw women as 'bait of Satan, by-products of paradise, poison in our food, source of sin, temptresses, whores of lust, sirens, and chief witches'!

This tradition of linking women's 'bodiliness' with sinfulness led to particular attacks on women's dress. Cyprian's 3rd century work, *De Habitu Virginum*, was the first in a long line of attempts by male clerics to control their own *libido* by insisting on drab, functional dress in women. In 1931, an anonymous Christian pamphlet, *Modest Apparel: An Earnest Word to Christian Women*, found shorts and sleeveless dresses immoral.

This image of women as constant temptation and danger, pulling males down into their 'lower' nature, has infused more recent debate in my own Church of England over the ordination of women to the priesthood. One Anglican bishop actually stated, as recently as the 1980s: 'Women, unlike men, radiate sex, and their temperament is inappropriate in church . . . their ordination would introduce distractions and earthiness into worship.'

For a substantial part of Christian tradition to the present day, women have been explicitly linked to the 'sins of the flesh'. They are temptresses, their provocative clothing leading astray otherwise rational (meaning sexless) males. They are the very antithesis of 'spirituality'. Unless, that is, they are well-draped nuns.

Changing and Unchanging

The idea that reason and spirituality are somehow more to do with men than women has been accompanied by a view of God as utterly transcendent. He is way up there, somewhere over the rainbow, beyond the clouds, above the trivia of daily life and petty concerns of the world and, most significantly, above the vacillations of earthly time. He is characteristically *atemporal*: he never changes and is wholly outside time.

That is to say, not only is God not limited by time as we are, but he has no experience at all of what we know as past, present and future. He transcends time utterly. He has no capacity to remember yesterday's news, or anticipate tomorrow's party. Passages used to bolster the picture of God as living in a time-free zone include Malachi 3:6: 'I the LORD do not change'. Divine atemporality and complete transcendence are assumed and reinforced in a range of popular hymns:

O let me hear thee speaking
In accents *clear and still*
Above the storms of passion . . . (*O Jesus I have Promised*, emphasis mine)

Immortal, invisible, God only wise,
In light inaccessible hid from our eyes . . . (*Immortal, Invisible*)

Similarly, much modern writing on spirituality and mysticism assumes a dualistic framework in that the aim of prayer and silence is to pull our minds or spirits up out of the realm of the temporal and changing, into a realm of transcendence, changelessness, atemporality. We strain, eyes tightly shut, teeth clenched, to pretend we are not on earth at all, but floating in some kind of heavenly blue jacuzzi. Such a view is to my mind dangerously sub-Christian. But it has exerted a considerable influence over many Christians.

If we idealise atemporality, we can only have a negative assessment of fashion. Styles change. Each garment wears out.

Clothing adorns the body, which itself wears out. Fashion embodies the transience of material existence.

The point also affects the issue of clergy vestments. In recent writing on ecclesiastical dress, sentences such as the following abound: 'The use of such dress over the course of the centuries and in all parts of Christendom gives a sense of *stability* and *continuity* which are essential in a religion concerned with eternal verities' . . . 'vestments should reflect the *continuity* of Christian worship rather than the discontinuities that at times have *afflicted* it' *(emphases mine)*.

The way we assess dress reveals our fundamental approach to the issue of time. Is it something to be escaped and transcended, or is it something to be celebrated? The solemn tradition of bifocal Christianity holds that time (and our embeddedness in it) is a bad thing. No surprise, then, that fashion as its most vigorous symbol has been correspondingly belittled. But is this inevitable? Is the only Christian response to time and change one of escape? The answer is an emphatic 'no'! In fact, there is a strong case for saying that an escapist Christianity is a defective Christianity, as we shall see below.

High and Low Art

Just as Christians have sometimes glorified the reason and the intellect, so too they have glorified 'high' art. Art is deemed worthwhile if it makes a 'serious' point. We like the 'classics', but the comic book is out of bounds. It follows logically: if truth is transcendent, way 'out there' somewhere in the spiritual realms, and approachable through the mind or some other invisible, spiritual capacity in mankind, then art has a function as a signpost to something beyond itself. High art is frequently (and I believe misleadingly) seen as 'ennobling', 'mystical', because it elevates the viewer beyond the physical world into a higher realm of truth and beauty.

By contrast, 'low' art is deemed popular, commercial, serving materialism. The art of the advertisement, magazine layout, or suit pattern is frequently not graced with the name of art at all. Rock concerts and raves are automatically suspect since they not only tease the ears and brain, but also vibrate the stomach. How unnervingly physical. Even *haute couture* is rarely bracketed with art. This attitude has been especially true of Christians, many of whom are deeply suspicious of all art. They feel they can only allow themselves to enjoy works which can be defended because they are didactic – they teach a moral or spiritual point. Not one of the recent books on art from a Christian perspective so much as mentions fashion. It is considered functional, popular, 'lowbrow'. As such, it is rarely considered justifiable from a purely artistic perspective, even by devotees of the arts.

Yes to Botticelli, no to Biba; yes to Dürer, no to Dior.

Binning the Bifocals

It is hardly surprising that Christians wearing the bifocal spectacles of a dualistic world view reject fashion, which finds itself at the negative pole of every single binary opposition. As long as the bifocals are in place, fashion is out. The Christian wardrobe will remain bare. So the crucial question then becomes: how essential are the bifocals? If we bin them, are we in fact binning the heart of the historic faith?

In the rest of this chapter, we shall discover that binning the bifocals is not only a necessary precursor to a proper Christian understanding of fashion, but it is essential if we are to understand the Christian message itself. We shall see that the bifocal mysticism many of us have been sold as Christianity is in fact a sub-Christian parody of biblical faith. Much rethinking might be necessary. As we proceed without bifocals, we shall discover that in searching for an alternative, world-affirming, culture-affirming Christianity we have overwhelming biblical support, not to mention some unexpected allies.

Body and Soul Reassessed

There is no single reason why so many Christians today continue to peer out through the lenses of a distorting, bifocal faith.

However, several different factors have encouraged its development.

One is the simple fact that bifocal religion is so much easier than the real thing. The God of the Bible is so demanding, so personal, so relentless in his desire to touch every dimension of our lives. How much easier to believe that spiritual reality is in a special compartment, for set times of the day or particular times of life, and that spiritual truth is away, 'out there' somewhere, distant and largely unknowable (a characteristic of much bifocal religion, from the earliest times to the present, has been the claim that God is remote and can only be defined by negatives). And how much easier to get our bearings for everyday life by absorbing uncritically the values of the culture around us, rather than using the word of God as a yardstick for criticising these same values.

Another reason for the prevalence of bifocals in the church has been the intellectualism of so many leading church thinkers throughtout history and today. So many have assumed that if your doctrine is right, the rest will follow. The church is led by 'brain' people, whose faith is thought out rather than danced out. The nitty-gritty of living, eating and dressing somehow seems less significant. Ironically, this can also be true of those advocating a more holistic Christianity. Those whose holistic, biblical theology rightly demands the full integration of faith and everyday life can turn even this into a head-trip, something to be debated rather than lived, eaten or worn. Tragically, there is little evidence that right ideas do lead to right living, and this is perhaps the single main reason why most people in our culture have deserted the church. Head-trips do not necessarily filter down into such mundane areas as how much I drink, what films I watch, or where I buy my shirts.

A third reason for the success of dualistic religion is that many people's faith has grown from roots which are as much non-Christian as Christian. The rigid separation of body and soul owes almost nothing to the Hebrew thought-patterns of the Bible, but a great deal to Greek philosophy and eastern mystical religions.

Bifocal dualism is found in particular in the thinking of Plato and his followers, and in forms of Hinduism. Perhaps its most virulent expression came in a second-century heresy called Gnosticism, which has spawned and influenced a wide range of modern offshoots, including Christian Science, Theosophy and much New Age thought. Gnosticism sees the only hope of salvation as lying in escape from solid matter – including the earth, and our human bodies – which is unredeemable. For the gnostic, 'spirituality' is the rekindling of a divine spark which has been trapped in base human flesh. Spirit is wholly good, matter wholly bad.

But historically, how did the early church handle the challenge of gnosticism? Far from seeing it as a logical development of the gospel, it condemned it as heresy. Rightly so, because the separation of spirit and matter that is prevalent in gnosticism is alien to the Hebrew mindset in which Old and New Testaments alike are cast.

Far from seeing the material world as evil, the Bible vigorously asserts that it is intrinsically good. The Scriptures strongly affirm the creational goodness of the cosmos in general and the human body in particular. When God created the earth from nothing, he saw with joy that 'It is good' (Gen 1). The psalmists repeatedly and continually celebrate creation (Ps 148, 19). The Song of Solomon is a frank and sometimes steamy celebration of sex between two young lovers, full of erotic innuendo. Even if one allegorises it, it remains true that sex is used positively as a symbol of the relationship of a human and God. The doctrine of the incarnation tells us that in Christ, God becomes a first-century Jewish male, and not, as the Gnostics would have it, only *appeared* to be really human, since they believed that divinity and human flesh cannot meet.

The Christian hope of life after death is the resurrection of the body , and not the immortality of the soul (an idea foreign to the Bible). The major theme of Jesus' preaching was the kingdom of God, or the rule of God in human affairs (not an escape from human affairs). One Old Testament vision of wholeness or salvation is a future Day of the Lord, on which

God asserts his rule over all creation, and celebrates it with very down-to-earth, material images: lions and lambs lying down together, people sitting under fig trees, people walking up mountains.

The biblical hope of eternity is always of a renewed earth, not an escape from the earth to remain in an ethereal heaven. This very solid picture of the after-life is endorsed by Jesus in his Sermon on the Mount, in which he states that the meek shall inherit not a private cloud, harp or translucent nightshirt, but the physical earth (Matt 5:5). Paul speaks of the future redemption of the physical world (Rom 8:18–22).

Likewise, the future hope in the Book of Revelation is not (as some Christians have fondly imagined) in being snatched away from the earth, but in the New Jerusalem (a vivid, colourful city) being established on the earth (Rev 21:2). Those Christians whose badges, T-shirts and car stickers boast that they are 'only passing through', that 'this earth is not their home', or that they are 'only visiting this planet' are in for a shock. The Bible says they will be here for the rest of eternity.

Some argue from Revelation 21:1, 'Then I saw a new heaven and a new earth, for the first heaven and the first earth had passed away . . .' that the end times involve the end of all physical life on earth, and the end of the earth itself. This is not true as this passage, and similar passages in the Old Testament on the renewal of the created order, can be interpreted in one of two ways, neither of which implies that our present earth is unimportant and is to be wished away or escaped.

One interpretation is that the 'new earth' is a renewed earth, the present earth with all the evil removed from it. On this basis, there is continuity between the physical world as we see it now, and the life of eternity. The discontinuity, of course, is that we shall die first; but afterwards, we shall live on this same earth. This view accords well with the Old Testament visions of the future kingdom of God on a redeemed earth (Is 11:6–9; Joel 3:18; Amos 9:13–15), as well as the apparent expectation of Jesus and Paul that the Christian hope lay in God's renewal of this present material world. It is also supported by the fact that when the author of Revelation 21:1 describes the meanings of the cosmos, he uses not the Greek word *neos* (new in time), but *kainos* (new in quality). This profoundly affects what is being said. John envisages not the destruction of the cosmos and the creation of a new one, but the renewal of the present cosmos. He describes a 'renewed' heaven and earth.

The second line of interpretation holds that the old earth is completely destroyed, and a new one brought into being. This claim is considerably weakened by the fact that the Greek word *kainos* is used, as explained above. But even here, the vision is of an embodied life, resurrection bodies on a physical earth. And the constant biblical emphasis that the new earth fulfils perfectly everything which is good in the present order of things implies that there is significant continuity between our earth and the future earth. Both are material creations of the same Creator. Jesus himself (after his resurrection, the prototype citizen of the renewed earth) returns to first-century Palestine with a resurrection body, and is able to walk along roads, eat food and break bread. There is no sense in which the new makes the old obsolete or irrelevant, or that the new is incompatible with the old. Quite the opposite. As we grow in the fruit of the spirit in the present age (Gal 5:22, 23a), we are learning now how to be citizens of the new age to come.

Nor is there any hint at all that our work in the present order for love, mercy, justice, creativity and so on are wasted effort. On the contrary, we do each of these at the explicit command of our Lord, and each becomes a brick which builds the New Jerusalem, as yet being constructed behind the scenes by God.

The writer to the Hebrews admits that 'here we do not have an enduring city, but we are looking for the city that is to come' (Heb 13:14), but what does this 'looking' involve? Surely, it is about embodying in the here and now the values of the city which is to come; it is an active seeking, not a passive resignation to the status quo. God does not write off the old order of things: he brings it to fulfilment in the new. The new earth is the logical extension of the present earth, even if it is a separate creation. Either way, the picture is clear. Eternity is a bodily existence, in a culture, in a city, on a solid, material earth, and its reality is already being foreshadowed in the present order of things.

But the strongest argument against bifocal Christianity lies in Hebrew anthropology in the Bible's understanding of what it is to be human.

Greek and Gnostic thought, and much modern western thought, assumes that people 'have' bodies. In other words, the essential person is a non-material soul or spirit which then inhabits a material body. Not so in Hebrew thought. The Hebrews, if anything, reversed the thought-process: the essential human being is a body, which then has life breathed into it (see, for example, God's creation of Adam, Gen 2:7; and Ezekiel's vision of dry bones, Ezek 37). I do not 'have' a body, I 'am' a body! There is no sense in biblical thought that the soul is the essential person, while the body is incidental; nor is there a sense that the soul (Hebrew-*nephesh*) is immortal, while the flesh (Hebrew-*basar*) is mortal.

Quite a contrast with Gnosticism, Greek thought, and eastern mysticism, not to mention modern western popular 'folk' religion, with its half-baked concepts of transparent, shiny souls floating around for eternity. Judaeo-Christian thought is inescapably material in its focus. 'Souls' are not saved, if by that we mean something non-physical. Whole, physical people are.

So how did confusion creep into Christian thinking and lead to the Bible being read through Gnostic eyes? The cause lay partly in the Septuagint, the Greek-language version of the Old Testament. The original was in Hebrew, but when certain Hebrew words were translated into Greek, the new Greek words came already wearing bifocals. They were already loaded with a weight of Greek philosophical dualism. The Hebrew *nephesh* was translated *psyche*, which in turn became *soul*. The Hebrew *ruach* became *pneuma*, which became *spirit*. So, at the stage of transition from Hebrew to Greek, the words began to carry clear dualistic overtones, which was rigidly fixed by the time the words were translated into English, not least because of the historical influence of Greek philosophy on the

English-speaking world. For us, soul and spirit are by definition non-physical – even if the Bible says otherwise.

However, in the original Hebrew, *nephesh* ('soul') is just as likely to be bodily. In Job 41:21, a particular animal's *nephesh*, or physical breath, is said to kindle coals. Similarly with *ruach*, which is often translated 'spirit': the same word can equally well mean the wind, or breath in the sense of life or animating force. In fact, *ruach* hardly ever corresponds to what we understand by 'spirit' – something ghostly or non-physical.

To cap it all, in Hebrew poetry, concepts such as heart, soul, flesh, spirit, ear, mouth, hand and arm are frequently used interchangeably! Each refers to the whole, physical person: 'bodily' aspects just as much as 'spiritual'. The distinction between spiritual and material is meaningless. The real biblical distinction is between whole, physical people who respond to God's call on their lives, and those who do not.

We might put this another way, since it is an area which many Christians today find confusing, not least because of sub-Christian dualisms which have seeped into the church pretending to be authentic Christianity.

We can take the issue of what happens when a person dies. Many Christians (and even more non-believers) hold to an appallingly anti-body view of it all. They say only the body dies, the body which is a mere 'husk' or 'overcoat', whilst the true 'spiritual' self (the 'soul' or spirit') lives on eternally in a disembodied form, in heaven, or some 'spiritual' realm. This is the view of the afterlife assumed in a wave of late 1980s and early 1990s Hollywood epics about death, such as *Ghost*. This rather confused idea is usually known as the 'immortality of the soul', and is based partly on a few vague hints given in the Bible about the intermediate state of the believer between death and the final resurrection. The trouble is, the immortality of the soul for all eternity is not a biblical idea.

The biblical position is quite different. Now, before death, I am an *embodied* person. My body is good and an essential part of who I am. It is not incidental, separable, secondary. It is me, created by God and unique. My body matters. What I do with it matters. My body is a temple of the Holy Spirit (1 Cor 6;19). I am to honour God in my body (Phil 1:20). So good is the physical body that it becomes the central New Testament image of the church (Eph 4:25; Col 1:24).

So much for the present, what of the future? The Christian hope for life after death is a future resurrection of the body. Eternal life is an *embodied* existence. Just as Jesus himself had a new resurrection body which was so physical it could eat barbecued fish for breakfast (Jn 21:12), so we too shall live as embodied people on a renewed earth. We shall be given new, physical bodies to live in a new, physical city. The caterpillar sheds its old body and receives a new, glorious body – that of a butterfly. Our bodies not only matter and are intrinsic to us now. They will matter and be intrinsic to us after the coming day of resurrection too. For the present, and for eternity, we are embodied. John Brown's body lies a-mouldering in the grave, but one day he will be given a new one by his maker. It may not fit the metre, but it is a good deal more biblical.

But what about the interim period, the time between my death and my resurrection? Here there is room for legitimate debate among Christians where biblical support can be found for any one of three positions:

1   The whole person dies and completely ceases to exist. What happens on the day of resurrection is in fact a 'recreation' of a whole person. I experience no conscious continuity between my present life and the future, resurrected me (although in both states I experience myself as 'me').

2   The whole person dies, but at that very moment, leaves what we experience as the passing of time. He or she immediately experiences being present at the day of resurrection. So one moment I experience being 'me' in my present embodied state, the next in my resurrected embodied state.

3   Only the body dies, and a disembodied aspect of myself continues, incomplete and perhaps in some state of

'sleep' for a limited period of time until the day of resurrection, at which point it will be united (or 'reunited') with its new, resurrection body.

Each of these may be inferred from the biblical teaching. Each has attractive points, each has its problems. But one thing emerges: these are the only three viable positions on the 'interim' state between death and resurrection. The possibility of an eternity without a body is never contemplated by the biblical writers.

From this brief survey, one thing becomes abundantly clear. Even if it is possible for some aspect of my personality to exist in a disembodied state (and this is far from being the only biblical option), it could only ever be for a temporary period. For the present I have a body. After the resurrection I shall have a body. As for what happens in between, two of the three options involve no separation of the bodily and other components of my make-up, not even for a short time. The other involves a separation for a strictly limited period.

Only one conclusion is possible: matter matters. It is no accident that I am embodied. Present and future embodiment is a glorious gift from my Creator. My body is unashamedly good, and is not to be belittled, transcended, or otherwise wished away. To do so is to diminish the pinnacle of God's good creation.

Bifocal Christianity: Adam and Eve Reassessed

Nevertheless, biblical passages cited throughout this chapter might on the face of it appear to support dualism; the splitting up of reality into categories of 'worldly' or 'the flesh' versus 'religious' or 'the spirit'. Perhaps one of the biggest bones of contention is Adam and Eve.

Many writers on clothing and fashion quote the two key passages on the origins of dress, from the third chapter of Genesis, as if the message of both passages were self-evident. These two passages (the couple's clothing themselves with fig-leaves and God's clothing them in tunics) are automatically assumed to be about bodily shame and guilt. In particular, it is assumed they are about sex:

> Then the eyes of both of them were opened, and they realised that they were naked; so they sewed fig leaves together and made coverings for themselves. Then the man and his wife heard the sound of the LORD God as he was walking in the garden in the cool of the day, and they hid from the LORD God among the trees of the garden (Gen 3:7,8).

> The LORD God made garments of skin for Adam and his wife and clothed them (Gen 3:21).

One commentator amongst the many who read these passages as being about the sinfulness of the body is Elizabeth Rouse of the London College of Fashion, who states it as plain fact in her otherwise helpful book, *Understanding Fashion*:

> It is quite commonly believed that we wear clothes because certain parts of our bodies are shameful and need to be covered. Attitudes of this kind have their origins in the religious mythology of Judaeo-Christian tradition, in particular in the story of Adam and Eve (p8).

The American sociologists Stuart and Elizabeth Ewen make this same assertion the foundation of their case that clothing is 'the mark of sin', or 'the trappings of sin' (*Channels of Desire*, p82).

Such critics tend to assume a scenario something like the following. Before the Fall, Eden was innocent and perfect. This meant there was no sexual activity. The Fall introduced awareness of sexual organs, and a corresponding sense of the 'naughtiness' of them. Therefore the couple rushed to cover up their nakedness, taking fig-leaves, and draping them over their pubic regions. They are embarrassed to have their genitals seen by each other, and they are embarrassed to be looked in the eye by God, now that they know about the 'forbidden fruit' of sex and are no longer pure and innocent. Henceforth, the naked body has been sinful and dirty because of its sexuality.

Such, at least, is a popular reading of the two passages, among secular critics and bifocal Christians alike. The only problem with such an interpretation is that there is no evidence at all to support it, and all the clues point to a completely different meaning.

Clearly, their desire to cover themselves up *is* due to some new sense of guilt and shame. But this cannot possibly be due to the discovery of sex, or the 'sinfulness' of sex. In the first chapter of Genesis, God has made the animals, fish and birds in two genders, and told them to pair up for sex. He has done the same with human beings. They too were made as male and female, with an express purpose of having companionable and procreative sex (Gen 1:28; 2:24). The unfallen world was teeming with sexual activity, including that of naked human beings, but nobody found this at all shameful or guilt-inducing, least of all God, the inventor of sex (Gen 2:25).

What then, is the real significance of their realisation that they are naked, if it is not to do with the discovery of eroticism or bodily shame? This is explained by the significance of the 'tree of the knowledge of good and evil' (Gen 2:17), from which the fruit was plucked. The idea that this refers to knowledge of sex is ludicrous (there was sex before the Fall). Nor is it even the capacity for moral judgement as the pair are treated as morally responsible before the Fall (Gen 2:16,17). From other uses of the Hebrew phrase, 'good and evil', it appears to be an idiomatic way of saying 'complete knowledge', or 'knowledge of everything'. In other words, it means the kind of knowledge which is God's alone, the knowledge which brings power and autonomy. To eat the fruit of such a tree is to claim to be like a god. In the light of this, the couple's nakedness has a straightforward explanation.

Before the Fall, they are compared to dependent children, who run about naked, free from the embarrassment which characterises adults. The change from unselfconscious nakedness to guilty nakedness is a sign of their change from childlike dependence on their Father, to wanting to be all-knowing, self-sufficient, independent adults. Independent is the one thing Adam and Eve were never supposed to be; they were to live in loving dependence on their Father, tending the earth at his behest, not just for their own gratification.

This interpretation is supported by another place in Scripture where small children are explicitly said not to know 'good from evil'. It comes as Moses tells the people of Israel that it is not the wayward parents who will enter the Promised Land, but only their innocent children (Deut 1:39). The parallels with Adam and Eve are strong: those who pretend to know better than God forfeit his blessings. Those whose childlike innocence leads them to trust him receive the blessings.

The couple's unashamed nakedness is an evocation of a certain childlike innocence. This is not childlike in the sense of pre-sexuality, since their innocence includes sexual activity, but childlike as dependence on a parent. Adam and Eve hide from God in shame because they know they have flouted his one rule for life in Eden: they are there as God's children, looking to him for all they have. It is significant that up to the Fall, God has made everything Adam and Eve need for life on earth. Their first act after the Fall is to usurp God's role by making their own clothing. Little surprise, then, that they feel shame when they hear God himself approaching. One who has pretended to be a god feels uncomfortable at the prospect of dialogue with the true Creator of the universe.

The central point is that when the couple cover themselves, it is not to shield themselves from each other's gaze, but God's. None of their desperate actions, from sewing together the laughably unsuitable material of fig-leaves to hiding behind the trees, are mainly attempts to cover up their nakedness from each other. They are hiding from God. When Adam tells God that he hid to cover up his shameful nakedness (Gen 3:10), this gives the game away. God knows their naked bodies are good and not shameful – indeed, he had made them and saw they were very good (Gen 1:31). The fact that the couple now see evil where there is only good sets warning bells ringing. They have grasped at the omniscience which only God can handle, and the result is that they can no longer even handle their own humanity.

To summarise: the 'fig-leaf' passage from Genesis equates nakedness with shame and guilt, but this is nothing sexual. It does not say that the naked, sexual body is in any way shameful. The whole point of it is that the couple's bodies are not shameful. They suddenly start to experience guilt, faced with something which ought not to be guilt-inducing. Their shame before something shameless is a measure of how far they have fallen from a state of childlike dependence, from the childlike innocence which can run naked in a garden and not feel self-conscious about it.

Likewise, when God himself clothes the couple (Gen 3:21), this has nothing to do with covering up something which is sinful to look at. It is not that God is disgusted by their discovery of eroticism and gets them covered up to hide their nudity.

The true significance is quite different. He is, firstly, reasserting his own rights as Creator: their first act of independence was to make their own, inadequate, clothes. Now, God restores the true order of things. He made clothes for them, and makes a much better job with his suede tunics than they had with their fig-leaves.

Secondly, God is announcing to the rest of creation that his original plans for Adam and Eve will not be thwarted by their disobedience. God himself turns tailor and provides them with an outfit worthy of their station and calling. These tunics are not to cover shamefully sexual bodies, nor are the tunics ever presented as a functional guard against the weather. The couple are being installed (despite the Fall) as viceroys of creation, elevated above the beasts, plants and inanimate matter. Their new tunics are robes of office.

An examination of the other uses of the same concept of 'clothing' in the rest of the Old Testament points clearly to this interpretation. The Hebrew noun used for this particular garment is *kuttonet* a tunic worn next to the skin. It is used regularly in the Old Testament. In particular, it is used eight times as a token of fatherly love in the Joseph stories, ten times in Exodus and Leviticus in connection with priestly garments, and twice in 1 Samuel, as a gown worn by princes. In practically all cases, the 'garments' are used by God to elevate the wearer above others. So to have such clothes put on for the very first time is seen as a kind of ceremonial investiture. In Exodus

28:40, the 'garments' are explicitly said to give the wearers 'dignity and honour'.

The grounds for holding that the Hebrew verb *wayyalbisem* ('clothed them', Gen 3:21), refers to a grubby, shameful covering up as the pair scurry away in sexual self-revulsion are extremely shaky. Far more likely that it means God 'robed' them, just as God robed the priests in Exodus 29:5,8 and 40:14, as Jacob robed his son Joseph as a sign of favour (Gen 37:3), and as Pharaoh robed Joseph for high office (Gen 41:42).

The same image recurs throughout Scripture. Saul robed David in his own tunic, to be the chosen champion to fight against Goliath (1 Sam 17:38). Jonathan gave David not only his robe, but also his tunic and belt (1 Sam 18:4), as a sign of intimacy and honour. King Xerxes in the Book of Esther honours Mordecai with a fine robe (Esther 6:6–11), and Jehoiachin is honoured by a new set of fine clothes (2 Kings 25:28–9). Through Isaiah, God says he will depose a man called Shebna as steward in Jerusalem, and instead clothe a character called Eliakim for the office (Is 22:20,21). King Belshazzar promises to robe Daniel in fine purple clothing and gold jewellery and make him third highest ruler in the kingdom if he can interpret his visions (Dan 5:16).

The father of the prodigal son robes his son in his own robe (the best robe in the house would always belong to the father), as a sign of restored sonship (Lk 15:22), and he put him in sandals (which servants did not normally wear). The message is clear: in the symbolism of the Bible, to clothe somebody is to honour them.

Too Sexy For My Shirt?

Back to clothing and sexuality. What then, should be the Christian's approach to the sexuality of dress? Two extremes are to be avoided. One unhelpful extreme, frequently trotted out by preachers and youth group leaders, is that the Christian is to aspire to sexlessness. Best be on the safe side, they say, and go for the most shapeless, drab, contour-disguising sacks the chain stores have on offer. That way we can avoid any reminder that we are created as sexual beings. But we *are* sexual, and to deny our sexuality is to reduce our God-given personhood.

The other is the extreme encountered daily on the streets of our cities: the sad sight of a human being reduced to a walking erogenous zone. This is happening at every level of society, from penthouse to pavement. The fabulously wealthy don the outrageous see-through dresses, plunging necklines and super-stud suits of the Italian designer Gianni Versace. In Versace's London store a gold mesh mini-dress currently costs £4,000, and a pair of velvet, mock leopard-skin thigh boots, £400. Then there are the bizarre conical bras and outrageous basques of Jean-Paul Gaultier.

The once-taboo fetishist garb featuring rubber, leather, metal and body piercing is increasingly rising from the underground, partly through the voyeuristic media coverage of events such as the kinky 'Skin Two' balls. Ann Summers sexwear parties are becoming increasingly a haunt of the bored middle classes, and PVC underwear and metal-tipped bras are blossoming on market stalls. The Marquis de Sade is alive and well, and living as a respectable citizen in your own town.

Versace, Skin Two and the like are in the business of turning people into erotic cartoons. But each of us is a miraculous, multi-faceted being. Our glory is our God-given complexity: we are each a wonderful blend of intellect, spirituality, sexuality, creativity, humour, tears, and more. The way we present ourselves in everyday life needs to express this multi-dimensionality. To single out one single aspect of our make-up and limit our appearance to that alone is a tragic reductionism, reducing complex harmony to a monotone.

The growing acceptability of 'bondage' styles into the mainstream conveys only one message about the self: I am sexually available, and that is all you need to know about me. A man or a woman whose conversation consists solely of blue jokes and sexual innuendo is a sad case, where we long to tell them there is more to fullness of life than sex. So, too, with our clothing. If all we communicate is sex, all others will hear is sex.

If Christians cannot accept the public wearing of styles which only shout out 'sex' to passers-by, it is not because we are anti-sex. We are pro-sex, when sex is one part of the lives of whole persons. It is because we believe the wearer is more than a one-dimensional erotic image. They are worth more than that. Sex is one part of our glorious, multi-faceted make-up, inseparable from all our relationships – with God and other people. Our clothing needs to reflect that.

So we can be neither frumps nor vamps. Our approach to clothing and sexuality must avoid these two extremes, both of which reduce our full humanity. In the broad middle ground lies a mixture of factors to bear in mind in deciding how provocatively to dress: the culture we live in, where we are, who we are with, the response we want to evoke from others. There are no hard and fast rules for the Christian in assessing the erotic potential of our dress, except the avoidance of these two extremes, and Paul's principle that while some things might be allowable, concern for another person can mean we hold back from exercising our personal freedom (for example, 1 Cor 10:23,24). Ultimately, we are given not a rule book. Rather, we clothe ourselves in the indwelling Holy Spirit, who renews our minds and guides our feet . . . and our wallets and wardrobes.

Bifocal Christianity: Paul Reassessed

We referred earlier to Romans 12:1,2, noting that this is one passage used to bolster the case for a bifocal Christianity:

> Therefore, I urge you, brothers, in view of God's mercy, to offer your bodies as living sacrifices, holy and pleasing to God which is your spiritual act of worship. Do not conform any longer to the pattern of this world . . .'

However, there is absolutely nothing in the text which, viewed against a background of Hebrew thought, implies that Paul was an advocate of bifocals. Some Christians have read Paul's injunction to 'offer your bodies as living sacrifices' as addressed to one's mind, soul or spirit, and telling it to keep that nasty physical object it inhabits under control. They have seen it as advocating the pleasures of the spirit or mind, but denying the pleasures of the body.

This completely misses the point Paul is trying to make. Paul is referring to the whole person, calling for full, holistic surrender to the will of God, submission in every aspect of our being. It is inconceivable that Paul, with his rigorous Hebrew background, could possibly be saying that because the body is more prone to evil than the 'mind' or 'soul', therefore it had to be kept tightly reined in, like a horse being driven along by some spiritual coachman. Paul knows that every aspect of our make-up can be tainted by evil, and that every aspect can be used in service to God. So the mood of the passage, far from being one of grim asceticism: (Batter your body into submission! Strive for spiritual and not the material!) is one of liberation, joy, ecstasy and wholeness: (Let every single part of your make-up respond to the call of God! Hold nothing back!).

Likewise, when Paul condemns, 'the pattern of this world' (v2), this has sometimes been taken as a condemnation of matter or human culture *per se*. But this too is an inadmissible interpretation in the light of Paul's Jewish background. Paul is using the negative sense of 'world' or 'present age' to designate the human being in its state of temporary rebellion against the Creator. The 'present age' means the totality of what we might call 'spiritual' and 'physical' phenomena alike, all turned in opposition to God. Both 'spiritual' and 'physical' alike are capable of redemption and being used in the service of God, and it is this to which Paul exhorts his readers.

In, Out, In, Out, Shake it All About

So much for the unhelpful bifocals of spiritual and physical. What about categories of 'inner' and 'outer'? This too proves to be a misleading set of opposites, which does little to move us towards a healthy, biblical Christianity relevant for today. To be sure, many Christians believe that true devotion means a plumbing of inner depths, an attempt to do away with distraction and find God as a 'still, small voice' in solitary silence. On this account, prayer must mean the exclusion of the outer world including the closing of the eyes, the motionlessness of the body, the silence of the atmosphere.

But why should this be? Is this ideal of devotion an inevitable consequence of Christian faith? Hardly, but there are historical reasons why it has been the case, and the recent surge of interest in popular psychology, particularly the study of 'psychological types' offers some provocative insights as to why. One method of psychological analysis currently used in business is the Myers-Briggs Type Indicator. One of the key distinctions between personality types made by Myers-Briggs is between *introverts* and *extroverts*. While introverts are energised primarily by their own inner world (by reflection) extroverts tend to focus on the outer world of other people and the external environment (by action).

Recent studies reveal that the populations of most modern Anglo-Saxon cultures are roughly divided equally between introverts and extroverts. However, the same studies reveal that no less than 80 per cent in the Christian churches are introverts. In other words, the sort of people who go to church, the sort of people who lead churches and teach in theological colleges, and the sort of people who write theology and works of spirituality, tend to have an inbuilt bias towards reflection and contemplation, towards the inside of their own heads, rather than outwards to the world.

This has profoundly shaped the churches' ideals of 'holiness', especially in the Anglican and Catholic traditions. A man who exudes an air of silence and mystery, and who appears to shun worldly haste – even if they are, frankly, rather 'wet' – is far more likely to be considered 'holy' than an outspoken activist who blasts out heavy metal on her car stereo, even though the latter might actually be more fervent to see the reign of God coming on earth, more enthusiastic to have her mind moulded by the spirit of God.

The greater part of the Christian tradition has been shaped by introverts. Consequently, the half of the population who are extroverts enter a largely alien culture as they enter church or embark on a Christian retreat. They are made to feel unholy, loud, superficial or glib. This conspiracy of the silent is a scandal.

Not that there is anything wrong with silent retreats, contemplation, deep thought or a capacity for quiet empathy. Of course not. It is just that the introverts have had it their own way for much of Christian history. Half a picture has dominated the whole Christian screen for far too long, and it is the half which sometimes veers perilously close to dualism. Are we seriously saying that holiness, devotion, and prayer are only possible for half the population? Surely not, when a study of godly devotion in the pages of the Bible is a fertile field for working out an extrovert spirituality: from the action-centred holiness of the Old Testament (holiness as a godly lifestyle, the performance of Temple and synagogue ritual), to the New Testament, where all the references to the basis of God's judgement of individuals concern faith in action, trust lived out in the real world (see the 'sheep and goats' of Matt 25:31–46).

Unlike most modern conceptions of prayer, prayer in biblical times and in the early church was usually performed standing up, eyes wide open and spoken aloud – open both to God and his world. Today, too, Christians should use the methods of spirituality, prayer, and holiness which best fit their own, God-given, character. Many of the difficulties people have with prayer are unnecessary. They are so often caused by people adopting models of devotion which are suited to somebody else's temperament, but not to their own.

There is no reason why Christian spirituality has to be about the 'inner' as opposed to the 'outer'. A biblical faith demands that both be offered to God in loving obedience.

Bifocal Christianity: More Reassessment

We have already noted that the anti-creation tradition puts an emphasis on God's atemporality and transcendence. For this reason, Christians have sometimes elevated those qualities in human beings which have been considered to approximate most closely to these qualities in God, qualities such as reason, masculinity, and mysticism. It has also led to the phenomenon of the other-worldly Christian, that unnatural hybrid: part human, part fluffy white cloud.

However, this tradition is open to two serious challenges: that its dualisms stem from non-Christian roots, and that there is a strong biblical case to be made for the temporality of God. Then, if that is true, it follows that we really ought to be concentrating on those aspects of humans which relate most closely to that.

As with other sub-Christian doctrines which we have already noted, the idea that God is wholly outside the limitations of space and time owes more to ancient Greek religion than to biblical Christianity. It is true that in the Hebrew tradition God is awesome and holy (ie 'set apart' from humanity). And it is true that in his own being, God is separate from his creation; he is in a completely different order of existence from us.

Nonetheless, he is repeatedly presented as acting *inside* time and space, even being limited by them. Even allowing for the different literary styles (poetry, metaphor etc) used in the relevant biblical passages, it is hard to get away from the fact that the God of the Bible is constantly involved in earthly space and earthly time. Even if he is not ultimately bound by space and time (least of all, by the human construct of hours, minutes and seconds – God does not wear a watch), he acts in them and respects their limitations.

Many biblical passages show how God interracts so closely and dynamically with the created order that the unfolding of events on earth actually changes God's intentions. Sometimes this is in response to intercessory prayer. Moses successfully pleads that God will relent and not destroy the Israelites (Ex 32:12), and Abraham successfully haggles with God over the fate of Sodom (Gen 18:23–32). At other times, God is presented as changing his plans in the light of human activities. When Nineveh repents, God relents (Jon 3:10). It is hard to read the Bible and not conclude that God is open to being changed through his relationship with his creation.

Passages such as Malachi 3:6, which appear to say that God does not change, are actually saying nothing about God's place in or out of time. They are a simple reassurance about his faithfulness to his people. He will not let them down. The most natural way to understand the biblical picture of God is not as atemporal but as everlasting, not aloof from time and space but intimately involved in them, from beginning to end.

This all has implications not only for fashion, but also for the debate over church vestments which we discussed earlier. It becomes clear that the advocates of 'traditional' vestments have arbitrarily selected atemporality and transcendence as the attributes of God and goals of Christian worship. From this, they have argued that vestments should likewise reflect loftiness and lack of change. However, it would be more justifiable to argue from the principles of God as creator, God as temporal, and God as incarnate, that clerical dress should be vibrant, artistic, colourful, up-to-date, culturally attuned and unashamed of regular change.

Time, change and transience have value. Far from being transcended and escaped, they are to be celebrated. Our limits of finitude and temporality are irremovable. They are good and God-given. Far from being something to be escaped, the limited, temporal and culturally-bound are where we meet God himself. Ask any of the gospel writers.

Finally, we noted that the distinction between high art and low art has been used in order to belittle the value of dress. The view that only 'high' art is worthwhile is open to criticism on two counts: that it is historically relative, and that it is biblically suspect. In most cultures before pre-18th century Europe, the artist was primarily a craftsman. It was not till the 18th century that the definition of 'art' became restricted to fine art, and the crafts were set aside as something inferior.

However, there is no reason why a Christian should accept these more recent definitions of art. If God himself became incarnate, the material world is a legitimate sphere for human creativity. Art should not be considered a way to be 'lifted' above the 'merely' material to some 'higher' realm of spirit. Quite the opposite. Art is an encounter with the physical world, touching our senses. It is the physical interaction of human with paint, strings, paper, stone and ink, that constitutes art. God celebrates and blesses the material for its own sake. Why should we belittle the earthiness of art, seeing it merely as a vehicle for some abstract truth? Truth is concrete.

Of course, to say there is no valid distinction between high and low art is not to say we cannot discriminate good from bad art. There can be bad oil painting and bad classical music, just as there can be good magazine layout and good shoe design. We do not want to abandon criteria of good taste and discrimination, simply to apply these criteria to the whole range of human creativity, not just a narrow section of it.

Christians in Bifocals: Some Alternatives

To some, all this will sound natural and self-evident. But to others, raised to see the bifocals as essential, it might sound astounding. Some will ask where throughout the Christian centuries, they could find such interpretations expressed and supported in the orthodox faith.

We have already noted how a holistic, body-soul unity is axiomatic to mainline Jewish thought. Hence, it is not so much demonstrated as everywhere assumed by the biblical writers. The separation of spirit and matter would have been unthinkable. Their inseparability was also assumed by the central tradition of the early church. The bifocals of Gnosticism (far from being embraced as authentically biblical) were rightly binned as being incompatible with the historic faith. Roman Catholicism has sometimes been guilty of dualism. But equally, Catholic sacramentalism can be an enthusiastic reminder that God meets us in the mundane elements of the material earth: water, bread and wine, and that the very earth radiates glory; it is not to be escaped or belittled. Furthermore, a major and central strand of the Roman Church has advocated a vigorous, earthy faith which seeks not so much escape from the earth as its renewal by Christ. Major Catholic celebrators of creation have included St Francis of Assisi, the wonderfully sensual poetry of Gerard Manley Hopkins, and the rollicking novels and essays of G.K. Chesterton.

Another church tradition which has always held to a high view of creation as good in itself is Celtic Christianity, the native tradition of the British Isles and Ireland. The goodness of the natural world features prominently in the Celtic faith, perhaps not surprisingly in its geographical context of hills, valleys, lakes, islands and coastlines. The Celtic church, like the Psalmist, celebrates the beauty of God's good earth, in its art and poetry, even to its central symbols. The most distinctive feature of the Celtic version of the Christian cross is the circle of creation, encircling the cross of redemption. The Celts have got it right: the earth is good but fallen. Creation and redemption are inseparable.

It is perhaps the Protestant tradition which over the years has been perceived as the most vehemently anti-world, anti-culture, anti-fun. It is time to help put the record straight and discover just how pro-world many in the Protestant tradition have been. In doing so, we shall come across a few surprises.

Early Protestant theologians ridiculed the Catholic ascetics who believed that bodily filth was a sign of a mind set on higher things, saying rather that our bodies are good gifts of God and should be kept clean and in good condition. Despite his widespread reputation as the founder of a world-denying movement in the church, Calvin himself (unlike some of his later followers) offers a positive framework for understanding the material world. He formulated this framework largely in reaction to the strong medieval ascetic tradition in Catholicism, which the 16th century Reformation in general was questioning. It is true that Calvin also has a strong emphasis on the fall of creation, but in his major work, the *Institutes*, this is never allowed to obscure the fundamental goodness of the world. His stress on the beauty of creation tempers his doctrine of the fall of that creation. He constantly uses imagery from the natural world, taking delight in the sheer sensuality of gifts such as food:

> If we consider to what end God created foods, we shall find that he wished not only to provide for our necessities, but also for our pleasure and recreation. . . . With herbs, trees and fruits, besides the various uses he gives us of them, it was his will to rejoice our sight by their beauty, and to give us yet another pleasure in their odours. . . . *Lastly, has he not given us many things which we ought to hold in esteem without their being necessary to us?* (emphasis mine)

This last sentence in particular ought to give pause for thought to those who write off Calvin as grim, functional and anti-pleasure. On the evidence, he can be precisely the reverse. In a striking phrase, Calvin elsewhere describes the physical earth as a 'Theatre of Glory'.

We might use a different analogy. Creation is an ancient, incredibly beautiful house, but one which has grown shabby and neglected. Medieval Catholicism and other bifocal traditions condemned the crumbling property to demolition, telling the inhabitants the only hope was to move away. Calvin's course was to exhort people to invite the builder to carry out repair work. The difference between these two stances is fundamental and crucial in terms of our present concerns. Calvin gives a basis for affirming the goodness and potential of the body and the created order.

Another group whose reputation is undeserved is the much maligned English Puritans, who also held a high doctrine of creation. They believed that God had created the physical world and it was good in itself, as well as pointing to the Creator. Again and again, Puritan writers repudiated centuries of 'sacred-secular' dichotomies in Christian theology. According to the Puritan William Perkins, the routine, practical tasks of daily life are the arena where we meet God. We can serve our Maker 'in any kind of calling, though it be but to sweep the house or keep sheep'.

For the English Puritans work, home, family and sex too, were all fully acts of worship to God, good in themselves and to be enjoyed with relish. The character of everyday Puritan life is described by the religious historian Philip Lee as a 'hearty earthiness'. So much so that a Roman Catholic critic, Thomas More (the famous Lord Chancellor to King Henry VIII), characterised the Protestantism of Tyndale (earliest of the Puritans) as the religion of people who 'eat fast and drink fast and lust fast in their lechery'. But for the Puritan there was no contradiction between 'spiritual' and 'material'. God was interested in every sphere of life, not just the 'religious' parts. This conclusion, that the Puritans provide a strong theological base for a positive assessment of not only the created world, but also the human body, sex and fashion, might be read with incredulity by many. The term 'puritan' is usually employed to refer to a revulsion of the body and a condemnation of fashion, style and ornament.

In reality, the English Puritans' high doctrine of creational goodness *did* lead to a celebration of dress. As a rule, they wore fine and elaborate clothes. Most of them dressed according to the fashions of their day. But, it will be countered, did they not go around wearing plain, black styles? They did, particularly on Sundays and special occasions. But their choice of sober cuts and the colour black for their best outfits was influenced by the leading edge of contemporary, secular styles.

European fashion from the late 15th century until well into the 16th century was dominated by the Italians, a style characterised by sumptuous silks and brocades (rich fabric woven with a raised design, often in gold or silver threads; from the Italian *broccato*, embossed fabric). The massive quantities of fabric used in dressmaking spoke of the wealth, luxury and privilege of the owner. The Italian style was complemented by a love of jewellery, embroidery and other decoration. However, around the middle of the 16th century, the cutting edge of fashion changed from Italy to Spain, and with it came a drastic change of mood.

The Spanish styles were rigidly stiffened, tight-fitting, and less ornate. The folds and creases in the fabric were removed, along with the flowing lines of the Italian styles. The watchword was stiffness, even to the extent of women's bodices being held in place by wooden boards, to heighten the impression of rigidity. Collars were high and stiff, and starched ruffs became popular. But, most importantly, the new 'in' colour was black, partly due to the preferences of the Emperor Charles V. Royalty and nobility across Europe, such as Henri II of France, took to wearing black with a vengeance. Even the flamboyant Henry VIII of England wore black in his later years. Under Mary Tudor, who married King Philip II of Spain in 1554, Spanish styles became all the rage, lasting well into the reign of her sister, Elizabeth I.

large white cufts

apron

'The Puritans' choice of sober cuts and the colour black for their best outfits was influenced by the leading edge of contemporary, secular styles' (p 58)

By the early 17th century, the fashion centre of Europe had shifted again, this time to Holland. The new Dutch styles kept the chic black of the Spanish, but their key note was greater relaxation. Out went much of the Spanish stiffness. In came greater simplicity, whilst at the same time keeping a distinct note of sober formality. The elaborate, flamboyant creations of former centuries (with their overtones of privilege and wastefulness) were out of fashion in the new, more egalitarian mood sweeping Europe, which was eventually to explode in the late 18th century, with France shaken by revolution.

The consequence was that the fashionable Dutch styles of the 17th century were predominantly black, formal and uncluttered in appearance, but more comfortable than the artificial rigidity of the earlier Spanish designs. Black, simple and plain, scrupulously clean and avoiding waste, the dress of a neat Dutch bourgeoisie. This was the height of European fashion which spread to Britain and was taken up by the English Puritans, partly because the Protestantism of the Dutch made their culture more acceptable as a role-model than that of Catholic Spain.

In this sense, the Puritans were ahead of their time. Their participation in the protest against aristocratic excess directly prefigured the simpler, starker styles in Europe which followed the French Revolution, including the immaculately clean, simple chic of English Regency dandies such as Beau Brummell, who changed his linen no less than three times every day.

One thing is beyond question. The Puritans were light years away from the asceticism of the Desert Fathers or the medieval monks. Far from rejecting style *per se*, the Puritans redefined it. While the Cavaliers looked to the aristocratic styles of France, the Puritans looked to the middle-class chic of the Dutch Calvinists. It was not a battle of style versus anti-style so much as upper-class style versus middle-class style.

It is all a matter of how we read the signs: why do we assume that James Dean or Jean-Paul Gaultier wear black out of a sense of style, but the Puritans wore black out of an absence of style?

After all, the Puritans not only believed in the goodness of creation, the body and sex: they believed that God gave his full endorsement to all of these. At the fashion shows in October 1993, Calvin Klein unveiled his 'New Puritan' look, its clean, straight lines and crisp blacks and whites prompting the *Independent*'s fashion critic to observe that 'the clothes of the prayer-meeting are on the streets'. The assumption was that Klein's sense of style comes from the ironic and self-conscious borrowing of old designs, from quaint and remote cultures, not in those old styles themselves.

When the new, sophisticated urbanite dons the garb of the Puritan it is considered chic. When the old, unsophisticated Puritan dresses like a Puritan it is considered an absence of chic. Why do we persist in viewing the Puritans as addicted to drabness? Perhaps we cannot believe that their choice of black was due to anything other than dour ill-humour or lack of imagination.

Again, the historical record indicates otherwise. We know for a fact that the Puritans had no aversion to strong colours. While black was the colour of their finest garb, the colour in which their portraits would have been painted and, hence, the image which remained most visible through subsequent history, most Puritans' daily dress was colourful. The most common hues were russet and shades of orange-brown, but inventories dating from the era show that wearing violets, yellows, greens and reds was quite normal. The American Puritan William Brewster is known to have worn coats of blue, violet and green. One historian of costume describes the regalism of the English Puritan General Harrison, in the House of Commons of 1650, as 'a scarlet cloak and coat both laden with gold and silver lace, and the coat so covered with cliquant (metal foil) that one scarcely could discern the ground'.

The English Puritan theologian John Owen is described by his biographer during his time as Vice-Chancellor of Oxford University (1652–1660) – a post given by Oliver Cromwell – in flamboyant terms: 'hair powdered, cambric band with large costly band strings, velvet jacket, breeches set about at the knees with ribbons pointed, and Spanish leather boots with cambric tops.'

Surely this ought to put in its place any nonsense about most Puritans being anti-body or anti-style. Here is a Calvinist Puritan, more extreme in some aspects of his Calvinism than Calvin himself, and a theologian to the top Puritan of them all – Oliver Cromwell. And he dressed like a fop. We have already noted how George Fox, founder of the Quakers and a contemporary of the Puritans, went so far as to denounce the Puritans for their 'ribbons and costly apparel'. Perhaps the pervasive image of the English Puritans as drab and unfashionable (in reality, their styles were in line with the latest trends across Europe), and with comical 'roundhead' hair-styles (in fact copied from the currently fashionable shorter styles of Holland) is due to the writing of history by the victors: in this case, the monarchists, who were hardly neutral in their assessment. Beware, we are victims of disinformation!

This is not to say the movement had no faults. As Leland Ryken points out in his reassessment of the Puritans, *Worldly Saints*, many of them were legalistic, verbose and partisan, with an inadequate view of recreation and often dismissive of the feelings of others. They did over-react to the excesses of their day which they found in the theatre and in the celebration of Christmas by banning both. And some, especially in New England and on the lunatic fringes of Puritanism, did lapse into a Gnostic-style suspicion of the physical body. But a condemnation of fine dress was never one of their failings. The verdict of C.S. Lewis remains a better epitaph than most presently on offer. He described the early Puritans as 'young, fierce, progressive intellectuals, very fashionable and up-to-date'.

Calvin and Calvin Klein may have been on the same side after all.

Conclusion

The Christian Church has frequently viewed culture through dualistic, bifocal spectacles, most centrally the dualism of body and soul. This profoundly colours how its exponents understand the message of the Bible, which is all too often seen as other-worldly, anti-culture and escapist. Such dualisms can only lead to a low view of human culture in general and of fashion in particular.

However, these dualisms are well overdue for reassessment. In the Jewish roots of Christianity, the Celts, sacramental Catholicism, Calvin and the Puritans (to mention just a few) we find the strongly pro-world, pro-body emphasis which will give us a firm foundation on which to build. The raising of the status of the temporal, the feminine, the physical, the transient and human culture in Christianity is long overdue. When performed, this forms our starting-point for exploring issues of clothing and style from a Christian perspective, stripped of unhealthy dualisms.

The bifocals need to be binned before we can start to see more clearly the way forward.

CHAPTER 3

NATURE AND CULTURE

'The youth of the present day are quite monstrous. They
have absolutely no respect for dyed hair.'

O. Wilde, 1892

Dressing up is a fundamentally artificial activity. This notion is
deeply rooted not only in the Christian mind, but also in
popular cliché. To be a 'wolf in sheep's clothing' is to wear a
disguise. It means being duplicitous, to have an external
persona at odds with a true, inner self. Behind such phrases lies
the assumption that nature, the 'true' self, is opposed to culture,
the 'false' self created by dress. Fashion is the art of telling lies.

The whole distinction has sometimes been put another way.
Christian moralists and others have frequently claimed that it
is acceptable to satisfy our basic 'needs', but frivolous 'wants'
are out. The true, authentic 'me' has genuine needs, say the
critics of style, and these include practical, functional clothing.
But fashion panders to the false 'me', the trivial, ostentatious
'me' who is duped by consumerism into a frantic attempt to use
my dress to impress.

In this chapter, we shall examine the history of this division
between 'natural' and 'artificial'. We shall start by showing how
widespread it has been among Christian and secular critics
alike, its claim to have a biblical basis, and its negative influence on the moral assessment of clothing. Then, in the second

half of the chapter, we shall argue that these very 'nature-culture', 'needs-wants', 'natural-artificial' categories are themselves deeply flawed and unbiblical, and that to do away with them removes another significant obstacle to giving the thumbs-up to fashion.

Nature Versus Culture

Behind much contemporary criticism of fashion is one big assumption, that the main purpose of clothing is practical and functional. People often assume that since dress clothes the body, it must be related mainly to biological needs: to give us warmth and protection from the elements. Thus, it is 'natural' to have solid, utilitarian clothing, but when this becomes 'style' for its own sake, this becomes morally questionable. It is strictly speaking 'unnecessary', an extra, a secondary stage beyond true needs. Sequins, silks and superfluous safety pins are to be shunned.

Nature Versus Culture: Christian Critics

In the battle between 'authentics' and 'artificials' in dress, Christians, especially those on the evangelical wing, have almost always sided with the 'authentics'. A 15th century poet and social commentator, Alexander Barclay, wrote of fashion as an unnatural imposition on God's handiwork. He addresses 'foolish men', telling them:

'(Ye) are not content
As God hath you made; his worke is despysed
Ye think you more crafty than God omnipotent
unstable is your mynde; that shewes by your garment.'

The flashier the dress, the further the fall from grace. In the mid-16th century, towards the end of Calvin's life, strict laws to regulate clothing ('sumptuary' legislation) were imposed on the people of Geneva by the pro-Calvinist city legislature, fearful of 'unnatural', worldly fashions. This included a ban on collars, embroidery, necklaces, silver chains and bracelets, as well as hair colouring. All styles held to be unnaturally showy were prohibited.

However, Calvin's sumptuary laws do need to be put in their historic context. It will not do, as some fashion historians do, to quote them as an example of how narrow the early Protestants were in their cultural outlook (and usually, by implication – how bigoted Christians are). The fact of the matter is that the Middle Ages had seen an unprecedented rise in sumptuary legislation right across Europe, reaching its height in the 16th century. Under England's Queen Elizabeth I, myriad laws were brought into force dictating the acceptable dress for all and sundry. An English law of July 1597 prohibits the wearing of purple silk to any below the rank of Earl or Knight of the Garter, and velvet to anybody of more humble estate than the wife of a knight, or the wife of a knight's eldest son. Another law, of 1582, prohibits apprentice-boys from wearing any hat other than a woollen cap. It further prohibits their wearing ruffs, cuffs, collars, silk and silver trimmings, and clothes of any fabric other than canvas, sack cloth, leather, wool and fustian (a blend of cotton and flax).

The goal of all such legislation was uniformly to keep the poor in their place. Stylish dress was to be reserved for the rich and noble alone, and harsh punishments were meted out to those deemed to be aping their superiors' dress, aspiring to a status higher than that 'given by God' at birth. For a peasant to wear the fine clothes of the nobility was not only considered heresy (denying one's God-given status), it was to disrupt the social order, and hence incur the penalty of the law of the land, which included public whipping.

Calvin's sumptuary laws exactly reversed these legally-safeguarded social hierarchies, which had been a weapon of the privileged since the early 14th century. In 16th century Geneva, none should dress to impress. None should flaunt an air of well-heeled nobility, as if they were a superior breed. We might with justification choose to condemn the Calvinists' zeal in banning silks, dyes and jewellery. But we must take into account that in an age where there was more sumptuary legislation than any other period in European history, at least Calvin's laws were ones which trampled archaic hierarchies, unlike the others,

which trampled the poor. In an age when fashion equalled privilege, there was at least something healthily egalitarian and dignifying to the common person about Calvin's sumptuary laws.
Unlike those of the surrounding nations, which legitimated
inequality.

There can be no doubt that the regular reminders in the histories of fashion that Calvin restricted stylish dress (when at the
same time the English government equally legislated dress
codes, to perpetuate the English caste system) owe more to anti-
evangelical bigotry than a dispassionate study of history. It
bears comparison with the oft-repeated (and true) assertion
that Calvin supported the execution of the heretic Servetus,
when his contemporary Thomas More (today universally
regarded as a saint of the first order) persecuted those who dis-
agreed with him with more vigour than Calvin. And we have
already seen how an anti-adornment stance is not a necessary
implication of the theology of Calvin, who had a high view of
the beauty of the created order, explicitly stating that sensuality is good in itself, a gift of a God who has 'given us many
things which we ought to hold in esteem without their being
necessary to us'.

Still, the fact remains that in Calvin's own day, and among
later representatives of the Calvinist tradition, curbs have been
placed on clothing which is other than plain and functional.
The laws of Calvin's Geneva have contributed to an assumption
(both inside the church and outside it) that the dress of the
Christian can only be stark and simple.

Likewise, the founding of the Quakers in the mid-17th
century was accompanied by a commitment to plain dress,
although here too a note of historical caution must be sounded.
Even in 18th century Quaker Philadelphia, plain did not equal
cheap or dowdy. Quaker businessmen may have worn 'simple'
styles of coat, but these were carefully designed by skilled
tailors, using the very best fabrics.

With the rapid spread of Evangelicalism in 18th century
Britain, utilitarian dress and conservative theology became even
more closely linked. Methodists, like Quakers, were firm

believers in bodily cleanliness and neatness of dress, but their enthusiasm for the body did not stretch to fine clothing. Early Methodists were mostly from the poorer classes and so elaborate dress would hardly have been an option. But converts from the aristocratic classes too were exhorted to follow the lead of John Wesley, who stated in his *Journal* that he only bought the most lasting and plainest clothing.

John's father, Samuel Wesley, had supplemented his meagre clergy salary in Epworth, Lincolnshire, by writing verse and essays. In one of his best known pieces, *An Epistle to a Friend Concerning Poetry* (1700), he stated that in literature,

> 'Style is the dress of thought; a modest dress,
> Neat, but not gaudy, will true critics please.'

His son took the same principles and applied them literally to style in clothing. Cleanliness and functional sobriety were paramount.

Today, too, 'gaudy' dress is frequently seized on by preachers and authors anxious to denounce what they see as the frivolous spirit of the age. Some go further, claiming that stylish clothing embodies a spirit of anti-Christ, or at least hostility to principles of wholesome living.

In contemporary Christian writing, this suspicion has found new support from the revival in environmental and social concern. The call for Christians to adopt a simple lifestyle appears in a range of contemporary Christian writers such as Richard Foster, a Quaker and best known as author of *Celebration of Discipline*. In this work, the first of his 'Ten Controlling Principles' of the disciplined life is to 'buy things for their usefulness rather than their status'. And in another work, *Money, Sex and Power*, true to his Quaker roots, he explicitly states that no Christian can participate in the commerce of 'things frivolous':

Fads will come and go; there is no need for the follower of Christ to participate . . . We value people more than ostentatious clothes and gaudy homes. So long as the gospel needs to be preached, so long as children need to be fed, Christians cannot afford to have any part with the 'Vanity Fairs' of this world (pp. 67, 68).

In Section 5 of the influential *Lausanne Covenant on Simple Lifestyle* of 1974, Ronald Sider and other evangelical thinkers state their resolve to renounce waste and extravagance in clothing, based on a distinction between necessities and luxuries.

Sider uses needs-versus-wants as a framework in his own *Rich Christians in an Age of Hunger*, and this idea of basic human 'needs' is unquestioned in much of the current wave of Christian 'green' literature, such as Catherine Von Ruhland's *Going Green*:

> God does not want us to be over-concerned about something as fleeting as fashion; there is no need to worry about what we are going to wear. They are not as important as the fashion industry likes to suppose (p 52).

Such writers rightly want to stress the positives of not living wastefully, and of showing compassion for the planet and its poor. These are vital truths, as we shall see in Chapter 9. The problem is that these authors then go on to imply that all fine or stylish clothing is by definition wrong. In a range of contemporary Christian writers, bodily adornment is at best unhelpful; at worst it embodies hostility towards the compassionate lifestyle.

Nature Versus Culture: Biblical Evidence

A text constantly cited by these authors is the 'lilies of the field'. The conclusion is drawn that Christ himself supports only functional dress:

> I tell you, do not worry about your life, what you will eat; or about your body, what you will wear. Life is more than food, and the body more than clothes. . . . Consider how the lilies grow. They do not labour or spin. Yet I tell you, not even Solomon in all his splendour was dressed like one of these. . . . For the pagan world runs after all such things, and your Father knows that you need them (Lk 12; 22,23, 27, 30; cf Matt 6:25–34).

The passage appears to base its argument on the concept of 'need' and condemn any preoccupation with ornamental dress as the lifestyle of unbelievers. Another biblical theme used in polemic against 'worldly' style is the 'image of God' (see Gen 1:26,27). If humans bear the image of the Creator somewhere in their deepest being, in their 'true self', then to be preoccupied with the superficiality of artificial adornment is to neglect the image. It is to replace the image of God with an image from the fashion glossies. These passages will be reassessed below.

Nature Versus Culture: Secular Critics

It is not only Christians who have operated with a nature-culture distinction. In doing so, they have simply reflected a wider cultural mood in society as a whole. The rise of the 18th century Enlightenment in particular saw the popularising of the nature-culture polarity. It became the major pair of 'spectacles' through which people viewed the whole of human activity, including fashion. The French writer Rousseau and the subsequent Romantic movement did much to elevate 'the natural' over 'the artificial' and advocate a return to nature, hence all the wandering through leafy glades and contemplating daffodils. The Romantic legacy exercised a profound influence over 19th- and 20th-century cultural attitudes. In 1814 a certain C.H. Smith was writing about the history of clothing. Imposing his day's cultural categories on pre-Enlightenment garb, he commends Anglo-Saxon dress for its 'native simplicity', and for not being subject to a 'restless desire for variety'. Such a verdict tells us more about the aesthetic judgements of Smith's own day than the dress of Anglo-Saxon Britain.

In the 1880s a Dr Gustav Jaegar of the University of Stuttgart became a household name across Europe for his theory that humans should wear 'natural' wool next to the skin, since animal fibres alone could prevent the body's retention of 'noxious exhalations'. Dress reformers from the mid-19th century onwards reacted against what they saw as the artificiality of women's clothing. Largely influenced by the plain dress of the Quakers, dress reform began in American Christian communities and early feminist groups. Elizabeth Cady Stanton, feminist and author of *The Woman's Bible* (1895) popularised the wearing of 'bloomer' trousers under a wide tunic. In 1880 the Rational Dress Society was formed, with the aim of eliminating all artificiality in dress; and the British artistic movement known as the Pre-Raphaelite Brotherhood developed a 'natural' style of women's dress based on their understanding of the simplicity of medieval clothing, banning the use of artificial dyes. The Pre-Raphaelites were direct ancestors of today's boom in 'natural' products.

The rise of Marxist cultural criticism in the early 20th century offered a new impetus to the condemnation of fashion. Marxist writers, such as those in the 'Frankfurt School' of thinkers, claim that capitalism has produced a uniform, mass culture of trashy goods which threatens 'authentic' individuality. True selfhood is invaded by plastic pseudo-selves, real needs blurred by the creation of false consumer needs. Other left-wing groups have been similarly suspicious of consumer style. The Chancellor in Britain's 1945–1950 Labour government, Sir Stafford Cripps, stated that he wished that people's desire for fashionable clothes and jewellery could be eliminated altogether.

A similar suspicion of fashion exists in some strands of feminism. A writer to *The Guardian* complained: 'I can't be the only woman who reaches for the first T-shirt and skirt or trousers that come to hand . . . adding a jumper (knitted by Mum from an age-old pattern) when it looks chilly. . . . I have absolutely no idea what is going on in the distant, nonsensical world of fashion.' Such sentiments would be echoed by many Christians. But many feminists add the complaint that the whole fashion project is exploitative of women, imposing man-made definitions instead of 'authentic' self-understanding.

For many today, influenced by Christian, Marxist, Socialist, Green or feminist thinking, to participate in style or fashion is to take a conscious step into the realm of the unnatural, the artificial, the externally imposed confines of false consciousness. For many Christians, this is all made much worse by the 'unnatural' way they believe dress is used to blur 'natural' gender distinctions, an issue we shall return to in Chapter 4. For all these critics, fashion is just *not natural*.

But the question has to be asked: is this 'natural-unnatural' polarity the most helpful way to analyse fashion? Is it even accurate? Because if not, a central argument used against style in dress by Christian and other critics, especially over the past 200 years, is shown to be flimsy.

We shall argue that what was already a questionable distinction, with little biblical support, has been undermined completely by certain changes in modern society.

Identity in Today's World

We begin by looking at the ways people go about forming a sense of their own identity, in particular the ways in which the culture we live in profoundly shapes the way we view ourselves.

Shaping My Identity

Western culture since World War II has seen a decisive shift in the popular understanding of personal identity. Since around the 16th century, identity had been considered a given, the product of upbringing, neighbourhood, education. It was related to one's social status and profession, both of which an individual was likely to keep for a lifetime. Clothing, made in one's own home, was used to express your place in society, a stable, unchanging self. It was not until the 20th century that clothing was generally bought, as opposed to being home-made. Traditional identity was fixed, and communicated through dress.

But now all that is history. Today's identity is more likely to be seen as actively-formed, fluid, open to being shaped and changing. Economic changes helped bring about the shift.

Before the war, most disposable income belonged to the over-20s. However, the post-War years saw the rise of the spending power of the 'teenager'. Previously, most adolescents had left school early and entered the adult job market. Teenagers were not viewed as a distinctive group in their own right. This was changed by delayed entry into the job market through longer education, and increased spending power. In the immediate post-War years, the spending power of the large, unmarried group between the ages of fifteen and twenty-one increased at twice the adult rate. Adolescence became a time of economic emancipation for a group with few dependents and (most crucially) for a group desperately in search of personal identity.

There was also new-found free time and consequent boredom. One response which emerged to this boredom and the teenage quest for identity was subcultural style. Fashion elements in themselves meaningless (hair length, shoe shape, brand of jeans) became carriers of an extraordinary range of subtle messages. If the skinhead would wear his trouser-bottoms turned up with neat, split-millimetre precision, the mid-70s Northern Soul boy might have flares of up to 40 inches, whereas the zoot suit wearers of early 1940s America had trousers some 30 inches round the knee, but tapering rapidly to just 12 inches round the ankle.

But the new messages conveyed by such dress, unlike those in earlier periods, were not about fixed class and status. From the early 1950s onwards, clothes became about choosing a sense of who you really are – whether as a ted, mod, goth, punk, skinhead, new romantic, hippy – or, as today, an eclectic combination of a number of such styles. Or else a chosen conventionality of appearance expressed a deliberate rejection of the aberrations of subcultural style.

After the war, purchasing became a means of establishing identity, off-the-peg personae for those desperate for both a sense of who they are and for peer-group affirmation. During the 60s a range of specialist 'boutiques' was pioneered by the likes of Mary Quant and Barbara Hulanicki (of Biba), where young sales assistants sold rapidly-changing fashions to teenagers against a backdrop of loud music and experimental lighting. The new boutiques were a statement of rebellion and difference, sharply differentiated from adult chain stores whose more conventional designs communicated middle-class respectability and 'normality'. London's Carnaby Street became the swinging world centre of rebellious youth style.

Another factor which contributed to the shift from people seeing identity as a fixed 'given' to a more fluid or malleable commodity is the character of today's urban life. The modern city-dweller sees more people in an average day's shopping than most medieval peasants might have seen in a lifetime. Urban life is fast and anonymous, and it is impossible to communicate anything meaningful to the hundreds of people with whom one has the ultimately superficial relationship of a glance. But communication may be made at the level of image. A personally-chosen identity may be spoken through clothing.

If economic and social factors produced a ready market for subcultural style, changes in methods of production and retailing were able to supply the goods. It is important not to neglect the importance of what *can* be done in shaping what *is* done. Until the 20th century, most fashion had only been for the wealthy and aristocratic. This century (in particular after the war) the shift downmarket was dramatic.

The ground had been prepared in the previous two centuries: the rise of the UK textile industry in the 18th century and the invention of the sewing machine in the mid-19th, enabled the changes in the mid-20th century to occur. But it was such factors as post-war techniques of mass production, the rise of the low-brow department store (previously they had retained an air of exclusivity and snobbishness), and the rise in disposable income for working women, which meant that affordable, off-the-peg styles became available to almost anybody. For the first time, expressing identity through clothing purchases became a possibility.

What technology made possible was then made desirable by the popular media. Throughout the 20th century, the images popularised in magazines and the Hollywood movie industry have had an enormous impact in teaching people how to dress, stand, walk and talk, drink and hold a cigarette, in shaping what is widely considered stylish, fashionable and desirable. For the first time, people could choose who they wanted to be: Garbo, Taylor, Monroe; Dean, Brando or Wayne. The fashion industry, like the American dream, is based on the premise: I can be anybody I choose. Today's consumer of off-the-peg styles is like the early American settlers. He sees in clothing his own America, a death to the burden of past identity, and a promise of a future self with new, unlimited potential.

Newspapers have also unwittingly helped disseminate each new style as it arrived, by the sensationalised manner in which each has been reported. The most common news-angle in popular journalism is conflict. Consequently, each trend has been 'slammed', 'hit out at', 'condemned' and 'blasted' by a range of reactionary interviewees sought out by a journalist in search of headline aggro. One group who are usually a reliable source of moral outrage are the clergy. There can scarcely be a trend, from teds onwards (no! Make that the 14th century onwards), which has not been denounced by somebody in a collar or cassock. The mass media have simply made such reactions available to a wider public. The style duly receives all the more publicity and draws more adherents from a fascinated wider public.

The arrival of 'psychographics' in advertising from the late 60s onwards hastened the shift from identity as given to identity as chosen. Until this period, the main method of market segmentation (dividing up consumers into separate, targetable categories) had been demographics. This categorised consumers by age, income, education, occupation and ethnic background. In the 50s and early 60s the method had succeeded. However, American marketers increasingly saw demographics failing to reach the growing 'Woodstock' counter-culture, which rejected the conspicuous hedonism of its parents' generation. Enter psychographics, the point where advertising meets psychology in an attempt to reach this growing and disillusioned sector. A new concept was introduced: that of personal 'lifestyle' as a critical variable. The self-concepts and aspirations of the potential consumer were seen to be crucial to purchasing decisions.

New categories for targeting consumers were introduced, such as VALS (Values and Lifestyles), resulting in a method which was essentially reactive (it identified existing lifestyle patterns), but which then became proactive. As lifestyle groups or subcultures were identified and reflected in advertising images, outsiders were initiated by these same images into the styles of the groups. It became possible to buy into a lifestyle image. Psychographic advertising reflects subcultural fragmentation, but it also affirms and hardens this very process. One consequence of all this is that the concept of 'lifestyle' is increasingly replacing old social boundaries (age, class, gender, locality) to create a 'sociology of aspiration' (the phrase of sociologist Dick Hebdidge). Life is there to be shaped and styled. Identity can be chosen off-the-peg and ready-to-wear.

Subcultural Identity Today

Today, western (sub-) urban society is tribal. Our culture is no longer monolithic. It no longer makes a great deal of sense to speak of 'English culture', because this is itself composed of a mass of diverse subcultures, each with its own fashions, music and magazines. This subcultural fragmentation is no longer the youth phenomenon it might once have been. The teenagers of the 1950s and 60s are the parents and grandparents of today. The passage of time has rendered the 'generation gap' caused by the bewildered reactions of 50s and 60s parents to the new (and at the time rebellious) subcultures largely obsolete. The custom-designed lifestyle is no longer the province of youth.

As I look out of my front window onto a suburban street in west London I see identically-shell-suited-families. I see leather-and-denim metalheads aged from fifteen to sixty. I see Sloane Square-ites in striped blouses and pearls aged from two to eighty. Today the generation gap is dead, replaced by a bewildering range of subcultural groupings sending out messages of identity to anyone who will hear, the heraldry of the pavement. The custom-designed lifestyle is no longer the province of youth. In the words of style critic Robert Elms, nobody is a 'teenager' any more, because everybody is.

Identity is a game where the rules have been replaced by choices. I can be anybody I choose to be. Out of the window go notions of an unchanging 'essence' of personal identity. Rather, today's identity is a malleable commodity, an aesthetic product to be shaped through lifestyle purchasing. Even if this is not done by buying into one particular subculture, it is likely to involve raiding several of the subcultures of the past and present, to construct a self from the fragments. Since the mid-1980s, the creation of street style has increasingly meant a browsing in the museum of tribal styles and mixing and matching one's own look. It is as if all the permutations of hair, dress and bodily piercing have been tried, and today's fashion is essentially retrospective, an art of quotation. Some, such as the modern-day punk, only quote from a single textbook. Others, more eclectic, display a full dictionary of quotations, creatively juxtaposing old and new, conventional and outrageous. We at the end of the 20th century are witnessing what the London style critic and fashion historian Ted Polhemus terms the 'supermarket of style'.

Either way, the motto of contemporary style is the same: I shop therefore I am. Here is the crux of the issue. Today, purchasing fashion is not generally considered a secondary, 'artificial' stage which overlays a natural, pure self. Rather, it is essential to the very creation of personal identity.

As we shall see in Chapter 6, this cannot be the final word on the matter for the Christian. Style can never be a substitute for identity. Nevertheless, we shall argue that the Christian is as free as anybody to use style to express and shape an identity securely rooted in God. And today's Christian has to live in and relate to a culture of 'off-the-peg' identities. Retreat to the mindset of an earlier generation, for whom identity was an uncomplicated 'given', is simply not an option.

'Nature-Against-Culture' Under Attack

We have noted that society has shifted. It is a simple matter of fact that for most people in today's society, there is no unchanging 'authentic self' which is clothed as a secondary, separable act. Clothing creates identity as much as reflecting it. At this point the reaction of many Christians is wholly negative: they write off modern culture. Yet another contemporary decline from the true, Christian stances of the past, they claim.

But are they right to see the old way as the better way? Irrespective of which direction society is moving, was the old nature-against-culture distinction helpful? Was it even true? Was it at all Christian? There are good reasons for saying that this particular set of opposites, so prevalent since at least the 18th century, actually never was particularly true, helpful, nor Christian. If we are right to claim this (and we shall look more closely at the case for it) this has important implications for the moral assessment of style from a Christian perspective.

For one, talk of meeting basic 'needs' over against the 'artifice' or 'luxuries' of culture is a historical fad, only becoming widespread in the West over the past 200 years. The sociologist Tony Walter, in his book, *All You Love is Need*, explodes the myth of nature-versus-culture, needs-versus-wants. In it, he states that the distinction is historically recent and geographically limited:

> Factually, it is hardly correct to say that people have always been pre-occupied with their needs. There is evidence that 'unsophisticated' tribes are usually very concerned with religion and ritual, with community and family life; for these are what enable them to make sense of what appear to us as prior states of need such as hunger and sickness. (p8)

Our culture, over the relatively recent past, has tended to assume that 'needs' are unchanging and definable because they are based on biological functions. This is open to question on several counts.

Firstly, clothing has never been primarily functional. There is a great mass of anthropological data to show that aesthetics is more ancient than wearing clothes at all. In some cultures, tattooing and painting the body appear to have existed before dressing it.

The anti-'wants' stance also ignores anything which does not have an obviously biological function. Out of the window go music, literature, art, faith and love. All the things, in fact, which make us most human. A functional view of clothing cannot be kept in isolation from the rest of our approach to life. To condemn ornament and design as frivolous is to inhabit a drab, sad little world of grey uniformity. And the crowning irony is that many of the poorest people of the world are those who most value ornament, beauty and celebration. An encounter with the bright, vibrant fabrics, the fabulous jewellery and the strong heritage of dance and ritual in traditional Africa leaves one in little doubt whether it is African culture or ours which is the more impoverished. Or try telling a proud Asian father who has saved up for a lifetime for his daughter's dowry, and wishes to see her (if only for one day) as a princess, that he is wrong. That clothes should be only for keeping the wearer dry and warm, and that he is wasting money which can be better spent on his 'real' needs.

Furthermore, the boundary between what is culturally deemed 'natural' or 'artificial' is wholly arbitrary. The Body Shop sells 'natural' products, but the very concept of packaged toiletries is itself 'unnatural'. Rastafarians wear their hair in 'natural' dreadlocks, while Presbyterian ministers tend to have a 'natural' short-back-and-sides. It is patently false to play off culture against nature. All human culture is 'artificial' in that it is the product of human artifice or creativity. Plain dress is equally the product of design, technology and marketing as 'fashionable clothing'. Anyway, what is this 'pure', 'natural' self which is pitted against culture? Surely, it is already in great measure the product of genes, environment, education, peer pressure and parental influence.

To speak in such earthy, culture-bound terms is not to leave God out of the picture, to deny that we are each created by God and fully known by him as unique, distinct persons. It is simply to acknowledge that the main ways in which God makes us who we are is through being in a family, a culture and so on. The autonomous individual, standing aside from all cultural influences, pure, natural and unsullied by the oddities of any given culture, able to view all cultures objectively – is a myth of the fevered, misanthropic brain of Jean-Jacques Rousseau, the French founder of Romanticism and author of the tellingly-titled, *Rêveries of the Solitary Walker*. The anti-culture, anti-people dreams of Rousseau, who is said to have given up his own children to an orphanage, are hardly to be held up as a blueprint for a healthy society. The isolated individual has never existed and never could.

There is another dimension to the problem. The criticism of stylish dress for being 'artificial' is challenged by the shifts in society outlined earlier. Today, there is no escape from the use of personal expressive style, no possibility of retreat to 'nature' from the artificiality of 'culture'. All clothing communicates identity. As the fashion writer Elizabeth Wilson notes, in her book *Adorned in Dreams*, 'Even the determinedly unfashionable wear clothes that manifestly represent a reaction to what is in fashion. To be unfashionable is not to escape the whole discourse or to get outside the parameters' (p5). Today, every attempt to defy the system is itself a statement of style, an attempt to express the wearer's own conception of 'normality' as opposed to 'deviance'.

Even the bowler-hatted London city gent, the 'young fogey' and the 'sloane ranger' today know they are dressing up. Gone are any past notions that the wearers are simply dressing 'normally'. With all the style self-consciousness of a punk's mohican haircut or teddy-boy's Edwardian revival jacket, the bowler hat is donned and the rolled black umbrella wielded as tribal insignia, badges of identity for a watching world. Different 'looks' now have names, their components studied and codified by everybody from one's friends to style magazines and university lecturers in popular culture. They have been identified and labelled in a way they never were previously. Elizabeth Wilson tells of a relative who confided to her: 'I'm afraid I'm wearing my sloane ranger outfit today!' Such style self-consciousness is a characteristic of life in the late 20th century. It is inescapable, part of the very air we breathe.

This has implications for the Christian's faith in a nature-culture distinction. To today's mind, the wearing of functional dress is not a rejection of the artificiality of fashion (such distinctions are invalid), but a chosen cultural conservatism. The church warden in sensible brown shoes, who questions the new youth group member's preference for rainbow-painted Doc Marten boots, might think he is alerting her to the trivialities of modern consumerism; that she need not be a victim of fads. But that is emphatically not how it is heard. A message is given that to convert to Christianity will involve adopting the conservative cultural stances of the church warden.

It is not a battle of 'natural' dress as opposed to 'artificial' dress. It is the battle of conservative culture as opposed to more radical culture. The pastor who questions a punk's clothing as 'artificial' means well. He is affirming his faith in the reality of an authentic, God-given self underneath the trappings of subcultural style. However, for the punk, such criticism is heard as a full rejection of her chosen identity, of all that she is. The result is that an expression of concern is heard as the very opposite, that God himself is a cultural conservative, that God might wear sensible shoes and a tie-pin.

Perhaps the key concept at stake is not so much 'nature' as time. Dress history is a constant battle against new styles, deemed 'immoral' until their novelty wears off with the passing of time. What is felt by conservative Christian critics to be a rejection of the artificial or hyped may in reality be a preference for styles a decade out of date. It is an expression of a purely cultural conservatism, a desire to wait until the novelty value of the item has worn off so that the wearer no longer stands out. The central, defining instinct of a conservative person is personal security. One may have an item of clothing as long as most other people have it, as long as it has been rendered 'normal' by the passing of time.

It is perhaps worth pre-empting some objections to this criticism of the nature-culture polarisation. Firstly, it might be objected that the freedom to create an identity from cultural bits and pieces such as clothing is actually an illusion; that while we may believe ourselves free, in reality advertisers and producers are pulling the strings.

There is some truth in this: our choices are drastically limited by whatever is available. But the argument shares the weakness of the Marxist approach: it is elitist and idealistic. The person advancing such an argument is claiming that he is an enlightened arbiter of taste, surveying culture 'from above', denying

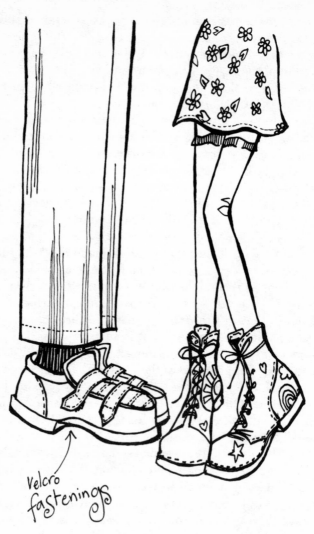

Velcro
fastenings

'The church warden in sensible brown shoes, who questions the new
youth group member's preference for rainbow-painted Doc Marten
boots, might think he is alerting her to the trivialities of modern
consumerism. But that is emphatically not how it is heard. A
message is given that to convert to Christianity will involve adopting
the conservative cultural stances of the church warden.' (p 80–81)

the validity of popular culture because it celebrates the disposable, standardised and marketed. But is this valid? Surely not. We all stand 'below' a culture, and can only use the cultural tools to hand. The argument assumes a naive, idealised view of human independence, as if people in any age have ever shaped their own identities without reference to their surrounding culture.

In which society has there been a single person who has not created a personal identity out of elements created by others, or aside from choices constructed for him? To suggest otherwise is to fall for another, purely cultural, seduction: the myth of the enlightened, autonomous individual, who uses calculating reason to weigh up all alternatives objectively. Such objectivity is illusory. The conversation of a man who can only speak in clichés may lack creativity, but it is not thereby made meaningless or inauthentic. A girl may choose a 'get-well' card from a range of 10 on display, or from a range of 300. But in either case she will use the card to communicate authentic sentiment. My choice of clothing is not made freely, but is dependent on external pressures. This is simply to say that I am a normal human being. I make my choices from whatever options are to hand. That is to say I am a normal creative human being.

There is another response to the charge that fashion, like other aspects of popular culture, is imposed, limited and, ultimately, false. It underestimates the playful, subversive character of today's style. A monolithic view of fashion as a narrow range of externally-dictated designs does not do justice to the lived experience of personal style, in which minor changes to dress codes and hair styles may be loaded with meaningful communication. The experience of wearing school uniform is not one of sameness. Imposed norms are constantly subverted by the angle of a tie, the bagginess of a cardigan, whether hands are pulled up inside sleeves or stick out, the cut of a shoe. No two punks or goths are ever exactly alike: minor changes and additions customise and individualise the common theme. Two punks will look no more alike than two middle-aged women in headscarves; probably less so. Identity is always playfully communicated by acts of sartorial subversion, whatever the broad parameters within which it is done.

Another argument against style is that fluency of communication in dress is only for those who can afford it. However, this claim usually proves to be exaggerated. The days are gone when styles were centrally dictated from Paris, a whole wardrobe of costly fashions had to be abandoned to keep up with the latest look, and any change in hem-line was front-page news. Styles today are more likely to be 'bottom up' than 'top down'. Styles such as hippy, punk and grunge may have been adopted by the fashion houses, but they began as street style. This is an issue we shall discuss at greater length in Chapter 5. But one thing is certain. Today, style is more likely to be about creating a personalised identity from diverse fragments: Oxfam jumper, sale shoes, cheap jewellery, than a conscious emulation of the wealthy and aristocratic. Indeed, to dress 'conventionally' may well cost more than to dress 'stylishly', and there is no guarantee that the quality of the goods will be any better.

The creation of vibrant, unconventional street styles, which demand more ingenuity than cash, is one of the areas in which Britain leads the world. International designers flock to the capital to seek out youthful, innovative inspiration for their collections. Quite why this should have become the case is hard to explain. It is perhaps due in part to the country's rich postwar art-college tradition, the earlier urbanization of Britain than most other countries in the modern era, the fact that the mainstream styles in Britain's high streets have had considerably less verve, colour and panache than their equivalents in France, Italy, Germany, Australia or the USA. So street style in the UK has been in part an act of desperation. It has also been, of course, a product of British eccentricity. David Bowie, Sid Vicious and Boy George are from the same stable as the Beefeater, Sherlock Holmes and Alice in Wonderland.

It was good to see such creative, 'bottom-up' style celebrated at London's Victoria and Albert Museum over the winter of 1994–1995, in a major retrospective on street fashions. In a V&A lecture to coincide with the exhibition Catherine

McDermott, lecturer at England's Kingston University, described the punk style as 'arguably Britain's biggest contribution to postwar culture.' In terms of its influence on the direction of popular culture worldwide, she may well be right.

It remains unlikely, however, that retired colonels in Esher or pastors in Eastbourne will ever see Johnny Rotten's dress sense as one of those things which has made Britain great.

Christianity Against 'Nature-Versus-Culture'

The attempt to view the world through the bifocal lenses of nature and culture is rightly under attack in our culture. However, there are strong reasons why Christians should also reject the validity of such bifocal distinctions.

The Idolatry of 'Self'

For a start, there are good reasons to see the categories of need and nature or wants and culture as an unchristian product of the Enlightenment era. A comparison with a more biblical perspective will highlight the difference. To the Hebrew mind, the concept of 'need' as understood today would have been alien, as Tony Walter points out:

> Things which we see as basic needs – food, health, life itself – were not seen as needs which people struggled to provide, but as blessings from a divine Creator. Rather than striving to meet our inborn lacks and needs, there is a vision in the Old Testament of a people and a land richly endowed by God. (*All You Love is Need*, p12).

In contrast to the biblical understanding of humanity's natural state of blessing and abundance, the 18th century developed the notion of human need as central. The 18th century Scottish philosopher Hume was searching for an objective basis for morality, a solid, universal answer to the problems of ethics which was valid for all times and all places, without reference to God. He believed that in the concept of 'need' he had found it. If one 'needs' to do something, then it should be done. Need appears to provide an objective view of myself. If I need to act in a certain way, then all debate over personal preference or desires is over. It just has to be done.

This human-centred version of morality was adopted by many of the early socialists, who set out to define basic needs, over against the 'false' needs or mere wants imposed by consumer capitalism. The language of need has appeared (falsely) to provide a totally naturalistic basis for morality, a version of ethics which can leave God out of the picture. Tony Walter goes as far as to claim that need is the 'religion of the religionless' (p125), and he claims that a key spokesman for the Christian left, Ronald Sider, falls into the simple trap of dismissing socially constructed and artificial needs such as those created by advertising, and counterposing them against supposedly objective and real needs which should direct our action. He shows little awareness that all needs are socially constructed (p162).

The widespread acceptance of need as a basis for morality amongst Christians actually comes close to idolatry. It looks worryingly like the decision of Adam and Eve that they themselves were the centre of their own universe. It accepts the Enlightenment's all-important self as the centre of all reality, that mythical being who can stand aside from her culture, upbringing and education, able to make detached, rational and objective moral choices. These are made on the basis that biological needs always come first. The mere 'wants' of personal choice, culture and art, are always secondary.

This is surely unrecognisable as the way any culture actually lives. The 'needs and wants' brigade who talk about meeting only needs and ignoring wants make the strange error of confusing the most basic preconditions of life with the whole of life, as if every floor of the house had to be a ground floor, every book a child's ABC, all ladders one-rung ladders. If, as we shall go on to argue, our being made in the image of God means we rule over the earth for him and use our creativity to explore the latent potential in creation, to say we deal with wants and not needs is disobedience. It is apostasy, a renunciation of our main God-given task on earth.

The acceptance of need as the basis of morality is a deliberate humanistic attempt to transfer to humanity what is by right God's alone. But only God should be at the centre of everything, not me. I might have a 'true self', but even so, this is limited, dependent, bound to a particular culture, a particular age, a particular upbringing. And that is all right. It is precisely in the middle of our limited and culturally-bound lives that God meets us. What matters is not what my autonomous mind tells me I need, but what God freely gives me.

We can proceed in one of two ways. Either we should abandon the common needs-wants distinction, based as it is on a biological reductionism, as unhelpful. Or else we should redefine our concept of human need so drastically that it includes hitherto excluded categories, such as love, art, friendship, creativity, the grace of God and even fashion.

Biblical Material Reassessed

Just how does the Bible view clothing? If centuries of Christian commentators and countless finger-wagging Christian moralists today are to be believed, we could be forgiven for assuming the Scriptures start by seeing dress as a symbol of guilt and shame, a reminder of our lost innocence, and culminates in Jesus railing against 'those of little faith' who are concerned with their wardrobes. But such a picture would be profoundly misleading.

We have come to a crucial part of our study: an examination of the symbol of clothing in the Bible. Far from being a mere protection against the cold or defence of modesty, clothing (fine clothing especially) is presented in such overwhelmingly positive terms that it even becomes a central metaphor for salvation and the human condition. If any reader has an aversion to passages peppered with biblical quotations, I would invite them to try not to let their eyes glaze over or skip to the next part in desperation! What follows is central to our case for a biblical, pro-style Christianity. The biblical references are offered for those who would like to follow them up.

We start not with ourselves, but with God. Throughout the Bible clothing is a metaphor for somebody's character and status. By looking at the clothing you discover something true about the person. This is even true of the Creator.

The Psalms make explicit what is implicit all through Scripture: that God 'clothes' himself in his creation: 'O LORD my God, you are very great; you are clothed with splendour and majesty./He wraps himself in light as with a garment' (Ps 104:1,2). 'He made darkness his covering, his canopy around him – the dark rain clouds of the sky.' (Ps 18:11).

God in himself is invisible to the human eye, but that does not mean that he is remote and absent from his creation (that would be 'deism'). Nor is he identified with the creation (that would be 'pantheism'). He is separate from the world, but indwells it. The 'splendour and majesty' which clothe God in Psalm 104 (and others, such as Psalm 93:1), are the observable evidences of God's presence in creation. The image being used is that of royalty, dressed in finest robes. Like a monarch, God is robed in splendour, but God's robe is his creation, the natural world.

Unlike much popular religion today, the Bible never sees the world as running according to predetermined, impersonal 'laws of nature'. God is present in the skies, the wind, fire, and the storms. Creation is charged up with the 'glory of God' the visible majesty which radiates out from him. God's glory is his self-revelation to humanity through physical phenomena, what the Hebrew Old Testament calls the *shekinah*. Creation is not merely beautiful or functional, it is the visible evidence of God's glory, his clothing.

Not only is God described as being clothed in light and storm-clouds. The glory of God was also seen in the cloud which led the Israelites through the wilderness (Ex 16), and Moses saw God's glory as a cloud and fire (Ex 24:15–18). Ezekiel saw God's glory in the form of a 'rainbow in the clouds on a rainy day' and as brilliant light (Ezek 1:28). God's visible glory in the form of fire was particularly associated with the hour of sacrifice in the tabernacle (Lev 9:24), and in the Temple, as a cloud (1 Kings 8:10, 11). As Moses discovered, the sight of God unveiled would be too overwhelming for human eyes, so

Moses sees his glory pass by (Ex 33:18–23). Isaiah too is given a vision of God, but it is as if his eyes are unable to rest on the majesty of God himself. His gaze does not rise higher than the train of God's robe (a symbol of his glory) filling the temple. The seraphs who address Isaiah remind him that this same glory fills the whole earth (Is 6:3).

Lest there remain any doubt at all that every molecule of the created order is charged up with the glory of God, because it is an extension of God, the Creator himself states it explicitly. As he speaks to Moses, he swears a solemn oath by the two most secure truths in all creation: 'as surely as I live and as surely as the glory of the LORD fills the whole earth . . .' (Num 14:21). The whole of the physical creation radiates it. The glory is always there, shining out for those sensitive to see it, people such as the Psalmist, who is constantly tripping over bits of this glory, and is so alive to its reality on earth that he sees the whole creation as alive, vibrant and responding to God (Ps 98; 148).

We too are touching glory daily, did we but know it. Calvin is right: the earth really is a theatre of glory. Some (the Psalmist, Isaiah, Calvin, the Celtic saints and the poet Gerard Manley Hopkins) have seen the glory. However, Habakkuk and Isaiah foresee a day when not just a few discerning individuals, but the whole earth will be filled with the knowledge of this glory (Hab 2:14; Is 40:5). The glory is never lacking, but our ability to see it frequently is. From the earliest days, our minds are trained in reductionist ideologies which tell us that nature is nothing more than the product of impersonal 'laws of nature'. Habakkuk reminds us that the glory, which is now real, but missing for those who refuse to look, will one day be overwhelming.

The symbol of God's glory as clothing reaches a climax in the New Testament. At Jesus' birth, the glory of God shines around the shepherds as a dazzling light (Lk 2:9), and it is welcomed by Simeon, who praises God that in Christ, God's glory has become visible in Israel once again (Lk 2:29–32). John underlines the point: Jesus is the visible embodiment of divine glory (Jn 1:14), and John constantly refers to Christ in terms of visible light. Jesus is the glory of God, the eternal Word clothed in flesh, visible to the human eye. In the words of the writer to the Hebrews: 'The Son is the radiance of God's glory and the exact representation of his being.' (Heb 1:3).

What has all this to do with human clothing? A great deal, because humans were created to reflect God's glory on the earth. We were crowned with the glory of God at our creation (Heb 2:7, quoting Ps 8). We were to be the chief visible pointer in all creation to the character of God himself, the one part of creation made in his image. The human body was to be the primary bearer of the glory of God in the world. The naked bodies of Adam and Eve radiated a reflected glory, a glory which was creative, sexual and purposeful.

But the choice in Eden to go our own way, and not God's, immediately meant that instead of being crowned with glory, we turned our backs on this glory and fell short of it (Rom 3:23). The result was a travesty. What is left when the thing designed to be the reflector of the glory of God no longer reflects that glory? What is left when the surface of the mirror loses its capacity to reflect? As Adam and Eve looked at their naked bodies, what they saw was not the shining out of God's own being, but something with the reflected glory removed. Something frail, limited, mortal. Their physical nakedness now represents their spiritual barrenness. Fired by their desire to usurp the role of God as provider of all they require, and perhaps also by some dim instinct that clothing brings dignity, they attempt to stitch together fig leaves to restore the lost glory, unaided. All to no avail as the glory had departed.

What is God's response to this? Rather than leave them naked and alone, he robes them for office. Although they no longer radiate his glory, they are still to be his deputies on earth. The tunics God makes become for Adam and Eve the remaining symbol of the glory which had been their covering. Their clothing now has a twofold purpose. It is a reminder of the glory with which they had been crowned. Their clothing is the symbol of status and honour. It is also a promise or foretaste of God's plan that one day humanity will be fully reclothed to reflect his own glory.

Clothing remains a constant and pervasive symbol in Scripture of dignity and authority. As we noted in the last chapter, dress is used to elevate a person above others, as a sign of blessing and honour on those who are counted worthy of such honouring, and as a robing for high office. Thus, the metaphor of clothing in the Bible, far from implying a 'cover-up' or falseness, always points to the truth about a person. It is a way of showing to the world what somebody really is.

So it is that Isaiah can call on God and say, 'Awake, awake! Clothe yourself with strength, O arm of the LORD' (Is 51:9). The prophet is not demanding that God pull on something alien or unfamiliar. Quite the opposite, he is asking God to be himself, and to show his true colours to the watching world. The point cannot be emphasised too strongly: the Bible's use of clothing (both actual and metaphorical) is always to do with showing somebody's true state, manifesting their true character.

This is why, throughout Scripture, individuals and groups who lose their liberty or dignity also symbolically lose their capacity for being 'robed' in clothes. Such types include slaves, prostitutes, the psychologically disturbed and demoniacs.

A potent symbol of slavery, captivity or defeat is the removal of a full set of clothes. Amos prophesies a coming day of judgement on Israel: 'Even the bravest warriors will flee naked on that day' (Amos 2:16), and Isaiah prophesies against Egypt and Cush that 'the king of Assyria will lead away stripped and barefoot the Egyptian captives and Cushite exiles, young and old, with buttocks bared – to Egypt's shame' (Is 20:4). The evil king Hanun of the Ammonites shames a delegation of David's men by cutting off their garments (2 Sam 10:1–4), while David's own cutting of the edge of Saul's robe symbolises a removal of kingly authority. Peter in prison loses his clothes (Acts 12:8), whilst the angel who rescues him brings them back.

Similarly, the prostitute is one whose personal dignity is no longer protected from public gaze. Babylon's 'prostitution' in Isaiah 47 is seen in terms of the removal of a veil, lifting up her skirts and baring her legs; and Israel's own infidelity to God is seen in terms of removal of clothes for adultery

(Ezek 16:36, 39). On the other hand, one of the most moving passages describing God's mercy is expressed in terms of dressing in fine, rich clothing:

> I clothed you with an embroidered dress and put leather sandals on you. I dressed you in fine linen and covered you with costly garments. I adorned you with jewellery: I put bracelets on your arms and a necklace around your neck, and I put a ring on your nose, ear-rings on your ears and a beautiful crown on your head. So you were adorned with gold and silver; your clothes were of fine linen and costly fabric and embroidered cloth (Ezek 16:10–13).

Let it be shouted out from the pulpits of the land: a sign of God's blessing in Ezekiel is the wearing of stylish clothes and a nose-ring!

Nakedness can also be a symbol of madness or the presence of demons. The insanity of King Nebuchadnezzar is symbolised by the removal of his splendid royal garb, and its replacement by the uncovered, wild appearance of an animal (Dan 4:32, 33, 36; 5:20, 21). Hardly some idealised, back-to-nature idyll here! Nebuchadnezzar's descent into uncovered bestiality (a sign of degradation) is discussed in the same breath as the elevation of Daniel by means of purple and gold robes, a sign of honour (Dan 5:16, 29).

The possessed man in Mark chapter 5 rushes about wild and naked amongst the tombs. But after his healing, his appearance is summarised in the beautiful phrase, 'dressed and in his right mind' (Mk 5:15).

The standard sign of grief in the Bible is tearing one's clothing, a symbolic rending of order and harmony. And the sign of true penitence is wearing sackcloth (1 Chron 21:16). It is true that nakedness can be used in prophecy or worship (Isaiah strips off to make a point, and David dances before God practically in the altogether). But the general point remains true, that nakedness is only good if accompanied by a prophetic word of God or in extreme and unusual circumstances.

The truth that fine dress equals dignity and blessing could hardly be expressed more directly than in Zechariah's vision of Joshua the high priest:

Now Joshua was dressed in filthy clothes as he stood before the angel. The angel said to those who were standing before him, 'Take off his filthy clothes.' Then he said to Joshua, 'See, I have taken away your sin, and I will put rich garments on you.' Then I said, 'Put a clean turban on his head.' So they put a clean turban on his head and clothed him, while the angel of the LORD stood by (Zech 3:3–5).

The first thing the father in Jesus' parable does at the return of his lost son is to dress him once again, to restore his true status: his former office of sonship and dignity: 'But the father said to his servants, "Quick! Bring the best robe and put it on him. Put a ring on his finger and sandals on his feet . . ." .' (Lk 15:22)

The son in the story ran away from home to chase the luxuries of life: fine clothing, jewellery, parties and drink. How ironic that on his shamefaced return home, these are the very things with which he is abundantly showered by his father – for free. It is not stretching the point of the parable too far to draw a parallel for today. Clearly, the father in the story represents God. So many people have felt that they had to leave their church and Christian faith to pursue a 'worldly' interest or career in fashion, whereas in reality there never was a conflict. The very things they left to find were on offer all along in the father's house, as free gifts for his beloved children, even if other relatives in the house can only stand by miserably, begrudging the father his colourful, extravagant generosity.

We could give more examples of the same fundamental point. Clothing, according to Scripture, is God's sign of dignity, honour and blessing on those who image him on earth. It acts as the human being's robe of office, a sign to the world of humanity's true status in relation to both God and the created order.

Here, perhaps, is a biblical response to the naturist (including the small number of sincere Christian naturist groups, such as the British-based NuNature) who insist that nakedness is a more wholesome ideal than dress. Modern naturism arose in the 19th century, along with other outdoor, health-conscious movements such as scouting and rambling. It was the product not of perverts, but Rousseauesque idealists such as George

Bernard Shaw, longing for a return to the simple life. They viewed dress as an artificial intrusion upon raw, unadorned nature.

However, from a biblical perspective, this understanding is misleading. Not because the naked body is sinful and evil. Of course not, the body is the pinnacle of God's good creation. Naturism is misguided not because the body is bad, but because clothes are good. It claims to want to return to a pre-Fall world, as if the fact that Adam and Eve's naked bodies were crowned with the glory of God meant they would never wear clothes. There is no indication that this is true. On the contrary, 'robing' is the biblical symbol of induction to high office, the evidence to the rest of creation that humanity is something special. God robes the couple because they are his managers of the earth, not merely as a shifty second best to replace the glory.

Where glory again becomes present in humanity after the Fall, it always co-exists with clothing: Jesus was the glory of God, but wore clothes, both before death and after, in his resurrected state. Life in the present kingdom of God and in the glorious age to come both involve clothes. When Saul in desperation seeks out a vision of the godly prophet Samuel, who has recently died and God uncharacteristically allows a conversation with the dead, (something condemned in Scripture see Lev 19:31, Deut 18:9–14), Samuel is wearing his prophetic robe (1 Sam 28:14). We assume that what Saul sees is Samuel in whatever 'intermediate state' the dead wait for God's final day of resurrection.

John's stunning vision of the future, glorified Jesus on the Island of Patmos sees him wearing a robe and gold sash (Rev 1:13), and an unidentified, Christ-like man in Daniel's vision (Dan 10:5) is dressed in linen, with a belt of finest gold. Even the two heavenly beings at the tomb of Jesus were dressed 'in clothes that gleamed like lightning' (Lk 24:4).

Naturism reverses biblical priorities by belittling human culture, dress and adornment (things which the Scriptures celebrate with vigour) and wrongly claiming that clothes are somehow artificial or unnatural, when the biblical use of clothing is always as a window into truth. The nudist owes this not to the Bible, but to 'back-to-nature' trends of secular thought in the era in which the movement was founded.

We have already noted that in some cultures, body-painting and tattooing have existed prior to clothing, and some have seen this 'nakedness' as a back-to-nature, unclothed idyll. However, the very existence of body-paint and tattoos points to an important truth: the universality of a sense of being 'naked' as opposed to 'covered' or 'adorned', which the Judaeo-Christian story can trace back to God's clothing of Adam and Eve. Of course, the ways this distinction is expressed will vary. In traditional Australian Aboriginal culture, for a woman to be properly dressed might mean wearing only a thin belt and necklace. In traditional Tahitian society no clothes were worn, but people felt naked if their bodies were not tattooed. In Islamic countries and in Victorian England it has involved leaving virtually no part of the body visible at all. We cannot be too rigid in our definition of what counts as 'clothed', since the specific outworking of the general principle will vary enormously from culture to culture. For this reason, we include jewellery and bodily decoration when we refer to 'clothing' as a universal, ennobling gift of God. The fundamental fact is this: all human beings (uniquely among creatures on earth) modify their appearance; all human cultures have a distinction between 'dress' and 'undress', although how this distinction is applied in a particular climate, culture, world view and so on will vary. Anthropology supports the biblical view of bodily adornment as the main visual component which marks out humanity as unique in creation.

Clothes are good. God says so. They have a vital, ennobling function for human beings this side of the Fall. But the Bible does not lose sight of the original intentions for humankind, the original promise of reflected glory. Chapter 60 of Isaiah presents a dynamic vision of the end times, a day when the whole earth is transformed by God. Significantly, it starts with a vision of the glory of God, his 'clothing', spread across creation:

'Arise, shine, for your light has come, and the glory of the LORD rises upon you' (Is 60:1).

Central New Testament images of salvation are expressed in terms of clothing. If Adam and Eve 'undressed' themselves of glory, Paul uses the language of clothing to declare that the way is now open for believers to be dressed again. The glory-image which was defaced in Adam and Eve is restored through Christ: 'You are all sons of God through faith in Christ Jesus, for all of you who were baptised into Christ have clothed yourselves with Christ' (Gal 3:27). They have 'put on the new self' (Eph 4:24). However, as believers, we still live in the time of tension between the 'already' and the 'not yet'. We already have the blessings of clothing-as-robing which followed the Fall; we have also 'clothed ourselves' in Christ, and tasted of the glory which was to have been our destiny, and one day will be. The church exists to reflect the glory of God as revealed in Christ, and to encourage the world to acknowledge it. And yet we still live this side of the final consummation of all things, that great day when God's glory will radiate all through the whole of creation with overwhelming brightness and clarity, in a city decked out in the most costly and elaborate style of all, as a bride (Rev 21:2). Our present 'clothing' is at best a real but incomplete foreshadowing of the stunning outfit which is to come.

Imaging God

Despite the wealth of evidence that clothing in the Bible is wholly positive, ennobling, and a sign of blessing, some Christians claim that the concept of the 'image of God' militates against the wearing of fine clothing. A contemporary author on spirituality, Philip Sheldrake, claims that the image of God lies in 'our deepest self', and that 'the movement inwards is where the essential self, or "image of God" within, may be encountered' (*Befriending Our Desires*, p17). In this he represents an emphasis common to much Christian devotional writing: that it is as we journey deeper than the superficial that we begin to encounter our 'true' selves, the image of God in us.

If the image of God is indeed treasure buried somewhere deep within, requiring some strenuous digging to uncover it, then clearly a preoccupation with the surface adornments of clothing is at best an irrelevance, at worst a hindrance in the life of faith. On this account, the lover of style is defiantly skating over the surface of life, dallying with the superficial, refusing to plumb the depths beneath.

The answer to this charge lies in a reassessment of where we locate this 'image' in the human person. A strong case can be made for locating the image of God not so much in some deep, hidden aspect of our inner being, as in the totality of who we *are* and what we *do*. The concept of the image of God is derived mainly from two practices in the ancient world. The first is the way coins functioned. Like the coins of modern Britain, ancient coins were imprinted with the image of the ruling monarch. The presence and authority of the ruler was represented by his stamped image on a common coinage throughout all provinces of his jurisdiction. Although the monarch could not be present in person, the coin-image could be, a constant reminder of his power. Even in Britain, images of the monarch cover the mail, as well as filling wallets: an ever-present reminder of the nation's constitutional monarchy.

Likewise, it was a practice of ancient kings to place an image or statue of themselves in provinces of the empire where they could not rule in person, a practice still carried out today in some parts of the globe. The image represented the ruler and his authority.

The profound statement of Genesis 1:26,27, that mankind is the image of God, is about something similar. Our function is to represent the presence of God in his world, to be the constant reminder of the reality of his rule, God's viceroy or ambassador on the earth, ruling where God is not himself visible to the naked eye.

In verse 28 of Genesis 1, God tells mankind to 'fill the earth and subdue it': to use our creative gifts to tend the world, to use its raw materials and to develop it. It is as if God has left us an unfinished globe, and the 'cultural mandate' of verse 28 tells us to carry on the creative work. We are the image of God, and the first thing the Bible tells us about God is that he is a creator. So it is precisely as we carry out our cultural tasks (including arts, sciences, fashion) that we fulfil our calling to be God's image on earth. We create, adorn and beautify because these are the activities of God himself.

So we cannot argue that we ought to avoid the artificiality of external fashion because it detracts from an inner, 'natural' image of God. It is precisely because we are made in his image that we must be dynamic, active and creative. We find the image of God in ourselves not by looking inwards, but outwards. Imaging God is not so much a state of being, as a task, which involves taking the raw materials of creation and fashioning them. The fashion designer, expressing artistic creativity by shaping materials, is closer to imaging God than the mystic who seeks to rise above the physical world as if it were a hindrance to his spirituality. Not only is fashion a valid calling for the Christian, it is hard to imagine a profession which is closer to the heart of God himself – the God who is the first designer and tailor, and who has delegated his work of creativity to people.

Reconsider the Lilies of the Field

Similarly, we noted earlier that Jesus' words on the lilies of the field (Lk 12:22–34) have been taken as a prohibition of adornment. But is this really what it means? In fact, the text implies exactly the opposite: a refutation of the purely functional approach. The analogy Jesus uses is a direct comparison between the way God clothes the flowers, and the way he clothes human beings. When Jesus refers to the 'lilies of the field', he was almost certainly pointing to wild flowers in general, rather than to a single species. If he were speaking in spring, he and his listeners could have looked down at the rich burst of wild, colourful flowers around their feet. Common flowers covering the Galilean hillsides at the time of Jesus included the poppy anemone, the crocus, the narcissus, the white daisy, the crown marguerite, and the yellow chrysanthemum.

Jesus takes it for granted that the way God clothes such flowers is in endless variety, rich colours and aesthetic patterns. To heighten the effect, he dramatically rises from the humble to the magnificent, drawing a parallel with the one figure in Jewish history whose name, more than any other, was a byword for wealth, luxury and colour: 'Yet I tell you, not even Solomon in all his splendour was dressed like one of these.' (Lk 12:27). The inference is inescapable. The same passage speaks of God knowing that we 'need' clothing, but it is scarcely the functionalism which has plagued Christian aesthetics. The 'need' in the passage is to be clothed in the rich, vivid variety of Solomon, more so, if that were possible: 'If that is how God clothes the grass of the field, which is here today, and tomorrow is thrown into the fire, how much more will he clothe you, O you of little faith!' (Lk 12:28)

We can go further, because Jesus' metaphor of flowers actually forbids us to apply a nature-culture distinction to clothing. There is no such thing as a 'pure', 'unadorned' flower which is then 'clothed' as a daisy or violet as a secondary act. A daisy is a daisy; its 'daisiness' is not a separable, artificial construct. In our study of the biblical metaphor of clothing, the point is reinforced that clothing is no 'merely' artificial, secondary act. If it were, then 'putting on Christ' would be something temporary and removable. In the words of media critic Marshall McLuhan, clothes are an extension of the body. The same point was discovered, to her delight, by the woman who touched the hem of Jesus' cloak and was healed (Mark 5:27–34).

The meaning of the lilies is to be found elsewhere. The principle Jesus is illustrating is that of trust versus anxiety. Those who do not know God are characterised by a fretful quest for even the most basic things of life. However, that is not to be the believer's attitude. The believer is to receive gratefully the abundant blessings of God (including vivid, celebratory clothing; God is no functionalist), and to focus energy on living a life fit for his celebratory kingdom.

I clearly remember sitting in a junior school assembly and being told by the headteacher about what he felt to be the best moral guideline for life. If we should ever be in any doubt about a course of action, he told us, we must ask ourselves one simple question: 'Would Jesus have done this?' Now, this was of some use when the dilemma, at the age of ten, was whether I should join the gang of boys who were to break into the vicar's garden and steal his apples. But applied to fashion, it raises more problems than it solves.

Would Jesus have bought Armani? Or dressed in a 1940s style zoot-suit? Or dyed his hair green? Clearly, the question has been rendered ludicrous by the cultural changes of two millennia. But this is not the only obstacle to using Jesus as some kind of role model in decisions about style. Our mental images of Jesus are profoundly shaped by the churches we have sat in, and sermons we have heard. The character so often called to mind is a drab, other-worldly Jesus, as preached by drab, culturally illiterate preachers. Of course such a Jesus would hate adornment.

But will the real Jesus please stand up? A fresh consideration of the lilies reveals a very different Jesus indeed, as does a survey of the kind of clothes that Jesus and his contemporaries would have worn.

Dress in Bible Times

How did the biblical emphasis on fine, creative clothing as a material blessing from God (and a metaphor for his other blessings) work itself out in the life of Israel? Wasn't biblical clothing plain, simple, unadorned, even a little dull? Far from it. The styles of dress covered by the 2,000 or so years of biblical history changed little, from the times of the Patriarchs to the New Testament churches, but styles remained mostly bright, vivid and often patterned. Over the loincloth, both men and women wore a (usually sleeveless) tunic of wool or linen, calf-length for men, ankle-length for women. This was frequently red, yellow, black or striped, often blue for females. The woman's tunic was usually embroidered in the traditional patterns of the village or region. Over the tunic, out of doors, men wore a light coat which was almost always patterned with

stripes or checks. Even the thick woollen overcoat worn as protection against the cold was usually striped. Weaving was a
skilled art in Israel, usually with dyed wool. And clothing was
frequently edged with fringes and tassels.

It is hard to imagine an understanding of clothing in the
ancient world which is less functional, plain and unadorned.
The people of God had very good reasons for not blending in
with nature or dressing with sober restraint. Clothing was the
major marker of humankind as rulers over creation. Humans
were not just another part of the created order, they had to be
marked out from the chaotic indistinction of nature.

Others might try to fit in with nature. The Egyptians might
wear dazzling white linen to appear clothed in the brightness of
Ra, the sun. (A fresco from the tomb of Khnumhotep III,
around 1890 BC, contrasts the plain white of the Egyptian's
dress with the multi-coloured, patterned clothes of Palestinian
labourers.) The Greeks might wear robes with many rippling
folds to reflect the waters from which they believed all life and
the heavens arose. The medieval monk might wear a functional
brown habit; and today's environmentalist, a 'natural', undyed
Aran sweater.

But the calling of the people of God was to be distinct from
nature, to be robed as princes and empresses, as befits the vice-
regents over creation. Creative use of colour, pattern and
adornment were not negative, or even neutral. Fine clothes
were, firstly, a badge of office for humankind; and secondly,
proof that humans were made in the image of a creative God.
There must be no hint that God's people were either blending
in with nature, or else trying to idealise and worship nature, as
did the Canaanites and other surrounding peoples. This, then,
is the authentic Judaeo-Christian verdict on clothes: they are
not primarily functional, either to do with protection against
the cold or modesty; they are to be dignifying and celebratory,
good in themselves and in what they represent, and the more
creative and colourful the better.

We have noted how Christians have historically sided with
'authentics' against the 'artificials' in dress. But this preference

has been a culturally-conditioned opinion, influenced by fashions in secular thought, particularly the relatively modern fad of opposing artificial against natural and needs against wants. The biblical material does not give warrant for such a boundary. In fact, it implies that we should be better off abandoning such unhelpful categories. We could go further. There is a strong case for the Christian to side with the French poet and art critic Charles Baudelaire who, in the 1840s, propagated the creed that (if we insist on keeping the distinction) the 'artificial' is actually a higher spiritual ideal than 'the natural'.

How ironic that so many drab, tut-tutting Christians refer the debate over fashion to Paul's great injunction that believers should not be conformed to the pattern of this world (Rom 12:2). They themselves are guilty of swallowing a sub-Christian world view whole, and they themselves are meekly conformed to a worldly image, only theirs is provided either by 18th century Romanticism, or else by Marks & Spencer.

Perhaps making a bee-line for the safe and predictable on a shopping trip is the kind of temptation the Christian should be praying against. The lure of the beige must be resisted at all cost. And when, as we rise, the voice of the tempter tells us that wearing socks under our sandals really is an acceptable option, we must not allow ourselves to give in to such apostasy. A trip for a pair of new trousers should be an adventure: an exploration of texture, colour, cut. Any pair of trousers which does not speak to us of the wonders of creation is to be shunned. A shirt which does not excite by its colour or its crispness is not a shirt worthy of the kingdom of God.

And if we do try to do away with the distinctions of artificial against natural, needs against wants, where does that get us? What would be the implications of doing this for the church and its mission today?

Conclusion: Incarnational Mission

Much of this chapter has focused around the analysis of modern western culture as being made up of tribal subcultures, each with their own styles, or else a post-modern eclecticism which raids and recycles past styles into an individual, creative 'look'. We have concluded that over recent years it has been those outside the churches who have tended to be more faithful to the cultural mandate of the Bible to be creative. Many church-goers have renounced this calling wholesale.

If there is any truth in the analysis of our culture as being comprised of creative, tribal subcultures, it ought to ring alarm bells for Christians. It is the same situation encountered by a previous generation of Christians as they embarked on foreign, cross-cultural mission. And, it appears, Christians are falling into the same trap which the earlier missionaries sometimes fell into, that of cultural imperialism, the insistence on one's own culture as distinctively Christian, as well as the content of the gospel proclamation you are offering. We have been offering not just our doctrine of unmerited grace, but our own undeveloped taste.

Pete Ward, youth adviser to the Archbishop of Canterbury, takes the same principle of cultural sensitivity in his book, *Youth Culture and the Gospel*, and applies it to the moral assessment of styles in today's youth subcultures: 'When we disapprove of a certain kind of music . . . or make a joke about a curious hair style, we are rejecting the young people's culture in much the same way as the missionaries were rejecting their converts' African culture' (p28).

The same lessons have to be relearned in a new generation: that effective mission is incarnational and costly. In the words of the Christian cultural commentator, Graham Cray, 'You've got to make the choice to cross that bridge to be part of that culture. . . . But you don't cross the bridge for a night a week and nip back into your old, comfy culture for the rest of the time. . . . You get to the point where crossing back is impossible for you.'

The approach outlined by Ward and Cray is precisely the opposite of that adopted by most churches, which assume that 'we' are natural, style-free, neutral, not obsessed with the 'artificialities' of the latest fashions, and that on conversion 'outsiders' will become like us. I clearly remember a conversation with one young Christian couple. They sat opposite me: she in striped blouse with the collar turned up, pearls, and navy blue hair-band; he in khaki pleated trousers, tie, brogues and tweed jacket, each the living embodiment of one of today's British sub-cultures. And they dared to criticise the 'artificiality' of today's youth sub-cultures as sub-Christian! They simply could not grasp that they were using one particular form of fashion in exactly the same way as a punk, no more, no less: as a badge of identity. They could only see it in terms of their own 'normality' and the punk's 'deviance'. So much for Ezekiel's reference to nose-rings as a blessing from God.

Closer to the mark was Robert Sweet, drummer of the Christian heavy-metal band, Stryper. As I interviewed him for a magazine feature, he sat opposite me in tight jeans, snakeskin boots and black eyeliner. But he denied that he was in any way simply aping worldly, sub-Christian styles. He was dressing like anybody else in the sub-culture in which he felt at home:

> In one sense, the evangelist who wears a suit and drives a Cadillac is aping the world too. It's the same suit the gangster from the mafia wears, the same Cadillac the atheist drives down the street. You see, most people take their own personal opinion about what is sin with regard to looks, clothing or hairstyles. Then they go and find something in the Bible and they pull it out of context to fit what they want to say.

The church has to recognise that all groups in society use artifice to communicate identity, and the best witness will emerge from a rejection of the nature-culture boundary, in favour of sub-cultural, incarnational mission. Pioneering churches achieving this include Holy Trinity, Brompton, just down the road from Harrods department store (upper and upper-middle class professionals), Willow Creek near Chicago (young adult, educated), the Late Late Service in Glasgow (young adult, urban, dance culture), and the Sanctuary churches across America (heavy metal sub-culture).

This is not to accept uncritically and wholesale the 'homogeneous unit' theory of church growth, which prescribes that worship and outreach occur best within one particular subculture. But it does demand that churches concede the following. We need to admit that most of our congregations are themselves *de facto* homogeneous units (of cultural conservatives at home in conservative dress), in which outsiders from other identity-groups feel culturally alien. We need to admit that homogeneous sub-cultural units are a given in today's society, so that cross-cultural mission is the dominant Christian agenda for Britain today. At the very least we need to accept that others' chosen styles are no more 'artificial' or 'unnatural' than those worn by conventional churchgoers. Let us have more nose-rings in church, please, not fewer. Style in today's world is an essential component in sensitive and relevant mission.

CHAPTER 4

BOYS AND GIRLS

'They're the prettiest girls I've seen all year.'
A Christian on seeing an album cover featuring the all-male Christian heavy metal band, Stryper

Male and Female: Blurring Boundaries

In many ways this chapter is a post-script to Chapter 3, in that it also refers to the tendency to pit what is supposedly 'natural' against the 'unnatural'. This time, however, we are looking not so much at the broader issues, but focusing in on one particular example: gender boundaries. The ways we show through our dress whether we are male or female. A major fear amongst Christian and other critics has been that the fashion industry frequently and gratuitously flouts such boundaries, that it participates in and encourages the general trend towards blurring boundaries, towards rejecting the natural 'givens' of our shared Christian past.

Blurring Boundaries: Christian Critics

For many conservative Christians the underlining of gender barriers has been a primary moral issue in the assessment of clothing. For a Northern Irish Free Presbyterian minister, Timothy Nelson (author of a leaflet on Christian dress) it is the central issue. In his leaflet, printed for limited circulation, he

106

cites with approval the argument of Matthew Henry (of biblical commentary fame) from the dictates of 'nature': 'Nature
itself teaches that a difference be made between the sexes . . . in
their clothes, which ought not to be confounded, either in ordinary wear or occasionally' (p3).

Among certain evangelical groups this principle has been
uncompromisingly applied. The 5,000 students at Bob Jones
University in South Carolina are governed by strict sumptuary
legislation and rules on bodily appearance. It is a home for the
terminally square. Women may only wear long skirts or pina-
fore dresses, and never trousers – to do so would be considered
immodest and an unnatural blurring of gender boundaries. One
former student was banned from returning to the campus when
officials heard she had been seen wearing trousers. Likewise,
men wear smart trousers (needless to say, no jeans), with their
hair cut in short back-and-sides, ears always visible.

Similar dress codes apply to many other Christian denomina-
tions among the estimated 30,000 currently in the world today,
notably at the evangelical end of the spectrum. Dress is a key
boundary marker, sometimes between the believer and the
outside world, more frequently as a mark of gender separation.
The head-scarves worn by women in some sections of the
Brethren movement fulfil both functions. The same is true in
many fringe Christian and cult groups, notably the Mormons,
whose ultra-conventional, gender-differentiated appearance is
their most obvious characteristic to outsiders.

Gender Blurring: Biblical Texts

Proof texts for being square and stereotyped are taken from the
Deuteronomic Law and Paul's letters. Most frequently cited is
Deuteronomy 22:5: 'A woman must not wear men's clothing,
nor a man wear women's clothing, for the Lord your God
detests anyone who does this.' This is taken as a plain statement
that any hint of what the critic believes to be gender blurring is
anathema to God.

Secondly, the argument over length of hair as a component of
personal style is often referred to Paul's statement: 'Does not

the very nature of things tell you that if a man has long hair, it is a disgrace to him . . .?' (1 Cor 11:14) Here, Paul appears to give full endorsement to the conservative Christian's own natural and unnatural bifocal classification to justify the need for men to have short hair. So Nelson can observe in his unpublished pamphlet that 'today there are many hairstyles which do not glorify God and are of the world'. A hairstyle which does not glorify God. Now there is a thought.

'Natural' Gender: A Historical Perspective

The wider, non-church culture, in which I and most readers are living is one in which grand, totalitarian statements about 'permanent' or 'unchanging' natures or essences are viewed with intense suspicion. Largely under the influence of feminist critics, this suspicion has been particularly marked in the debate over gender. Such critics rightly point out that contemporary perceptions of clothing as a primary marker of male and female are themselves culturally relative. It was not until as recently as the economic circumstances of the late-18th and 19th-centuries that gender started to become strikingly and unambiguously marked by dress.

It must be disconcerting for the conservative who insists on trousers for men and skirts for women to realise that Israel, along with most ancient cultures, had no such marker of gender. Men and women alike wore almost identical, sleeveless tunics, the only differences being that women's were slightly longer and tended to have more embroidery.

It is true that the major divide in clothing around the world has always been between 'draped' clothes on the one hand (such as skirts, togas, and tunics), and 'fitted' clothing on the other (such as trousers). But it is simply wrong to say that one is usually the dress of women, the other of men. That is an historical accident of the recent past. In the western world, for the whole of the lengthy period up to and including the Middle Ages, all poorer members of society (male and female alike) wore almost identical clothes, namely, long tunics which were simple, unadorned and loose-fitting. Social class tended to be marked by use of expensive dyes and different fabrics. But gender in dress was never a crucial issue, and for most people for most of human history, never has been.

From the mid-14th century onwards, in the higher reaches of society which had the luxury of experimenting with fashion, the sex of the wearer was gradually underlined more obviously. Women's dress became more restrictive and ornamental, involving tight bodices and long, hooped skirts. Men, on the other hand, wore tight 'hose' on their legs and items of dress, such as padded shoulders, which communicated mobility and dynamism. But even here, the differences were often less marked than the covers of sentimental novels and the costumiers for Hollywood epics would have us believe. Some 16th- and 17th-century styles were overtly androgynous. And for outdoor activities, such as sports and riding, women and men continued to dress alike.

Significantly, much fashionable clothing for both sexes remained almost identical. Until as recently as the late-18th century, the male city aristocrat wore the same embroidered silks, velvets braided with gold and hand-worked lace as his female counterpart. Both wore ruffs, bisexual curled wigs, and jewellery. The message conveyed was one of shared social status, not differentiated gender.

When change did come, from the late-18th century onwards, and the dress of the sexes became markedly different, it was in response to changing social conditions, and not due to any rediscovery of supposedly timeless truths. It was certainly not due to the sudden realisation that a male leg is more naturally at home in a trouser leg than a female one, or that the female waist is naturally more in need of being uncomfortably squeezed by her clothing.

In the late-18th century, city gentlemen began spending more and more time away from the city, at their country estates. This was partly for business reasons, but more importantly due to the growing influence of Romanticism, with its idealisation of nature, wildness and informality. The silks and lace of ornamental city life not only proved impractical for the great outdoors, they were considered symbols of an old, artificial existence. It was the era of the country gentleman: matter-of-fact, sober, masterful and businesslike. Not for him the bored ruffs, laces and affected mannerisms of *Les Liaisons Dangereuses*. Women, on the other hand, were slower to change. Changes there certainly were, but in the altering social scene, their roles were different: he out and about, off to the country estate, outdoors, doing; she, the mistress of the city house, indoors, being. His role became primarily functional, hers ornamental.

The shift towards a growing gender divide was accelerated by the early-19th century and the Industrial Revolution, which brought further change in social expectations placed upon the sexes.

Previously, most people had worked from home or close to home: on the land, in small-scale local enterprises. Suddenly a chasm began to open up between home and workplace. Men increasingly left home to go 'out' to work, often leaving the women indoors. The workers wore functional work dress, and the bosses practical, sober garments which would not hinder their mobility and which bespoke integrity and reliability. After all, who trusts a dandy and a fop in the real world of business?

Meanwhile, new expectations were placed on middle-class wives. Now, they were not to be out doing the manual labour which most women have always done, but to be a status symbol for their husbands. The successful gentleman's prosperity was reflected not in his own dress. This was impractical, due to working conditions and his desire to convey an image of sober industry and reliability. Instead, it was reflected in his wife's. The middle-class women of the 19th century marked a return in all but name to the aristocratic excess of pre-Reformation, pre-revolutionary Europe, with their lace, corsets and countless layers of skirts. One late-19th century survey of women's dress found that on average, indoor clothing alone weighed seventeen pounds, rising to thirty when outdoor clothes were added.

We are inheritors of the Industrial Revolution's legacy. From then onwards, it became 'natural' to see men dressed in sober, functional attire, and for women to indulge the luxury of aesthetic, non-functional 'fashion', which regularly changed due to boredom. This has held sway until extremely recently, with the youth styles of the 60s and 70s. But even then, 'real' men knew their place: in suit and tie, sensible cardigan, creased trousers. Even today, there is still no male equivalent of the vibrant, deep shades and textures on offer in women's clothing stores such as Monsoon. Deep down, we still believe that men should look more sober than women. The grey business suit, a weapon of drab conformity, has marked the widespread male renunication of *joie-de-vivre*, passion, spontaneity, colour, life itself. A friend of mine, now a senior figure in the Church of England, was once hauled up before the principal of his theological college for daring to wear bright red trousers.

But things are slowly changing. The aestheticisation of masculinity since the mid-1980s, has seen a gradual increase in the range of colours, styles and fragrances for men, not to mention the eroticisation of the uncovered male torso in advertising. The start of the shift can be dated fairly precisely to that day in March 1986 when the model Nick Kamen appeared on TV and billboards, removing his Levi's in the traditionally female preserve of a launderette, to the astonished and amused gaze of female onlookers. The rise of the male body and its coverings as potential art gallery is greeted by some Christian critics as a step into new, dangerous territory. When Jean-Paul Gaultier pioneered the male skirt (or should that be the non-tartan kilt?), and it became worn by males as diverse as London night-clubbers and Axl Rose, vocalist of rock group Guns'n'Roses, the sound of old Bob Jones turning in his grave was almost audible this side of the Atlantic. At the time of writing, the style appears unlikely to catch on in Brethren meeting houses.

But why is the aestheticisation of the male body viewed as new, dangerous territory? It is arguably a return to normal after the aberration of two centuries of artificially rigid gender stereotyping, a return to the days when if fashion, colour and style were an option at all, they were equally an option for both sexes. Masculinity today, unlike that of our Victorian fore-bears, is playful and malleable. Current statistics reveal that men now spend an average of twenty-three minutes a day on 'grooming', and the British industry in male beauty products stands at £469 million annually. Similar figures apply in North America and Australasia. Shocking? Trivial? Not really. Boys will be boys.

'Natural' Gender: A Christian Perspective

We have noted how a rigid separation of the sexes by means of dress was largely a creation of the Romantic and Industrial eras, and alien to the practice of Bible times. It is only to be expected that Christians who live in a culture which is heir to such attitudes might emphasise biblical passages which stress male and female appearance as polar opposites. Such separa-tion to them feels 'normal' because their culture has reinforced it all their lives. So what are we to make of a passage such as Deuteronomy 22:5, cited earlier? Surely here at least is a clear biblical principle for all time: that men and women should not wear clothes characteristic of the other sex?

Keeping the Law

However, the passage is more problematic than such a simplis-tic reading allows. It raises the whole issue of hermeneutics, or how we go about interpreting a biblical passage for today. It is just not possible to handle a verse or passage responsibly unless we take into account its literary and historical contexts.

The verse in question is one of over 600 commandments, spread across the books of Exodus, Leviticus, Numbers and Deuteronomy. These commandments were to be kept by the people of Israel in token of their loyalty to God. God had called and made a Covenant with Abraham, saying that he would make the old man's descendants into a great people, he would give them a land of their own, and a relationship of covenant blessing (Genesis chapters 12; 15; 18). If God's call and promise is one side of the Covenant, the other is that Israel will be

chimney pot hat

mutton chop whiskers

'*Masculinity today, unlike that of our Victorian forebears, is playful and malleable*' (p 112) faithful and obedient. This is to be evidenced by keeping God's laws. In other words, the Old Testament law, where the verse on cross-dressing is to be found, is given to a particular people at a particular time. This raises the crucial question of how such laws apply to us, if they do at all.

Old Testament law represented Israel's side of the Covenant, the Old Covenant (Covenant is another word for Testament) which is no longer binding on Christians. We now have access to God through a New Covenant made possible through the death of Christ, not by keeping Israel's side of the Old Covenant. So our basic assumption always has to be that specific laws are not applicable to us, unless there are good reasons for believing that we are dealing with a more universally valid moral absolute. Of course, God still wants a loyal, faithful people, and he still wants a people who take the ideal of a godly lifestyle seriously. But the ways in which that loyalty is lived out by individual believers, and by the Christian community, have changed.

A clear example of Old Testament laws which applied to Israel but not to us are sometimes known as 'badge' laws, because their purpose is to proclaim to the world the identity of Israel as the unique covenant people. Badge laws include ritual laws for animal sacrifice (God's chosen method under the Old Covenant for forgiving sins) and the civil laws for Israel, which specified penalties for crimes. These only applied to ancient Israel. Other badge laws include a mass of legislation which sounds bizarre to modern ears, but which had the express purpose of keeping the chosen people pure and uncontaminated by the beliefs and lifestyles of the surrounding nations.

One way in which the purity and faithfulness of Israel was to be maintained and symbolised was that all kinds of minor things in everyday Jewish life should be kept in order and not inappropriately mixed. Holiness was expressed through a recognition of God-given differences in the created order, in keeping things as God had first created them, just as Israel had to be kept separate. Thus, two different species of animals should not pull the same plough, and Deuteronomy 22:11

forbids the weaving together of different fabrics in the same garment. No polyester-cotton shirts if we woodenly apply that law to today, ignoring its original, intended context!

Much of the Law (functioning as 'badge laws') is not applicable to us today in any practical sense. However, there are sometimes good reasons to believe that the principles underlying some laws are of more universal application, and can operate as a moral guide for today's Christian. Major yardsticks which function as indicators of such ethical relevance are as follows.

Firstly, when there is a clear, common sense piece of social order or community morality which the law was designed to safeguard in its original context (the ban on sleeping with your mother-in-law, in Deuteronomy 27:23, seems a highly realistic bit of peace-keeping!). Secondly, certain moral laws and principles (as opposed to civil and ritual laws) are underlined elsewhere in the Old Testament itself as being more important than others. The Prophets constantly make a fundamental distinction between 'badge' laws and God's own moral priorities. Mercy is better than sacrifice (Hos 6:6), obedience is better than correct religious observance (1 Sam 15:22; Amos 5:21–27).

Thirdly, some aspects of Old Covenant law are explicitly renewed in the New Testament (such as in the teaching of Jesus), because the principles behind them are deemed of relevance to the Christian as much as to the Israelite. This is particularly true when the passage in question also involves a creational norm, something built into the structure of things at creation (such as human creativity and the complementarity of men and women – see Gen 1:26–28; 2:21–24).

So where does this leave Deuteronomy 22:5, which bans cross-dressing? It is clearly a 'badge' law, safeguarding the order of the community by preventing blurring and confusion of boundaries. Israelite dress is always to keep some element of gender-distinctiveness, for the same reason as their fabrics are not to be mixed: as an everyday symbol of the wider distinctiveness of the nation. But is it only a 'badge' law, or do any of our three pointers to wider relevance apply?

Firstly, there do seem to have been very practical principles underlying the Israelite ban on cross-dressing. One is the link with Canaanite cultic worship. There is historical evidence that cross-dressing was a practice in the worship of the Canaanite divinity Astarte. Another is that it may be addressed to women who wished to infiltrate areas of Israelite life which were at the time held to be a male prerogative because social order was at stake. Or again, cross-dressing may have been linked to particular homosexual practices in Israel.

Secondly, are there ethical principles underlined elsewhere in the Old Testament, such as by the Prophets? Certainly, there is material on the ethics of dress: not taking a person's clothing as payment of a debt lest they be left cold (Deut 24:12, 13, 17), the underlying moral principle being mercy. And there is condemnation of wearing fine clothing in a spirit of arrogance while deliberately treading down the poor (Is 3:16–26), the principle here being justice. Cross-dressing does not seem to figure high on the agenda: there are apparently more important issues on God's mind.

Thirdly, is the principle renewed in the New Testament? Certainly, the practical moral principles at work in addition to the law's function as a 'badge' of Israelite identity are reiterated. There is much material on worshipping the true God alone, and not being compromised with pagan forms of worship (1 Jn 5:21, 1 Cor 8). Paul also affirms the principle of order: that there may be times when contemporary custom prescribes different roles for men and women, and that for the sake of order and decency, Christians should defer, rather than stand on their rights (1 Cor 14:35). What about homosexual practice? The New Testament contains very few references to it, and none from the mouth of Jesus (a healthy corrective to today's lurid obsession with sex, and a likely indication that he was more concerned about issues such as pride and legalism, particular temptations of those who indulge in 'gay-bashing'). However, in the few references there are, there is an affirmation that heterosexual monogamy is the biblical pattern for sexual relationships, a reaffirmation of Genesis and the creational complementarity of men and women.

So where does that leave us? At most, we might carry over to today these principles behind the Deuteronomic ban on cross-dressing: namely, avoiding anti-Christian worship, upholding practices of good social order, and upholding the norm of monogamous heterosexuality.

We cannot even use the verse to condemn at a sweep Britain's estimated 300,000 men who cross-dress, since most of them are heterosexual and indulge their activities privately. Of course, such transvestism does raise searching moral and pastoral questions about wholeness of identity, reality and fantasy, and honesty with other people, such as one's wife. And serious questions must be raised about the practices of *travestis*, gay men who not only dress as women, but also undergo silicone implants and take hormones to bolster the illusion. The travesti culture is particularly prevalent in Brazil, perhaps due to the normalisation of sexually risqué activities and experimentation found in the country's carnival heritage. Many work as homosexual prostitutes. This practice of actually changing biological males into an illusion of femininity must surely be contrary to the creational complementarity of males and females. The attempt to create a 'third sex' is questionable, especially when the men involved are not among the small number around the world suffering from gender dysphoria.

Gender dysphoria ('dysphoria' being the opposite of 'euphoria') describes a genuine conviction by some people that they need medical help to change the appearance of their external sexual organs. They claim that they are in reality biologically of the opposite sex, but that their development in the womb went wrong, resulting in their being born with 'wrong' genitalia. From a Christian perspective, this ought not to be an unthinkable claim this side of the Fall, in a world where the original harmony of creation has broken down. And the story of the Ethiopian Eunuch (Acts 8:26–39; c.f. Is 56:3–5) certainly shows that the removal of genitals is no bar to being a believer. But, whether we are considering the transvestite, the travesti or the gender dysphoric, the wider point remains: we must handle Old Testament law responsibly, not piecemeal to bolster our own prejudices.

Certainly excluded from contemporary application are the majority of applications made by conservative Christians, such as women wearing trousers. Even if we hold to a principle of clear, unambiguous gender differentiation based on the complementarity of male and female in creation, this can only be applied within a particular culture. In some Arab countries, men have traditionally worn long tunics, while the women have worn 'bloomer'-style trousers. But nobody could claim that these men are therefore effeminate, and the women masculine. The principle of gender differentiation must be applied within a culture, not by an outsider looking in and applying alien criteria. Not even the most fundamental of the fundamentalists would wish to question Jesus's masculinity because he did not wear trousers. Indeed, as we noted earlier, Israelite culture (Old or New Testament) never had any of the clear gender markers in clothing which today's conservative insists upon. Clearly, the verdict on how to distinguish male from female must always be culturally appropriate.

If we were right to characterise contemporary western society as increasingly fragmented into 'tribes' and subcultures, the same principle must apply closer to home. It will not do for the outsider to appeal to Deuteronomy 22:5 to condemn the Mod girl's 'boyish' look, or the heavy metal boy's 'effeminate' look, since within the subculture, other meanings may be intended. Far from designating effeminacy, the long hair and tight trousers of the heavy metal guitarist are used to evoke a particular form of aggressive heterosexuality.

'Hairstyles which glorify God'

So much for Deuteronomy which, we have seen, yields far less ammunition than the advocates of highly conventional, gender-stereotyped dress would wish. The second passage cited earlier as a biblical warrant for applying a strict gender divide to personal adornment is 1 Corinthians 11:14: 'Does not the very nature of things teach you that if a man has long hair, it is a disgrace to him, but that if a woman has long hair, it is her glory?'

The verse is an important one. In it, Paul might appear to be a prototype Bob Jones, arguing not only for strict gender differentiation in hairstyles, but seemingly making out a case for this from 'nature'. In other words, he seems to be making a universal claim, not merely a local and provisional one. The case appears further strengthened with reference to the Greek understanding of the concept of 'nature' prevalent in Paul's own day. Under the influence of Stoic philosophy, many educated Greeks understood 'nature' in the same way as the Romantics of the 19th century, or the Green movement of our own day. The perfect state was to live 'according to nature', according to the natural, given order of things. And for the Stoics, one such natural 'given' was the distinction between male and female. For this group of Greeks at least, gender-bending was out.

It seems inconceivable that Paul, a highly-educated, Greek-speaking Jew, would not have known the Stoic overtones of 'nature' to his Greek-based readers: an idealisation of the 'natural' and a belittling of the 'artificial'. However, the issue at stake is whether Paul uses a Stoic term in a Stoic manner, or if he was using a common cultural vocabulary which he then filled with his own content and his own meaning. The commentator Gordon Fee, in his commentary on 1 Corinthians, opts for the latter. He notes that in the use of the concept of nature here, 'Paul makes no theological significance of the idea as one finds it in Stoicism. For him this is not an appeal to Nature, or to 'natural law', or to 'natural endowment'; nor is Nature to be understood as pedagogic' (p527). That is to say, Nature does not teach us what ought to be done.

So the content is not distinctively Stoic. But what about the context? This argues even more strongly against the Bob Jones approach. The whole sweep of thought leading up to the verse about hair length is about the issue of local propriety and custom. Between 1 Corinthians 10:23 and 11:1, the discussion is about respecting the customs and practices of others, and the

Christian responsibility to respect others' consciences. Paul's message, briefly, is that a believer should not cause unnecessary offence in a situation where common practice is different from that which he might personally observe.

The debate about hair length is likewise about not causing unnecessary offence to others, worshippers and outsiders alike. We know from ancient artefacts that to the Greek culture of Paul's day, long hair was customary for women, short hair for men. So the most likely explanation is that Paul means by 'nature' the sensibilities of his contemporary culture, what 'normal people' would consider to be 'normal' practice. The New International Version helpfully translates the word referring to 'nature' as 'the very nature of things', adding the slight note of provisionality and cultural relevance which Paul almost certainly intended. This is clearly underlined by the very next verse: 'If anyone wants to be contentious about this, we have no other practice. . .' (1 Cor 11:16). Here, Paul makes it abundantly plain that his whole argument has been about fitting in with the customs of his day. Even at the very climax of his argument he refuses to issue a timeless command. His whole appeal is to custom.

Other factors militate against a Stoic use of 'nature' as prescribing short hair for men here. Firstly, the claim would be ironic since, as Fee points out, a short haircut is the triumph of artificiality, of culture imposed on nature. Secondly, Paul would be strangely at odds with Jewish practice. Jewish men had always characteristically worn their hair long, probably including Jesus and most of the apostles. This had held sway until recent Greek influence had led to a tendency towards shortening. Would Paul, biblical scholar *par excellence*, have at a stroke denounced the practice of all his heroes of the faith? Would Paul, who met the risen Saviour in the most dramatic fashion in history, have had as his evangelistic theme that Jesus might bring salvation but sadly had an unnatural hairstyle?

Thirdly, for a period Paul himself appears to have grown his hair long as part of a 'Nazirite' vow to God (see Acts 18:18), the same sort which led the Old Testament hero Samson to grow his hair long, and which John the Baptist may well have taken too. Would he really denounce something which he himself had experienced as symbolic of a wholly positive self-offering to God?

The evidence is cumulative and strong. In context, 'nature' means the sensitivities of mainstream culture in Corinth. If we wished to infer a principle for today, it might be this: that the appearance and personal style of the Christian is a matter of personal freedom, but this freedom is to be moderated by one important factor. Your appearance should not hinder the reception of the gospel message among those around you. The gospel is too precious for you to put people off it by the way you look.

If this is the heart of Paul's meaning (and the evidence indicates it is) then there is a New Testament imperative for the heavy metal fan to keep his flowing locks. There is no universal, God-given law on hair length. The messages given out by hair will rightly vary from culture to culture: royal Egyptian women shaved their heads, the macho heroes of ancient Sparta had extremely long hair, as did the men at the court of the English king William Rufus, as did Hebrew men for the greater part of biblical history, and it is almost certain that God incarnate was crowned with the long hair of his day.

The issue at stake is cultural appropriateness and sensitivity. In many modern contexts, a dapper short back-and-sides might well be 'a hairstyle which does not glorify God'; a visit to the barber's, could be a sign of backsliding. Ask Samson.

CHAPTER 5

PRIDE AND HUMILITY

> 'The tulip, and the butterfly,
> Appear in gayer coats than I:
> Let me be dressed as fine as I will,
> Flies, worms, and flow'rs, exceed me still.'
>> Watts, I. *'Against Pride in Clothes'*, *Divine Songs for Children* (1715)

The 'Essential Vice'

A Christian condemnation of stylish dress as far back as the early Church Fathers has been that it is inextricably bound up with pride. And, in the Christian tradition, nothing more damning could possibly be said of it. Pride is the first of the traditional seven 'deadly' sins, and throughout church history it has often been characterised as the very essence of human sinfulness. This is the perspective of C.S. Lewis in his classic, *Mere Christianity*:

> According to Christian teachers, the essential vice, the utmost evil, is Pride. Unchastity, anger, greed, drunkenness, and all that, are mere fleabites in comparison: it was through Pride that the devil became the devil: pride leads to every other vice: it is the complete anti-God state of mind (p107).

Fashion, communicating wealth, rank, beauty and sexuality, has been readily identified as the embodiment of pride. For many Christians, such as the early Quakers and Methodists, so intimate was the link between fashion and proud human nature that levels of ostentation in dress were considered a reliable marker of an individual's saved or unsaved state. Pride has been inseparable from prejudice.

Two separate but closely related examples of pride in dress have historically been identified by Christian and other commentators: vanity ('ostentation occasioned by ambition': *Collins English Dictionary*), and narcissism ('an exceptional interest in or admiration for oneself, esp. one's physical appearance': *ibid*). We shall re-examine both.

Vanity: Christian Critics

Christian invective against dress as vanity becomes prevalent in the early Middle Ages. The great Catholic theologian Thomas Aquinas describes dressing through vanity as a venial sin (in the categories of the day, an offence which is serious but which can be forgiven), advising men and women to avoid 'excessive expenditure and parade'.

In 1303 the Gilbertine Canon Robert of Brunne wrote *Handlyng Synne*, in which he condemned sartorial excesses of the aristocratic women of his day, notably their voluminous skirts which, he said, were long enough for devils to sit on. Many other medieval Christian moralists compared the elaborate 'horns' on the fashionable women's head-dresses to the horns of the devil. In similar vein, the Elizabethan Puritan Samuel Ward wrote in his College Diary that one of the 'sins of the University' was that of 'excess in apparel'.

In 1615 the Puritan Massachusetts Bay Colony set fines for those deemed guilty of aping their social superiors by dress, vainly declaring themselves something that they were not. The leaders proclaimed:

> utter detestation and dislike that men and women of meane condition, educations and callinges should take uppon them the garbe of gentlemen, by the wearinge of gold or silver lace, or buttons, or poynts at their knees, to walke in great bootes; or women of the same rank to wear silke or tiffany hoodes or scarfes.

'Medieval Christian moralists compared the elaborate "horns" on the fashionable women's head-dresses to the horns of the devil' (p 123)

John Wesley, in his 1817 *Sermon on Dress*, likewise drew attention to the vanity of fashion, stating that 'Nothing is more natural than to think ourselves better because we are dressed in better clothes', which 'have a natural tendency to make a man sick of (ie with) pride'. For many contemporary Christian authors, the charge is unchanged: that any dress other than the grimly utilitarian equals vanity. Richard Foster is outspoken in his bestselling *Celebration of Discipline*:

> Hang the fashions. Buy only what you need. Wear your clothes until they are worn out. *Stop trying to impress people with your clothes and impress them with your life* . . . And for God's sake (and I mean that quite literally) have clothes that are practical rather than ornamental. (p79, emphasis mine)

Vanity: Secular Critics

But these criticisms are not only made by Christians. A seminal work claiming to establish a link between fashion and vanity (which still exercises significant influence over many social commentators today) is Veblen's *The Theory of the Leisure Class* (1899). Influenced in part by Marxist and Nonconformist Christian thinking, Veblen (an American sociologist) says dress is essentially about communicating status. So deep-seated is the desire to communicate affluence that this overrides more mundane matters such as utility. He notes that even in cold weather, people will go around in skimpy clothes in order to appear well-dressed. According to Veblen, two principles of vanity are at play in fashion: conspicuous waste and conspicuous leisure.

The principle of conspicuous waste centres on affluence. The fashionable person is the one who can afford to wear elaborate garments, and without such wealth the fashion project is impossible. Consequently, the public's very conceptions of beauty in clothing are moulded towards desiring the costly status-symbol. How much more is clothing a statement of affluence when constantly discarded and updated.

The idea of conspicuous leisure logically follows. Costly dress, regularly updated, communicates not only affluence, but further implies that the wearer is wealthy enough not to be engaged in any productive labour.

> If he or she is not under the necessity of earning a livelihood, the evidence of social worth is enhanced in a very considerable degree ... It goes without saying that no apparel can be considered elegant, or even decent, if it shows the effect of manual labour on the part of the wearer, in the way of soil or wear (p170).

Echoes of Veblen's critique appear as recently as 1992, in Colin McDowell's *Dressed to Kill: Sex, Power and Clothes*. For McDowell (a British fashion critic) as for Veblen, fashion is a statement of rank for those who possess status and a statement of aspiration for those who desire it. Thus, he criticises those of the middle classes who go to Henley in blazers and boaters, since these items are merely aspirational emblems:

> They have frozen as fashion has moved on not because they are the most practical or suitable forms of dress, but because they are so closely associated with the class for whom the events were originally created . . . they immediately betoken a level of privilege and confidence that precludes others (p108).

For McDowell, class and status still form the essence of fashion, from the mass-market aping of the Country House style in the early 80s, to the wearing of designer labels on the outside of clothes.

Narcissism: Christian Critics

One could be forgiven for thinking that the worst possible sin was looking in the mirror, especially if you are a woman. Wearing attractive clothing may be bad enough, but to admire one's own appearance in them is simply beyond the pale.

From the Church Fathers onwards, one tradition of Christian thought has consistently accused women of being narcissistic, that of being excessively preoccupied with their own image. The term comes from the name of Narcissus, a mythical Greek youth of great beauty who was so taken with his own reflection in a pool that he stayed there looking at it, and eventually pined away. The charge of narcissism levelled at women has usually been linked in some way to the Fall.

The sin of pride and satisfaction in one's appearance is considered as embodying a repetition of Eve's primal sin of pride which expelled our forebears from Eden. Tertullian draws conclusions for the dress of his early 3rd-century contemporaries, condemning all silks, jewellery and other lavish adornment: 'Woman should dress in humble garb walking about as Eve, mourning and repentant . . . that she might more fully expiate that which she derives from Eve – the ignominy and odium of human perdition.'

An identical argument against narcissism in dress is advanced by the 18th-century hymn writer Isaac Watts, albeit this time aimed at both sexes: 'all our ornaments and clothing are but a memorial of our first sin and shame, and when we take a pride in our garments, it looks as if we had forgotten the original of them, the loss of our innocency.'

So convinced was he of his anti-fashion case that he felt even the smallest child should know it by rote. Consequently, he versified his link between Eve and narcissistic pride in dress in his 1715 bestseller of popular piety, *Divine Songs for Children*. Song number 22, *Against Pride in Clothing*, begins:

> Why should our garments, made to hide
> Our parents' shame, provoke our pride?
> The art of dress did ne'er begin,
> Till Eve, our mother, learnt to sin.
>
> When first she put the covering on,
> Her robe of innocence was gone;
> And yet her children vainly boast
> In the sad marks of glory lost.

In similar vein, the 1695 Philadelphia Yearly Meeting of the Quakers had advised that all members wear plain dress, lest they succumb to the sin of narcissism. The 19th-century evangelist Charles Finney recalls how one woman could only accept salvation after renouncing all her fine clothing, and countless Christian writers today similarly apply the same dichotomy: narcissistic self-absorption versus the mind set on God.

Narcissism: Secular Critics

Narcissism is not only a Christian obsession. It is also central to the analyses of a range of secular critics. The most important and influential of these are Flügel and Lasch, who each offer differing accounts of it.

In *The Psychology of Clothes* (1930), Flügel adopts a Freudian approach to dress. He sees all human behaviour as motivated primarily by an impulse to pleasure-seeking. In particular, he links this hedonistic urge to our naked human bodies and our desire to exhibit them to the world. This, he claims, leads directly to narcissism. For Flügel, the role of clothing is as the object of 'displacement'. Narcissism, which he defines as the tendency to admire our own bodies and the wish to display them to others, is 'displaced' onto our dress. So the things we wear are a kind of substitute for flashing our actual bodies to all and sundry. Clothes also draws attention to our bodies, helping the display along.

An alternative understanding of narcissism is provided by the American culture-watcher Christopher Lasch, in his seminal 1978 work, *The Culture of Narcissism*. For him, narcissism is not so much about self-admiration as an inadequate sense of self. The insecure modern narcissist demands constant admiration from other people, and if this is not forthcoming, then all sense of his own self-esteem vanishes. Unless others 'reflect back' to me positive images of myself, I see myself as worthless.

It is in this context that he discusses fashion. While once the preoccupation with personal appearance and the regular discarding of showy dress was the province of bored aristocracy, it is now (due to mass production) the prerogative of everybody. Fashion is part of the 'Banality of Pseudo-Self-Awareness' (the title of one of his chapters), it does not help us to know ourselves as we are, but instead creates pretend selves. We then look at the public fronts we put on, and think we understand who we really are.

For Lasch, advertising is a particular culprit in encouraging such narcissism. He writes disparagingly of the increasing incidence of seeing 'in ordinary men and women an escalating cycle of self-consciousness – a sense of self as performer under the constant scrutiny of friends and strangers' (p90). And he joins the Marxist social critics in attacking the artificiality of mass culture. For Lasch, the 'New Narcissus' is 'imprisoned in his pseudo-awareness of himself', a prison of self-absorption worse than the physical gaols of previous ages, since at heart it is occasioned by an utter collapse in self-image. In this sense, Lasch's definition of narcissism is less a kind of pride than a kind of insecurity.

Dress and Pride – Biblical Passages

In discussions of the link between clothing and personal pride, certain biblical passages constantly recur. Perhaps most frequent is 1 Timothy 2:9: 'I also want women to dress modestly, with decency and propriety, not with braided hair or gold or pearls or expensive clothes, but with good deeds, appropriate for women who profess to worship God.' Another, similarly contrasting inner and outward beauty, is 1 Peter 3:3–4:

> Your beauty should not come from outward adornment, such as braided hair and the wearing of gold jewellery and fine clothes. Instead, it should be that of your inner self, the unfading beauty of a gentle and quiet spirit, which is of great worth in God's sight.

Other writers have examined the end-time ('eschatological') visions presented in Scripture and drawn conclusions that the dress of God's ultimate kingdom (and, by inference, God's ideal for all human dress) is spartan white.

In Revelation, the saints are all clothed in white as they stand before the throne of God (Rev 7:9, 13, 14), as are the faithful martyrs (6:11); white clothing is the promised dress of those in Sardis who are uncorrupted (3:4,5); white is the colour of clothing counselled to the Laodiceans (3:18). The twenty-four elders seated around the throne of God wear white (4:4); and white linen is the dress of the armies of heaven (19:14). By contrast, the Whore of Babylon is 'dressed in purple and scarlet, and was glittering with gold, precious stones and pearls' (17:4).

Consequently, most utopian writings by Christian authors presuppose the absence of fashion and universal wearing of white or neutrally-coloured linen. Thomas More's *Utopia* (1516) was influenced by biblical apocalyptic literature, but was also written in reaction to the sartorial excesses of the Tudor court. *Utopia* presents a society without fashion, tailors or dress-makers. In Tommaso Campanella's *City of the Sun*, the utopian vision of a 17th-century Dominican monk, men and women all wear identical white clothing; and in *Christianopolis* (1619), by Lutheran minister Johann Andreae and influenced by the regu-lated dress of Calvin's Geneva, the uniform clothing of all is simple white or ashen grey. Even today, uniformity of dress is taken by some Christians to have an eschatological warrant (they suppose white or grey will be the uniform of the New Jerusalem) and they assume that sumptuous dress will be done away with. These biblical passages will be reassessed below.

Pride: A Reassessment

We have noted that both Christian and secular critics continue to berate fashion as an essentially proud enterprise. However, the argument of this chapter is that if we examine how fashion is used nowadays, the moral boundary of humility versus pride is increasingly unhelpful, as we consider both vanity and nar-cissism.

Vanity Reassessed

The argument that fine clothing is inseparable from vanity rests on on a central assumption: that dress is a primary indicator of wealth, class or status. It assumes that those who have attained cash and status use style to belittle those without them. It also assumes that those people still without status use clothes as a statement of aspiration. Garments show what sort of person I should like to be, and what rung of society I should like to be standing on, even if I am not there yet. It seems beyond ques-tion that at least until the turn of the 20th century this criticism was accurate. For most societies in most places, the wearing of fashionable as opposed to functional dress has indeed betok-ened privilege.

And this use of clothing has not entirely disappeared. If once fashionable dress in general was worn as a badge of privilege, now it is just specific types of fashion which send out messages of wealth: the so-called 'designer labels'. Certain labels can command such extortionate snob-value prices that nobody who lacks the wealth of Midas or the self-importance of Herod could ever hope to stock their wardrobe with them. A Ralph Lauren polo shirt costs £65, whilst the equivalent item in Marks & Spencer is £15. A Versace denim shirt retails at £105, over five times the price of the Marks & Spencer version. And nobody can seriously justify denim jeans by Vanderbilt or Armani (at the time of writing, the latter on sale at a local men's fashion store at prices from £85 to £129), when Levi's make them with about as much style and retro chic as any legs can carry (from around £35 in the UK, far less in the US). A trip to the department stores in London's exclusive Knightsbridge area reveals a depressing sight: the unapproachable in pursuit of the unaffordable.

The critics of today's high fashion are right: it is all too often a rather silly game of big egos, extravagant ostentation, bulging wallets and corruption in high places. In 1994 the Italian taxman caught up with a number of leading figures in the fashion industry, including Giorgio Armani and Gianfranco Ferré. Each admitted to bribing the Guardia di Finanza, the Italian tax inspectorate, to the tune of tens of thousands of pounds, to turn a blind eye to their audits. Later that year, the designer Gianni Versace's brother and business partner, Santo Versace, admitted to a reporter from Britain's *Independent on Sunday* (23/10/94) that he too had paid the Guardia a figure of £100,000.

Haute couture is rife with the sounds of clashing egos, empire-building design moguls with fragile self-esteem and armies of yes-people. Each bitches about the other, and courts the rich and famous. Front seats at catwalk shows are granted to those currently in favour, over against the lesser mortals, who fight it out for their small patch of turf in an unseemly rugby scrum. Many a journalist has been banned because she dared criticise some garments the previous year. Christians in particular have good reason to shun a sector of the industry whose motto might well be 'Vanity, Vanity' in the sense both of proud ostentation and empty futility.

However, we can no longer take it for granted that all stylish clothing is a visible expression of overstuffed egos and Swiss bank accounts, or the lower classes deliberately aping the ways of the rich. The technological and commercial shifts charted in an earlier chapter have led to a democratisation of style. Fashion in its broadest sense is no longer the prerogative of privilege. It is a game of identity played by almost all people living in consumer societies. The mass production of clothing from the late-19th century on (but especially in the post War era) has been a decisive step in bringing to the masses something previously reserved for an aristocratic elite. It closely parallels the introduction of the printing press in 15th-century Europe. No longer was the product (books, clothing) to be produced laboriously, by hand. Now, it could be made quickly and cheaply, and became available to all. If the one democratised the intellect, the other has democratised the body.

In this sense, McDowell is surely wrong to view the Henley blazers and boaters or the 'Brideshead' style of today as aspirational statements, an emblem of the Oxbridge 'wannabe'. They are, rather, a part of the playful aesthetic of today: a 'trying on' of identities in the museum of styles, a 'grabbing at', and an enjoyment of, cultural and historical allusions for their own sake. This simple fact cannot be underlined too often in any study of modern fashion: today, style is no longer primarily to do with rank or status. It is to do with expressing personal choice and communicating identity.

Today, fashion does not always conspicuously emulate the aristocrat, from 'above': many of its styles are taken directly from the workplace and street, from 'below'. Denim may have originated in 17th-century France (the word is from the French, *serge de Nîmes*), but it became popular as the hard-wearing fabric worn by American miners and black slaves from the 1850s on. Even the idea of the rivets in denim jeans was taken from the rivetted horse-blankets of the West Coast, pioneer and gold-prospecting era.

Or take the T-shirt. Its first recorded use was in the US Navy at the end of the 19th century, becoming standard Navy issue by the 1940s. It was standard issue to all seafarers, but such were its overtones of work and sweat, that officers were only allowed to be seen wearing them underneath another shirt! After the end of the war and demobilisation, the T-shirt caught on in civilian use, its military overtones adding a note of rough glamour to the garment. But perhaps the moment which most fixed the identity of the T-shirt in post-war America was the Marlon Brando film, *A Streetcar Named Desire* (1951). On the character of Stanley Kowalski, a carworker, Brando's white T-shirt became an emblem of marginalisation, affinity with the working man, masculine grit and grime.

When Calvin Klein walks down the catwalk at the end of a show, dressed in blue denims and white T-shirt, his look is deliberately plugging into a certain set of historical associations: with the marginal, the unacceptable, the risqué. The marginalised origins of blue denim and T-shirts are used by a range of groups, from bikers to gay men, to convey a message that they too are 'on the edge'.

Likewise, industrial-type boots, lumberjack shirts, boiler suits, 'grandad' shirts, 'donkey' jackets, fisherman's smocks, cowboy boots, army surplus trousers, gypsy headbands, peasant smocks, unbleached linen, and more recent trends in torn and patched clothing, not to mention a range of other components in popular style, all refer not upwards but downwards, to their origins among the 'have-nots' rather than the 'haves'. Since the arrival of the 'teds' in the 1950s, 'anti-fashion' has been a major element of the fashionable.

Even the boundary between 'high fashion', street-wear or work-wear has become blurred over the past four decades or so, as leading designers of haute couture have plundered the creativity of the streets for inspiration. The young Yves Saint Laurent looked to the black jackets of bikers and counter-cultural Left Bank existentialists to inspire his early collections.

Designers such as Vivienne Westwood, Zandra Rhodes and Jean-Paul Gaultier have adapted the punk look for the catwalk. Gianni Versace and Karl Lagerfeld have made the biker's black leather jacket an object of high fashion. Such is the intensity with which today's designers scour the streets and clubs of the major urban centres that the grunge and hippy-revival looks of the early 90s were adapted for the catwalk almost as soon as they graced the backs of teenagers in Seattle and Manchester. If once fashion trickled down, today it is more likely to trickle up. The real style creativity of today comes from the streets, while the rich and famous desperately run to keep up.

Furthermore, in a cultural mood such as ours, it is equally likely that deliberate and self-consciously aspirational state- ments will be looked down on and ridiculed. In a day and age where most of us see clothing as an expression of somebody's identity, we become minutely sensitive to spotting ill-fitting *per- sonae*. Arline and John Liggett, authors of *The Tyranny of Beauty*, remind us that most of us can readily spot mutton dressed as lamb. Rather than admiring the aspirational mes- sages given off by somebody who clearly wishes to look younger, richer, and more glamorous than they are, we cringe inwardly:

> Declarations about wealth and class are often attempted through jewellery and ostentatiously expensive clothes. Unfortunately, diamonds and designer-labels tend to sit uncomfortably and unnaturally on over-ambi- tious wearers. The outcome, all too often, is the uneasy, haggard face of striving – the very opposite of effortless elegance (p176).

If my neighbour were to bring home a Rolls Royce and park it outside his west London terrace, the rest of us would peer through our lace curtains and snigger at his presumption. Far from envying him, we should be more likely to pity his misjudg- ment. 'More money than sense', as they say in these parts. So it is with clothing. In a culture acutely sensitive to the expression of identity through dress, conspicuously inappropriate masks are hardly an object of envy.

Narcissism Reassessed

The argument from narcissism up to and including Flügel similarly has an underlying assumption: that self-analysis and adoption of *personae* through dress are expressions of unhealthy self-admiration. This is a charge which, we noted, has historically been levelled at women in particular. However, there is reason to question from a psychological perspective whether this is true, especially today. Could it be that Christians and other critics have been wrong to see in clothing a blatantly narcissistic pleasure in one's own appearance? Might not a more helpful, and more accurate way into the subject today be that of role-playing?

Most of us in the West play out a range of roles every day, depending on the social settings we are in. The same woman might wear a two-piece suit for work, a seductive dress for evening-wear, a track-suit for weekend leisure and jeans for playing with children in the park. We each have a range of images we want to present. Our clothing dresses us in appropriate *personae* for each place and occasion.

But have we not claimed earlier that identity today is largely subcultural? That we tend to form our self-image in relation to particular groups, with certain looks? So how then can we reconcile these two ideas: that individuals can belong to a subculture with a fixed image, but that we might each *change* our image many times a day?

In fact, the apparent contradiction is only superficial. The 'big picture' of style is essentially subcultural: style used as a badge of affiliation to a subcultural group (large or small, clearly defined or eclectic). However, within this classification, some identities are fixed (punk, skinhead, goth, 'new age traveller', many clergy), while the great majority contain serial *personae*. The business executive, the 'Sloane', the young fogey, the permed secretary, and the tweedy spinster all dress differently for different occasions. The metamorphoses of serial identity do not extend to blurring subcultural identity: the country house gentleman may dress differently for riding and for dinner, but he will probably not become a purple-haired goth for weekend leisure.

Such serial identity is a normal consequence of social inter-action in the modern world. Elizabeth Rouse states that we all dress to gain a certain level of approval from others, and that this is simply inevitable:

> Children learn very early in life that their own appearance and clothes evoke certain responses from others . . . They also become aware of the fact that approval is given to people and children with particular types of appearance and is withheld from those who lack the necessary attributes or clothes (*Understanding Fashion*, p62).

As we grow, the opinions of others are central to the develop-ment of a sense of identity. We form a self-image by imagining how we appear to others in different circumstances, whether we are 'dressed for the occasion'. This is particularly true in a culture where most of us (unlike the medieval peasant or Victorian labourer) appear in a wide range of social settings.

To ask a friend for an opinion on a garment, or take time over selecting an outfit for an occasion is less an expression of ego-centricity than a desire for affirmation. It is a consequence of being social creatures. Under normal circumstances, others rarely praise our character or attributes ('You know, you really are one of the cleverest people I've ever met', 'I get a buzz just from being in the same room as you'). However, they might readily comment on our appearance ('That dress looks nice on you', 'You do look better with your hair shorter'). Such com-ments function as a basic reassurance mechanism that *persona* is being acceptably adapted for new circumstances.

This concept of affirmation in serial identities might sound identical to Lasch's definition of narcissism as the product of a personality which is insecure and consequently wholly depen-dent on the opinions of others for its very existence. But the difference is one of degree.

Lasch puts his finger on a vital problem. He rightly identifies the possibility of narcissism as idolatry, when it becomes the sole focus of our self-esteem, when we feel we are nothing at all unless other people are constantly telling us how wonderful we are or how good we look. This danger must not be downplayed and we shall return to it in Chapter 6. However, anything good in itself (family, work, sex, a hobby) may become an idol if it is absolute. That something may be used idolatrously does not mean it must not be used at all: it implies rather that it should be used appropriately. In the case of dress, there can be no harm in a Christian, whose identity is securely rooted in God, joining in the normal ways of life in a culture which uses dress as one means of interpersonal affirmation.

There is also the important, but often neglected, issue of differing personality types which we discussed in Chapter 2. It simply will not do for introvert Christians to insist that at the end of the day, the external world of material objects and other people's opinions are unimportant in the Christian life. The introvert might well be able to develop a spirituality and self-esteem in isolation from others. It will feel natural for the introvert Christian to encourage others to root their 'true' identity in a withdrawal from worldly distractions: in silent prayer, contemplation, reading and retreats. Even the notion that we all have a 'true, inner self' which is subsequently overlayed, and often corrupted, by the world of culture and material goods smacks of the influence of introvert psychologists and theologians.

However, to the half of society broadly classified as extroverts, this approach will be unhelpful. The extrovert is far more likely to form a self-image in relation to other people, to shape a spirituality which involves other people's contributions. The extrovert, in other words, is more likely to take seriously the biblical image of the Church as the Body of Christ, whose members are incomplete without one another. Extroverts should not be denied their outer-directedness. It is an emphasis the Church urgently needs to retrieve.

However, as we shall see in the next chapter, the individual whose total self-esteem completely collapses without the affirmation of others is pushing extroversion to an unhealthy degree. For now, we are simply noting that many people, including some Christians, naturally look to the opinions of others in formulating a healthy self-image. And this, far from being an expression of pride, is a simple difference in personality type, not to be gainsaid by others whose psychological makeup may be different.

Healthy Self-Esteem

Too often it is assumed that looking in the mirror, or asking for the opinions of others on personal appearance, is either 'self-worship' or idolatry, especially in women. This has left women in a cleft stick. They are accused of arrogant pride if they dress well. This assumption is particularly ironic, since arrogant, self-sufficient pride (as outlined by C.S. Lewis and a tradition of male theologians) may well be a more distinctively masculine tendency. If men are tempted to confident arrogance, women (on the evidence) often appear to be more tempted to self-deprecation and self-effacement.

In biblical terms, the essence of sin is not pride, vanity or excessive self-esteem. The essence of sin is a falling short of God's ideal, or a brokenness in God's creation. This is evidenced by an excessively *low* self-esteem just as much as by having too *high* a view of oneself.

Some common assumptions need to be knocked firmly on the head. One is that beautiful women, such as models, tend to be vain and proud of their appearance. In fact, exactly the reverse is often true, some of the humblest people you could hope to meet are professional models. Contrary to popular mythology, the model is not constantly puffed up with a sense of her own beauty. In her professional life she is constantly criticized and reminded of her flaws by those in search of the flawless image. In an average day the model receives far more messages of rejection than affirmation. Consequently, many in the profession live lives of insecurity, in need of constant reassurance. If they look in the mirror regularly, it is because they genuinely see only their physical shortcomings, and know that the slightest blemish could lose them the next precarious job. They are all too aware of their faults, of which their profession reminds them daily.

Many women share the basic insecurity of the model, albeit to a lesser degree; and, paradoxically, the greater the beauty, the greater the anxiety. So how has the church responded to the challenge to help rebuild a secure self-esteem for women? The result of the constant reminder in some conservative churches that pride is 'the essential vice', traceable back to Eve, has been Christian women with a pitifully poor self-image, believing this to be humility; craving love and affirmation but believing their craving to be wrong because it is misplaced pride. And if dress is used by women to help compensate for this inadequate sense of self-esteem, they are caught in the other fork of the cleft stick: guilty of pride and sinful idolatry. They cannot win.

But the ways some churches have sternly exhorted women to give up fashion and instead don self-denial and self-effacing humility are highly ironic on at least two counts. Firstly, this view of humility (woman as doormat in a dress) is a grotesque parody of the biblical understanding. The true meaning of humility is well expressed by the great 19th-century Baptist preacher, Charles Haddon Spurgeon: 'Humility is to make a right estimate of oneself'. Biblical humility includes a healthy, balanced self-esteem, which strives to remedy shortcomings, but which also basks in the gifts, personal dignity and adornments lavished by a loving heavenly Father on his children.

Secondly, the accusation that women are guilty of pride if they dress well is particularly cruel and ironic in view of the historic reasons why women since the 18th-century have tended to dress more sumptuously than men. The major reason has been the hypocrisy of religiously-minded, moralistic males.

Post-Enlightenment Europe had seen a reaction against the sartorial excesses of the court. Earlier courtly fashion was universally deemed frivolous, indolent and wasteful. The new breed of industrialists and businessmen dressed in the 'virtuous' styles of simple cut and plain, sober restraint. How, then, to flaunt their wealth? Through an ornamental wife, piled with costly, layered fabrics, constantly swooning due to the constrictions of impossibly tight corsets. The men thus simultaneously wore both an air of personal virtue on their own bodies, and the trappings of success on their wives. Not much has changed: compare the sober dress of most male politicians, millionaires, royalty and media stars with the conspicuous excess covering their wives or girlfriends.

However, this strategy has enabled 'virtuous' men to berate women for their vanity and preoccupation with the fripperies of fashion, something which has continued unabated till the present day. It has enabled the grim, black-clad preachers to denounce women for vanity and exhort them to self-effacing humility, when it was the very moral and economic stuctures of male-led, and sometimes Protestant-led, capitalism which encouraged their crinoline and lace imprisonment in the first place.

However, a middle path is possible: a moderate use of appropriate dress as a part (not the source or entirety) of a healthy, well-balanced self-esteem for a Christian. Clinical evidence has shown that clothing as affirmation can play a constructive role in the rebuilding of lost or precarious identity. Some mental health centres in the United States and elsewhere have experimented with 'fashion therapy', in which clothing and cosmetics have restored feelings of self-esteem and promoted social confidence.

In 1982 Nellie Thornton, a Yorkshire textile designer, teacher and practising Christian, set up Britain's first fashion consultancy and fashion manufacturing centre for disabled people. In her moving book, *Fashion for Disabled People*, she notes how appropriate, attractive clothing can transform the self-confidence of people with a disability. This in turn can lead them to try new things, go to new places and meet new people. Clothing can be directly responsible for helping to enhance a self-esteem which a disability, wheelchair or crutches have removed. This should not come as any surprise to the Christian. We have already seen how clothing in the Bible is all about conferring honour, dignity and favour. Scripture tells us that the very purpose of clothing is to give us a sense of our importance and value, and to communicate this to others. That is not vanity or narcissism, it is God's grace.

We have already noted in earlier chapters how the 'plain' styles of the Puritans were in fact up with the leading edge of fashion in their day, and how even the Quaker businessmen of

18th-century Philadelphia, for all their invective against the frivolity of sumptuous dress, had their 'plain' coats made from the finest fabrics, by the best tailors. Even 'plain' is a style, which can be just as luxurious as any other.

It is ironic that the truth that appropriate dress is used as a way of gaining personal affirmation is best illustrated by ostensibly the most militantly anti-fashion of all Christian groups, the North American Amish. Hostetler's 1963 study of Amish communities highlights the extraordinary extent to which members of the groups use the 'right' hats to gain social acceptability:

> Hat manufacturers produce at least 28 different sizes and a dozen different styles of Amish hats. . . . The outsider may never notice these differences, or if he does he may regard them as accidental. But to the Amish these symbols indicate whether people are fulfilling the expectations of the group. A young man who wears a hat with a brim that is too narrow is liable for sanction. The very strict Amish congregations can be distinguished from the more progressive ones by the width of the brim and the band around the crown (p136).

Dressing appropriately is good. Having a glance in the mirror to check that I am appropriately dressed is good. Enjoying the experience of being told I am appropriately dressed is good. The way I dress is a vital part of any healthy social interaction. It is not by definition arrogant or idolatrous, though (like anything good in itself) it may become either.

Fashion as Pride, or Fashion as Art?

If we are not seeing fashion as pride, then what is it? We already know it is about conferring dignity and status on people. But it is also about personal creativity, it is a way that each of us can be artists in our everyday lives. Many, however, doubt that creative fashion is a real option for Christians. They cannot accept that the aesthetic dimension is worthwhile *per se*. But the anti-art brigade are mistaken.

The Bible and Aesthetics

In Chapter 2 we examined the concept of the 'image of God' in Genesis 1:26,27, and concluded that it is about humans representing God on earth. In the physical absence of the Creator, we stand here as reminders of his rule, as God's delegates to manage his creation. This gives a strong basis for starting to consider human creativity, in that the God whose image mankind bears is a Creator. The novelist Dorothy L. Sayers wrote helpfully on this theme in her 1940s classic, *The Mind of the Maker*, in which the biblical passage to which she refers in the following extract is the first chapter of Genesis:

> It is observable that in the passage leading up to the statement about man, (the writer) has given no detailed information about God. Looking at man, he sees in him something essentially divine, but when we turn back to see what he says about the original upon which the 'image' of God was modelled, we find only the single assertion, 'God created'. The characteristic common to God and man is apparently that: the desire and ability to make things (p17).

Edith Schaeffer wrote a provocative book, *Hidden Art*, which challenges Christians to take seriously their creativity and to express it in all the business of life. She concluded similarly from the concept of 'image' that creativity is a primary calling of the human being before God: people were created in order to create (p24).

Not only are we creators because we are imagers of God, the Creator, but he has also given us the cultural mandate of Genesis 1:28, 'God blessed them and said to them, "Be fruitful and increase in number; fill the earth and subdue it. Rule over the fish of the sea and the birds of the air and over every living creature that moves on the ground".' This offers a basis for human *artifice* of every kind, including art and personal creativity: the creation of God is presented as unfinished, waiting to be used historically, and art is a way of responding to the call to cultivate the earth.

A range of other biblical passages and themes offers support for creativity. The first person recorded in the Bible as being 'filled with the Spirit of God' for a task is Bezalel, whose gift is 'skill, ability and knowledge in all kinds of crafts – to make artistic designs for work in gold, silver and bronze, to cut and set stones, to work in wood and to engage in all kinds of artistic craftsmanship.' (Ex 35:31–33).

Not only this, Bezalel and his colleague Oholiab are explicitly stated to have been filled with the Spirit to work as 'designers, embroiderers in blue, purple and scarlet yarn and fine linen, and weavers' (Ex 35:35). The point is repeatedly underlined that they are no mere jobbing workmen; in all aspects of clothing production they are 'master craftsmen and designers'. The first mention of the Spirit being sent for a specific task, then, is in connection with inspiring the creation of fine, stylish dress! Throughout Exodus there is a strong focus on the aesthetic dimension: in chapter 26 the plans for the tabernacle centre on rich colour, style and beauty, as do the priestly garments of chapter 28.

All of this means that, in the words of Hans Rookmaaker, former Professor of Art at the Free University of Amsterdam, for the Christian . . .

> . . . Art needs no justification . . . It has its own meaning that does not need to be explained, just as marriage does, or man himself, or the existence of a particular bird or flower or mountain or sea or star. These all have meaning because God has made them . . . So art has a meaning because God thought it good to give art and beauty to humanity.' (*Modern Art and the Death of a Culture*, p230)

For Edith Schaeffer, dress comes under the category of 'hidden art', art which is not the 'high' art of the gallery or professional expertise, but which each of us can express in mundane ways, in everyday life. Each person can use aesthetics in a range of ways, from cookery to gardening, to brighten and enrich daily life. And that includes dressing in the bright colours, textures and variety of the lilies of the field.

Gaudy? Ostentatious? Why not! The time has come for Christians to boycott the depressing rows of earth-tone trousers in Marks & Spencer, Dunns and Burtons. Today's Christian woman needs to resist the gravitational pull towards the safe end of Laura Ashley. We need to pray for a new revulsion at the bland and safe, to beg the Holy Spirit to renew our aesthetic sense, and stimulate our desire for the new, bright and unpredictable. Our clothes need to express our giddy delight at the sheer wonder of creation. We need to begin to walk, with a spring in our step, down the King's Road, in more senses than one.

However, other passages cited earlier appear to contradict this biblical warrant for creativity in personal adornment and these need to be reassessed.

The Bible and Pride in Dress

Biblical literature needs to be treated responsibly, not abused by taking verses out of context and reading into the text themes which the original authors could never have intended. We have already seen that the category of Old Testament Law needs to be read in a particular way, and that there are hermeneutical principles to be borne in mind as we read it and ask how the law applies to today. The same is true for all the other categories of literature in the Bible. Scripture is not all Law, so the principles through which we read the books of the Law will not be identical to those which we apply to other parts.

The verses at stake here are from the New Testament epistles, originally letters written to specific churches or individuals by key followers of Jesus: characters such as Paul and Peter. They were addressed to particular people, in particular geographical destinations, at particular times, usually in response to specific queries or requests.

Therefore, as we look to apply the message of such letters today, the first question we have to bear in mind is this: what would the words in the letter have meant to the letter's original readers or hearers? It cannot mean for us what it could never have meant to those who first received it. A lot of wasted breath and questionable exegesis might have been avoided in our churches, had this basic, sound principle been sensibly adhered to. Clearly, we will need the help of commentaries, Bible dictionaries and encyclopedias to help us ascertain the original context in which the letter was written. This process of common-sense exegesis is not a way of 'avoiding' difficult passages, or denying that God might speak to us directly through the pages of the New Testament. On the contrary, it is to take seriously the nature of Scripture, and to help us avoid misusing it by reading in personal prejudice.

The second step is this: if our context is similar to that of the original recipient, then the letter might apply to us just as it applied to them. In other words, if we share their problem, then we can share in the answer offered in the letter. We discover God's word to us as we discover his word to them. If, however, the contexts are dissimilar or alien (such as Paul writing, in 1 Corinthians 10, about food that has been offered to idols), then we need to look at the general principles which we might still apply to today. (In the example just given, this might include: freedom, conscience, sin, worship of false gods and giving a positive witness to unbelievers.) But here too, we must watch out that the principle we draw out is genuinely comparable.

We must also always bear in mind what the rest of the Bible has to say on the issue at stake: there may be creational principles which apply (something structural built into the very way God made us and our earth), or eschatological principles (the way things will one day be on the renewed earth), or else there may be other references to the same subject in the teaching of Jesus or in other letters.

As we look at 1 Timothy 2:9: 'I also want women to dress modestly, with decency and propriety, not with braided hair or gold or pearls or expensive clothes, but with good deeds, appropriate for women who profess to worship God', a reasonably clear picture emerges. The New Testament specialist Gordon Fee notes in his commentary on the letter:

> There is a large body of evidence, both Hellenistic and Jewish, which equated 'dressing up' on the part of women with both sexual wantonness and wifely insubordination. Indeed, for a married woman so to dress in public was tantamount to marital unfaithfulness (p71).

Some women in the ancient world braided their hair with gold in elaborate styles to attract the attentions of men – such braiding was considered sexually attractive. So, historically, the issue addressed is not about vanity or narcissism in dress. That is not what Paul is writing about, he is dealing with the question of what conduct is appropriate for Christians when they appear in public. Equally, the passage holds no condemnation of creativity in personal appearance. Paul is concerned here about one issue: that the women in question should not engage in conduct which might be deemed immodest or seductive. A contemporary parallel might be Christian women regularly wearing a basque and fish-net tights in public. That, says Paul, would send out the wrong sort of messages.

The same concern, incidentally, is behind Paul's insistence in 1 Corinthians chapter 11 that the Christian women of Corinth should wear head coverings. The reason lies in the way women's hair was viewed in the ancient world. Unlike today, hair was widely seen as provocatively sexual. In many countries of the eastern Mediterranean (including Palestine) to go about with your hair uncovered had about the same meaning as parading around in a see-through blouse or revealing mini-skirt today. Uncovered hair, like braided hair, was a turn-on for the men.

Despite this, some upper-class women were so keen to show off their latest styles that they flouted the sexual taboos of the day by going about with their heads uncovered, and the culprits appear to have included the Christian fashion-victims of the day. So Paul is partly addressing a class issue: some people believe that their money sets them above the normal rules of society and church. But more importantly, it is about sex. Not that Paul is anti-sex. He is simply saying that a worship service is not the place to do it. Again, it is the underlying principles which must be transposed to our own culture.

We need to apply the same set of hermeneutical principles to 1 Peter 3:3,4, which says 'Your beauty should not come from outward adornment, such as braided hair and the wearing of gold jewellery and fine clothes.'

However, the first issue we need to clarify before we can proceed any further is the most basic hermeneutical question of them all, the precursor to hermeneutics: what the text actually says. As it stands, in this NIV English translation, there is an apparent polarisation of 'fine clothes' against 'inner' virtues. This, in turn, implies a condemnation of unhelpful excess in dress. But this is a mistranslation of the original. In the Greek, 'clothing' has no qualifying adjective such as 'fine'. So, the text literally says, 'Let not your adorning be the outward adorning of braiding of hair and wearing of gold or putting on of clothing'. The implications of this extra adjective in the NIV (and RSV) fundamentally changes the meaning of what is being contrasted.

The point is made by Wayne Grudem in his commentary on the letter:

> It is incorrect, therefore, to use this text to prohibit women from braiding their hair or wearing gold jewellery, for by the same reasoning one would have to prohibit 'putting on of clothing'. Peter's point is not that any of these are forbidden, but that they should not be a woman's 'adorning', her source of beauty (p140).

Evangelical Bible studies might be a rather different experience if the faithful sincerely believed that Peter was actually banning the 'putting on of clothing' for all time!

The responsible hermeneutical inference from the passage is that today's woman, like the women in the churches to whom Peter is writing (his addressees are listed in 1 Peter 1:1), might well wear fine clothes and jewellery. But she must not root her entire sense of self-confidence in them. Her self-esteem must have a firm base: trust in God, and secure, reliable human relationships (1 Pet 3:4–6). Her public image must never become a substitute for a sense of who she really is. The biblical message could scarcely be more relevant to citizens of a modern, consumer culture.

Back to the Future

We must also reassess the inferences which have been drawn from biblical eschatology (pictures of the end times) about plainness of dress. The conclusion is usually drawn that white linen is God's ideal, and that colour, shape and pattern are deviations. However, we shall argue that it is equally legitimate (indeed, more so, given the biblical warrant for aesthetic creativity) to draw from predictive visions of the end times (notably in Revelation and Isaiah) support for even 'worldly' fashion.

Revelation 21:24 states of the New Jerusalem that 'The nations will walk by its light, and the kings of the earth will bring their splendour into it.' In this vision, we find a fundamental endorsement of the cultural artefacts of 'secular' culture: while once they were offered to the city of the antichrist, they are now brought into the city of God. The whole created order is being sanctified.

It is a vision strikingly similar to that of Isaiah 60, which pictures the Holy City as a centre of commerce, receiving the vessels, goods and currency of commercial activity. In this chapter we see brought into the New Jerusalem the gold and incense of Sheba (v6), the ships of Tarshish, laden with silver and gold (v9), the best animals from all nations (vv6, 7), and the 'wealth of the nations' (v11). It is a picture of all the commerce of the ancient world, and even the pagan kings of the ancient world (vv10, 11), redeemed for use by God's people. Pagan cultural artefacts (including, implicitly, fine clothing) are to be redemptively appropriated. The emphasis is not on the destruction of fine things, but on their transformation. But now they will be used for the purposes they were originally intended, instead of being misused by those who refused to bow to God as Creator and Lord.

This is a vision at odds with what many conceive as 'heaven' or 'the afterlife', a vapid, insubstantial place where we all drift around like nightshirts which have escaped from the washing-line. But in Isaiah 60 and Revelation 21 there is a biblical mandate for a belief that the ultimate Kingdom will not obliterate the riches of human culture and creativity, even the 'worldly'. Our present life is heading for a city, an embodied state in some sort of remarkable continuity with our present existence.

In this perspective, the colour white in Revelation is simply being used as a symbol of purity and victory, in the context of an apocalyptic vision. It describes in the imagery of colour the spiritual state of those in the presence of God. Surviving inscriptions from Asia Minor show that people were not allowed to enter some temples if their clothes were anything other than spotless, lest the deity be insulted. White is not intended to be a literal description of the dress of eternity. It is a symbol, not some utilitarian couturier's pattern. Whiteness is a positive assertion of purity, not a denial of colour or finery.

When the 'Whore of Babylon' is pictured wearing purple, scarlet, gold and jewels (Rev 17:4), this too is intended to be symbolic. The harlot mainly represents Rome (purple was the imperial colour) whose decadent emperors, such as Nero, surrounded themselves with riches, and lived in golden and jewel-encrusted palaces. It was the Roman emperors who threw Christians to the lions and burnt them alive, and who claimed that they themselves were gods. Purple and scarlet dyes were expensive in the ancient world, so the clothing of the harlot embodies earthly luxury, the fine robes of an authority which is not used to glorify God, but which denies God and slaughters his people. Purple was also the colour worn by high-class prostitutes to draw attention to themselves in public.

We cannot conclude from such precise, contextualised symbolism what colours and textures will one day robe God's own people, since elsewhere, rich purples and fine cloths are used as symbols of blessing from God himself.

Role Models

We noted above that the first time the Bible mentions the sending of the Holy Spirit on people for a particular task, this task includes the design and manufacture of fine, beautiful clothing, in rich colours (Ex 35:30–35). We read of a range of characters in the Bible (historical and metaphorical) who do just this, under the Spirit's inspiration.

The description of the 'wife of noble character' characterised at the end of the book of Proverbs was designed as a piece of parental advice for a young man in search of a partner for life. It has been held up for centuries as an ideal of womanhood. In the light of this, what we find there is interesting. The woman is an organiser, an efficient businesswoman. She is the very embodiment of a practical, efficient godliness in the ordinary things of life, a working mother who is creative, caring and stylish. She not only wears fine clothes and makes them, she also markets them to the high street retailers:

> When it snows, she has no fear for her household;
>> for all of them are clothed in scarlet.
> She makes coverings for her bed;
>> she is clothed in fine linen and purple . . .
> She makes linen garments and sells them,
>> and supplies the merchants with sashes (Prov 31: 21–24).

Lydia, a Christian woman whom Paul met at Philippi (Acts 16:14) was a 'seller of purple', almost certainly an overseas agent for a company based in her home city of Thyatira, which was a major centre for dyeing and clothing manufacture. She was a saleswoman for dyed clothing named after the colour of the dye, a rep for a foreign fashion wholesaler.

Dorcas, a disciple who was raised from the dead by Peter in Joppa, was a clothing producer (Acts 9:36–42), a seamstress who made fine garments. The widows who mourn her death show Peter some of her work. The original Greek even implies that the mourners were wearing some of Dorcas's creations.

It is these godly women and not the drab functionalists who more closely embody the biblical vision for clothing. They (stylish dressers, fashion wholesalers and seamstresses) contribute to the Christian mandate for dress as creative, vibrant and celebratory.

PART TWO

Dressed to Kill

CHAPTER 6

FASHION VICTIMS

'Peter held the door closed but did not shut it; for, of course, he remembered, as every sensible person does, that you should never shut yourself up in a wardrobe'
Lewis, C.S., *The Lion, the Witch and the Wardrobe*

Dress in Excess

Nike was the winged Greek goddess of victory. After centuries of neglect, she must be gratified that her cult is once again thriving on the streets of the modern world. Once again she, like her modern cohorts Reebok, Hi-Tec, Adidas and a panoply of other minor deities, demands faithful servitude. Even to the point of shedding blood.

Brand names on trainers represent far more than mere label snobbery, design preference or an index of affordability. To countless teenagers the world over they represent an adrenaline rush of street heroism, a full statement of personal identity. They are at the foundation not merely of one's legs but of one's very self. In some forms of street culture, trainer brands epitomise group solidarity, personal worth, aspiration. A *faux-pas* in one's choice of trainer can entail ostracism, collapsed sense of personal value, worthlessness.

The top brands frequently favoured by gangs and other groupings of young people often cost well over £100 a pair. If

'Trainers . . . at the foundation not merely of one's legs – but of one's very self' (p 153)

unaffordable, such is their iconic value and prestige, that they are stolen, mugged for and in the extreme murdered for. Some have even taken their own life rather than suffer the shame of being seen to do without the highly specific status symbol. An apparently innocuous item of footwear has been elevated to the status of a world view, an ideal, an absolute. Long gone are the days of pure functionalism, the days when a trainer was just a trainer: the current Nike catalogue features no less than 347 different styles, each of which is designed not just for sport but as a lifestyle accessory, a badge of identity.

Doreen is in her late 50s, lives in Yorkshire and prides herself on being well turned out. So keen is she to present an appropriate image to the world that in recent years she has never been seen in the same dress twice. Her wardrobes contain literally hundreds of dresses, hundreds of skirts and hundreds of blouses. Her shoe collection is well on the way to rivalling Emelda Marcos's tally of 1,060 pairs. The same with fashion accessories. Her grown-up children realise that if they give her jewellery, they will see it worn once and afterwards it will disappear into the Aladdin's cave of chains and trinkets, never to be seen again. Doreen's long-suffering husband wishes she would stop her compulsive clothes purchasing, but worries that if he speaks out, home might become unbearable and he prefers a quiet life.

Again, clothing is out of all proportion. On reading these two illustrations, most of us feel uneasy about such absolutising of dress, but in the light of Part One of this book, do we have to hold our tongue and refrain from criticism? Have we not already established that clothing is good and dignifying, that buying into a style or image can be a valid way of expressing ourselves and even helping to create an identity, and that an interest in fashion and looking right for each of life's different settings is fine? Indeed we have, but that is not the same as concluding that anything goes. It is one thing to celebrate the creative uses of fashion, it is quite another to condone its abuses and excesses.

This chapter, and those which follow, aim to show the other

side of the coin from that looked at in Part One. We need to look at the darker side of fashion, starting in this chapter with a look at what happens when we set too much store by our dress, when it assumes a significance out of all proportion. In Christian terms, we are looking at style as a modern idolatry.

But we are jumping ahead of ourselves so let's consider the two examples at the start of this chapter: teenage trainer-mania and middle-aged clothes addiction. Before we make any moral interpretation of what is going on, it is necessary that we understand what is going on. We need to put each in some sort of historical context, to show that each is simply the logical outcome of significant trends in today's world but pushed to an unhealthy degree. Firstly, the brand names on trainers.

Reading the Label

Labels in clothes simply did not exist before the 18th century. They were introduced, following the model of hallmarks on metal objects and stamps on ceramics, for two main reasons. They served to remind increasingly mobile buyers of the name of the store where the garment had been purchased. And, since producing labels was not a cheap affair, it implied that the garment in question was something of a luxury item. Some labels were stamped onto the garment, others glued or sewn in.

However, it was in the early-19th century that the use of the permanent label (as opposed to the ephemeral price-tag) took off. Since the Middle Ages, the only means available to the store for creating a brand identity had been the sign above the door. Who needed anything more? A largely static population bought its clothes locally, or (more commonly) made them at home. There was no point advertising, since such publicity implies mobility and distinguishing between a choice of goods on offer.

The early-19th century saw the rise of larger 'warehouses', supplying a larger range of goods than had previously been available under one roof. Some of the more exclusive garments were made by specialists, based further afield, and were labelled to prove their superior quality. This was the same era which saw the rise of other methods of brand and store identification, such as labelled paper bags and trade-cards, and patents were increasingly used to protect clothing designs from other copy-cat manufacturers, especially in the field of women's wear, such as front-fastening corsets.

By the end of 1839, with the introduction of Registered Design status in the UK, the legal protection and publicising of certain designs was already becoming a marketing strategy. As mass-production increased, so manufacturers would only register a small number of their products, in order to give these products an air of exclusivity, and this was enhanced by the use of royal, aristocratic or scientific names. Designer labels are not a late-20th century innovation!

In 1875 the introduction of the Registered Trade Mark helped promote the cause of brand labels. In an era when retail and manufacturing were increasingly carried out in separate premises, sellers were careful to cite only the brand name, and never to identify the manufacturer – lest buyers bypass the middle-man and buy direct from source. This rise in the importance of brand loyalty was helped at this time by the use of illustrated boxes from stores, emphasising the shop's name and bearing pictures illustrating its chosen 'feel'.

By the start of the 20th century, trade-marks, brands and labels were firmly established in the popular mind, and customers were becoming highly specific in their stated preferences for specific products. As the century progressed, advertising gradually became more and more sophisticated in its ability to lodge brand loyalty in the brain of the consumer. So much so that by the 1990s, certain brand names are far more than a convenient reminder of a mild preference. They embody a lifestyle, a chosen persona, an identity chosen off-the-peg and flaunted to the world. I create myself by acts of purchasing products which make a statement to the people I meet: I shop therefore I am. Because my identity, my very self is inseparable from this product, I am prepared to defend it to the grave. Or kill for it!

Fashion is the main place an identity is rooted by those most insecure individuals and in search of themselves, the modern teenager. The 1990s marketers have targeted sports fashion as a key area for the building of brand loyalty among the most insecure of fashion victims. The yearning for virility, belonging, heroism, group identity, achievement, aspiration, even transcendence are all displaced to the feet. Rarely are the desired items used for something as mundane as sport alone. Something far more subtle, more central to personal identity is afoot, and in the background lurk a range of social pressures, from gang culture to the sense of personal powerlessness engendered by unemployment and racism.

Addicted to Style

Doreen from Yorkshire is also a fashion victim, but in her case, she is a junkie hooked on clothing abuse. Not, of course, that clothing is a 'chemical' addiction, such as tobacco and other narcotic drugs. It is unlikely that even the roughest Aran sweater, shredded and rolled up, could produce that kind of dependency. Rather, it is an example of a different kind of addiction. Any experience which offers a momentary 'high' has the potential to lead to a craving for repeated sensation, be it gambling, sex, even certain types of charismatic religion . . . or spending. This kind of addiction is psychological. It is perhaps better described, as some psychologists describe it, as a compulsion.

In my previous book *Born to Shop*, I quoted the journalist Jeremy Seabrook, whose words are highly relevant here: 'The instant of buying is the most intense and concentrated experience that our culture offers to the individual.' Doreen has experienced such a 'high', and has become hooked. Pathological spending is a condition recognised as comparable to other forms of addiction. Across the USA, 'shopaholics anonymous' groups are being formed to help compulsive consumers kick the habit.

Not that compulsive shopping was unknown in previous centuries. One of US President George Washington's lesser-known activities was his mania for shopping. He not only indulged a passion for buying clothes; he also spent huge sums on fabrics, and would spend hours designing uniforms and accessories. A century later, Mary Todd Lincoln (wife of President Abraham Lincoln) was ultimately declared insane as a result of her excessive purchasing habits. In her day she was a notorious spender, just one example of her extravagance being her purchase of eighty-four pairs of gloves before moving into the White House. The French novelist Balzac was a notorious shopaholic with a passion for fine clothing, ordering fifty-eight pairs of gloves on one (unpaid) bill. The phenomenon is not new, but the scale of it certainly is. As shopping became an option for those other than the rich and noble, so too did the possibility of compulsive shopping. A *New York Times* report of 1991 estimated that today, around six per cent of the entire population of the USA is shopping addicted or has some similar problem with spending: some fifteen million people. If the figure is remotely similar in the UK, that means over three million Britons are victims of a similar compulsion.

Why? What is it about that moment when cash changes hands that feels so exciting? What is it that leads to the bulging wardrobes, some of whose contents have never been worn even once? Shopping addiction is almost always the combination of two factors:

a) Hidden inner motives. The compulsive shopper is usually the victim of hidden motivations inside himself. These might include a low sense of self-esteem, a sense of inner emptiness, problems at home, or simply boredom. Often such motivations are unconscious, and may reach back as far as early childhood. Shopping thus becomes a substitute for inner wholeness, a way of meeting inner needs, or else to distract from them.

A common fear found in compulsive shoppers is that of abandonment or loneliness. In many cases, this may stem from a lack of parental affirmation in childhood, or rejection by a teenage peer group. Such experiences of hurt can run deep, even after their causes are long forgotten, leaving the person in later life craving attention, yearning to be told they are worthwhile.

We referred in an earlier chapter to the fact that we all need reassurance that we are adequately playing the 'roles' demanded of us in all the different settings of modern life: this is normal and healthy. However, this reassurance mechanism can be distorted, particularly by experiences where affirmation was withheld in the past (bullying, parental indifference or pressure, unpopularity, friendlessness at school), leaving an individual with an insatiable craving for affirmation in the present. They then try to win this affirmation from others by only ever presenting the image they think will be acceptable to whichever group or individual they seek to impress. This may take the form of dressing in constantly new styles, a mania for always looking immaculately turned out, dressing in a sexually provocative way, even dressing excessively drably if that is what will impress their peers (churches take note).

Similarly, in the absence of personal affirmation, the acquisition of things can be used to mask inner pain. Those suffering from a low sense of self-esteem will purchase to obtain an external status symbol to make themselves feel more important in themselves: the bigger car, the flashier suit, the costlier jewellery. Despite popular perceptions, such acquisition is likely to reflect not an excessive sense of self-worth, but its absence. For others, normal life is felt to be so humdrum that the boredom needs to be alleviated with some regular moments of excitement. Shopping becomes the sensation which lifts life, the thrill which reassures you that monotony is not your only lot in this world.

In every such case, compulsive shopping is a mirage of hope. It may briefly alleviate the symptoms, but it will always leave the deeper issue of substantial inner healing of the true problems unattended. More than this, shopping addiction, like alcohol or narcotic addiction, makes matters worse by deadening your sensitivity to your true dilemma.

In some ways, a compulsion to shop presents an even greater threat than chemical addictions. It is possible to be a reformed glue-sniffer, heroin-taker or tobacco-smoker, and afterwards to cut out the addictive substance from one's life completely. But who could resolve never to shop again? Abstinence from shopping is clearly not an option for most of us!

Yet, because purchasing is not in the category of an all-or-nothing drug, it therefore presents a greater opportunity to the addict for self-awareness. Recovery is not about cutting something out, but rather about redefining your own relationship to the activity. It is about understanding yourself and your motivations so recovery becomes a journey of true inner healing.

b) Social Pressures. American authors Catalano and Sonenberg, in their self-help manual *Consuming Passions*, refer to compulsive shopping as a 'smiled-upon addiction'. Whereas alcoholism, excessive gambling or crack addiction might draw a concerned frown or sympathetic nod, shopping addiction will draw little more than a snigger. It is simply not taken seriously. It is trivial, fun, normal. Problem? What problem?

Shopping addiction is encouraged by every part of our consumer society. It is not only specific individual pressures to keep up with the Joneses, be as well turned-out as the girl opposite, or be in this season's colours. The pressure is from the very foundations of consumer capitalism: the more each of us spends, the stronger the economy, the happier we all are. Little surprise, then, that our culture does all it can to help you shop: from the ads on TV, radio, in magazines and on buses, to the architecture of shopping malls and the music played in stores and the scents increasingly wafted at you as you browse. This desire to facilitate purchasing is behind the current rise of home shopping: buying at the push of a few buttons and the flick of a credit card, all from the comfort of your own armchair.

So all-pervasive is the culture of consumption that those of us who are modern westerners believe that at the moment of purchase we are most truly ourselves. Like the French novelist and philosopher Jean-Paul Sartre, we believe that in some way, the choices we make determine who we are. But while Sartre dourly advocates choosing our way in life as a bulwark against the nauseating pointlessness and arbitrariness of the human condition, consumerism tells us that as we choose from the myriad ranges of goods on offer, we are making statements about lifestyle and identity. At the moment of purchase, I am not merely expressing who I am; I am creating the sort of person I choose to be.

The self has become plasticine, to be squeezed and shaped at will. It is a commodity to be designed and then realised through lifestyle purchasing. If the advert offers the hallucinatory image, then buying promises the realisation. If window-shopping and catalogue-browsing is the foreplay of consumerism, then buying is the consummation. The analogy is not a forced one. All our lives we are bombarded with countless consumer stimuli: dreams of possession and personal transformation, the titillations of avarice. In the words of media critic Raymond Williams, advertising is the official art of modern capitalist society, its function of creating dissatisfaction well expressed in the phrase of media critic Marshall McLuhan: 'keeping upset with the Joneses'. Buying is the central act in a consumer society. It is where the deepest values of our society are achieved, our world view expressed.

The shopaholic clothing addict is simply doing what comes naturally. Doreen is merely living out what her culture has told her that life is all about. She shops therefore she is.

Naming the Idols

To refer to the contemporary trend of wrapping up our identity wholly in our clothing as idolatry may sound extreme. Far from it. Indeed, it exhibits all the classic traits of idol-worship so abhorred by centuries of Judaeo-Christian prophets. We shall identify three major traits of any idolatry, and then focus in on the specifics of clothing as potentially idolatrous:

1) Idolatry uses an intrinsically good element in God's creation.
2) Idolatry mistakenly elevates this thing to a position of ultimate importance.
3) A person destructively roots his or her identity in this false god.

1) *Idolatry uses an intrinsically good element in God's creation.*
A major thrust of Part One of this book was to underline the
fact that our world has a good and benevolent Creator, who
rejoices in his creation. He is a God who loves the peoples,
places, plants and all he has made. He celebrates colour,
vibrancy, physicality – indeed, all that can be perceived by our
senses, because he is the Maker of it all. He loves his handiwork
to be enjoyed; art, nature, relationships, commerce, science,
sex, music and family life, all have their place in the richly
diverse world we inhabit. All are good in themselves, but of
course each has the potential to be used destructively. So too
with clothing, which is a gift: something creative, fun, serious,
artistic, which has a valid role in helping us establish our
uniqueness as persons.

2) *Idolatry mistakenly elevates this thing to a position of ultimate importance.* There is that in fallen human nature which is
not content to enjoy variety in moderation. Idolatry is the sin-
gling out of just one aspect of the good creation and elevating
it above all the rest. This one thing then becomes so significant
that other aspects of life begin to pale and diminish. Effectively,
the part of the created world has had attributed to it a power
and universal significance which by right belong only to the
Creator.

Examples are not hard to find in our society. One is the individual or government for whom the bottom line is only and
always, 'Is it economic?' Money and the structures of today's
employment market offer a total value-system and world view
which trample all else in their path. Or sex; an obsession with
the creational good of sexuality to the point where it dominates
all waking and sleeping thoughts is a prevalent cultural idol to
which millions are enslaved.

Another way to express the same thought is that idolatry is
reductionistic. It reduces the manifold wonder of life to a single
track. And we can see this with many of the major
'-isms' of the present and recent past. Freud made sex into the
golden key which was supposed to unlock the universe. Marx and
monetarism alike, each in different ways, claim that economics is

the foundation on which all else is built. Others idealise and idolise 'nature': if only we could get in touch with nature, then all our problems will be solved. Nature (sometimes personified as Gaia, the goddess of the earth) must be worshipped and appeased.

For many today, the cultural idol to which they give themselves wholly is personal image. You are the way you look and your identity is little more than the off-the-peg persona so carefully selected and purchased. This is reductionism. In biblical terms, it is idolatry.

c) *A person mistakenly roots his or her identity in this false god.* It is in the very nature of idol-obsession that the infatuation (or 'worship', for that is what it is) shapes the individual involved. The principle that worship forms identity is crucial to an understanding of why Christians worship God. We were made in his image and only find secure roots of identity with reference to him, as worshipping creatures. Our worship is an acknowledgement of God's rule in our lives and over the earth. Worship always shapes identity. If we worship God in Christ, this too shapes our very being: we are gradually being transformed into the 'likeness' of Christ himself, the best that humanity can become (2 Cor 3:18).

Any idol is an image claiming to be God. If we worship that idol, that not only demeans God; it demeans ourselves, since we alone were created to be God's image on earth. Idolatry effaces the likeness of Christ in us and replaces it with the likeness of our idolatry. The Psalmist is clear, with regard to idols of all types, that 'Those who make them will be like them, and so will all who trust in them' (Ps 115:8). And the wonderful, wise, wild words of Isaiah mercilessly parody the ways a person is demeaned by the worship of the wooden idols of his own day:

> No-one stops to think, no-one has the knowledge or understanding to say, 'Half of it I used for fuel; I even baked bread over its coals, I roasted meat and I ate. Shall I make a detestable thing from what is left? Shall I bow down to a block of wood?' (Is 44:19; see the whole of verses 9–22 for the full effect of the parody).

The cultural idol of personal image says: all that matters is how you present yourself. Style is a substitute for identity. The

hall mirror can become the wayside shrine, where we reli-
giously do our devotions each time we leave the house. The
Scriptures and iconography of consumer style surround us
daily. The self is constructed from the images found in style
magazines, billboards, films or the hallucinatory dream-worlds
of TV ads. In particular, women's magazines and men's style
magazines are more than diversion; they embody dreams and
ideals, offering images of the self as it could be: transformed,
perfected. It offers magical images of the self as hero, somehow
transcending the mundane. It is a quest which bears the
hallmarks of what a previous age would have recognised as
religion.

It is an idolatry of the self as spectacle. Its hallmarks are
unmissable in every mannerism and gesture as people walk
down the street with the self-conscious poise of the model, lean
against a bar with a carefully cultivated nonchalance, raise a
self-consciously debonair eyebrow, hold a cigarette, suck in the
cheeks, pull in the stomach, give the well-rehearsed flirtatious
smile. And, perhaps most of all, in the way people examine
themselves in the full-length mirrors of the fashion stores. The
music played in such stores is designed to bolster a certain
mental image of the self as work of art, urban hero, sex god. If
only I buy this jacket, we are persuaded, this dynamic self-image
evoked by the ads, the window-display, the mirror, the rock beat
played loudly over the in-store hi-fi, the fragrance being wafted
past my nostrils, will be my permanent possession.

As with all idolatries, the devoted are not spread equally
through all places, ages and temperaments. The cult of self-
image is focused in the larger urban centres of the west, and
particularly among young adults. A stroll through an area such
as London's Covent Garden might bring you close to its heart-
beat: an area teeming with those dressed up with no place to
go, those whose whole being is image without identity, style
without substance. It is a world where style talks loudest. The
streets of London have produced an intriguing new phenomenon: the T-shirt which is more fluent than its wearer.

But this is not to personalise the idolatry by scapegoating a few urban socialites. It is an idolatry we breathe in every day simply by living in a consumer culture. Sooner or later most of us dabble at the edges. Many become hooked. Ironically, countless people today have consciously rejected the Christianity of their grandparents' day, but unthinkingly swallowed whole a reductionist idolatry. They have exchanged the depth of true personhood for pure surface. No wonder that life seems superficial; they have become like the idol they worship. An idol is an image, and the modern urbanite adores an image, the reflected image of the beautified self.

Dethroning an Idol

How is an idol to be dethroned? By restoring things to their correct places. God needs to be restored to the position of ultimate authority which he alone has the right to possess. He alone is sovereign. The aspect of creation which had been singled out needs to be restored to its proper place, as just one of God's many blessings. Our identities need to be rooted again in a God-given variety of sources, which previous generations and other cultures today have frequently managed far better than we do. Our deep and genuine needs (for love, affirmation, purpose in life) need to be acknowledged and receive real, substantial healing.

Everything in my society and daily experience might shout out that my inner emptiness will be met by that next trip to the mall. The gospel tells me it will only be met in that strange, wonderful, life-changing encounter with Jesus of Nazareth. In the final chapter we shall examine some radical Christian responses to the identity crises of our culture in more detail.

Narcissus needs to leave the reflecting pool in which he sees only his own image, and engage with real people in a real world. He should visit his Granny or change a nappy. He needs to learn honesty in facing up to his true condition, and to restore the priority of relationships, with God and with other people. Such relationships, says Jesus, are what life is actually all about (Mk 12:28–34). It is as we learn these two forms of intimacy that we learn true personhood. We learn to give and receive love, forgiveness, vulnerability and openness. Narcissus needs to develop relationships which are not characterised by the need to impress: befriending somebody with learning difficulties or a disability, someone who might shortly die of AIDS. He needs to start getting down to the level of young children. The potty and the Armani suit sit uneasily together. He needs to explore personal vocation, a concept the Puritans understood well, but which we have rather neglected. He needs, in short, to become a whole person, robed in the reflected glory of his Creator.

Looking Good

Style is one of God's lovable, mischievous little creatures, but it makes a cruel master, leaving its worshipper (the fashion victim) with the emptiness and insecurity which are the eventual characteristics of all idolatry. Style is a component of identity, not a substitute for it.

Style can express my secure sense of who I am, and can enable me to communicate and creatively enhance this. It can never create a self *ex nihilo* from the diverse fragments of other people's identities collected in the High Street or mall. Style is not about following the current trend, it is about me dressing creatively and (above all) appropriately. Self-adornment is inseparable from self-awareness. For this reason, we each help dethrone the idol of insecure image-purchasing as we become more secure in our own sense of identity, and consequently in our own sense of style. Rather than being blown this way and that by the winds of whatever the latest fashion guru or magazine feature would have us wear, we need to know what genuinely looks good and appropriate on us. Even if that involves wearing colours and cuts which are defiantly out of fashion.

Some Christians scorn the likes of Mary Spillane's 'Color Me Beautiful' organisation. In March 1993 the Bishop of Aston, the Rt Rev Michael Whinney, invited the clergy of Birmingham to a talk on 'the language of clothes', by image consultant Jane Fardon. The talk was followed by a series of consultations for individual clergy, to help them analyse their own skin tones and hair colour, and from there to advise each on appropriate dressing for work and leisure. The day sparked a national outcry amongst other Christians (clergy and laity alike) who felt that the goings-on in Birmingham were unseemly, trivial and vain.

In reality, the work of such groups in raising people's self-awareness and teaching people how to dress to enhance their own natural features is extremely healthy. It teaches them when shopping to look only for the few items and colours which will suit them, irrespective of what the neighbours or the latest soap star may be draped in, or what happens to be on the sale rail that week. For the price of a pair of trousers or a skirt, one personal consultation can help clients avoid expensive mistakes in future. Such consultations actually help subvert potential manipulation by marketers, eager to sell this season's style, whether or not it suits us. It also helps us become secure in our own identity before God.

I am me, unique and precious. I know what sort of hair colouring, body shape and skin tones God has given me. As God's image on earth, I am to do with my appearance what all mankind is to do with the whole earth: to take the good gifts of God, and develop them creatively, responsibly and obediently. Getting appropriately dressed and having an appropriate haircut can be acts of creative stewardship.

Surviving the Sales

There are particular seasons of the year when the blood begins to race in even the most confirmed style-phobic, and every young man's fancy runs wild with passion and irrationality. We refer, of course, to sale time in the clothing stores. That season when the most passive housewife becomes a tireless hunter-gatherer, armed and dangerous, as she doggedly pursues that elusive bargain. That season when suburban civility is replaced by a violent recklessness which treads all obstacles underfoot.

It is that season when so many of us triumphantly return bearing our trophies of battle, and spread them out on the bed to admire them. But it is also that passionate season invariably followed by a bright, cold dawn in which we look again at our spoils of battle, and realise that every single one was a big mistake, never to be worn, something we would never have considered buying at any less hysterical season of the year.

So to help avoid the pitfalls of both seasonal and permanent shopaholism, I offer the following sales survival kit, each of the six points painfully learned in the heat of battle and the cold light of morning, by myself and other seasoned sales victims:

1) Always go clothes shopping with a list of things you actually require

2) Choose well-made, classic styles you are likely to wear for years

3) Only go to the stores where you know the colours and styles tend to suit you

4) Do not compromise on the fit, 'because it's a bargain'. Be every bit as fussy as you would if the garment were full price.

5) Do not ask, 'Will I wear it?' but '*When* will I wear it?' and avoid the trap of thinking, 'If I wear it once it will be worth it'

6) Do not feel you have somehow failed if you return empty-handed. You have actually won a victory.

CHAPTER 7

DYING TO BE THIN

'I don't want women bigger than a size 12 wearing my clothes'

Calvin Klein

Starving for Style

In the last chapter we examined compulsive shopping and label-mania as symptoms of a modern fashion idolatry. In this chapter we shift to some other instances of how things have gone badly wrong as a preoccupation with image and style have got out of hand: namely, body image and eating disorders.

Anorexia and Bulimia

The best estimates from the UK's Office of Health Economics reveal that in 1994, some 200,000 people in Britain suffered from anorexia (self-starvation), or its close cousin bulimia (binge-vomiting). They add that the cases on record were doubling every ten years, at an estimated cost to the National Health Service of £4.5 million a year. In the US studies have found that between five and fifteen per cent of female students on college campuses suffer from eating disorders. Each month over 100 new academic papers on eating disorders are published.

Among those with anorexia, around six per cent actually die, the most famous anorexic death being Karen Carpenter, vocalist of the musical group *The Carpenters*. But she is not alone: the anorexia death-toll also includes the actress Diana Wynyard and the ballerina Janet French, who committed suicide after wasting away to just six stones in weight.

The earliest medical records of self-starvation in anything more than isolated instances occurs in Europe in the early-18th century among rural, working-class, Roman Catholic girls. They appear to have been motivated by religious zeal to emulate popular Catholic female ascetics such as Catherine of Siena, who lived in northern Italy in the 14th century. The disorder became known as 'anorexia mirabilis' – miraculous or holy anorexia – stemming from a mystical belief that the denial of food might induce a state of ascetic sainthood. However, by the mid-19th century all religious overtones to the condition had vanished. It was now a condition peculiar to middle-class, urban and suburban females, and it is still among such groups that its rapid rise in recent years has been observed.

Explaining Why

Experts on eating disorders agree that behind the experience lie two separate but related factors: firstly, particular problems in the life of the individual, and secondly, wider social pressures on her. In this, the causes of eating disorders are uncannily like those of shopaholism, outlined in the last chapter.

1) Individual factors. Most researchers believe that a predisposition towards deliberate starvation or a compulsive pattern of bingeing and vomiting lie in some specific pressures or traumas experienced by the sufferer. That makes sense, as most women in our culture experience identical pressures from our consumer culture, but the majority do not develop anorexia or bulimia. As with any addiction or pattern of compulsive behaviour, the person has been in some way psychologically predisposed or prepared to be a victim. There is something in particular individuals which makes them pull the triggers offered by modern society.

In the case of eating disorders, the latest research strongly indicates that some people (women especially) *internalise* through their eating habits *external* circumstances beyond their control. The poet Elizabeth Barrett Browning is thought to have been in her semi-invalid state due to an anorexia brought on by the suffocating attentions of an over-zealous father. There are times when we all need to express feelings of anger or even violence due to circumstances. However, if such expression is stifled due to family or other pressures, there is evidence that some women push the anger deep within and take it all out on their own body. Excessive and destructive control over oneself can take the place of normal, healthy control of one's personal circumstances.

2) Social pressures. But if some people are prone to internalising pressures and taking them out on their own bodies, the 20th century has provided abundant reasons why this should be done in terms of food deprivation.

Ironically, the background to this has been the greater opportunities and aspirations created by the relative levelling out of old hierarchies in western society. Traditional society was rigidly stratified. Parentage dictated one's lot in life: whether university was a possibility or not; whether you had the front or back pew in church; whom you could mix with socially; whether you sat at table or served. Expectations were set from birth, from the nobility down to the working classes. Few escaped the constraints imposed by one's station.

Today, such constraints are less prevalent. We rightly pride ourselves that there is more or less equality of opportunity for all, encouraged by free state education. What, then, are the new yardsticks by which society operates? How do people evaluate themselves, if not by looking up and down a ladder? When the random blessings of birth cease to be a meal-ticket, what am I left with? Quite simply, my own physical self. The new measuring-stick is the body, its looks, fitness and style. The new comparison is how close I come to whatever society deems attractive, and for at least thirty years now that norm has been slimness.

The current pressures on young women are directly traceable to the mid-1960s and the rise of models such as Twiggy and Jean Shrimpton. This era saw a return to the emaciated ideals of femininity which had last been popular among the 'flappers' of the 1920s. With the decision by the editor of the *Daily Express* in 1966 to name 16-year-old, six-and-a-half-stone Lesley Hornby (Twiggy) as 'face of the year', the 50s ideal of the voluptuous, curvaceous girl was ended. True, Marilyn Monroe had followed the frequent Hollywood trick of self-induced vomiting as a means to instant weight-loss before a shoot. Even in the 50s, that tummy had to be flattened. But nobody had been in any doubt that *those* breasts and hips, squeezed into those size 16 dresses, were a well-rounded pack of sexual explosives.

Of course, the 50s film directors and fashion designers chose full-figured girls for the same reasons that most cultures in most places have preferred them. The reasons why the well-covered girl is celebrated by painters such as Reubens and exploited by pornographers, not to mention being the standard of beauty in early Hollywood and across Africa, is self-evident and logical. She is more obviously sexual, prosperous, fertile and mature. All of these are desirable properties to anything other than a culture which is anti-life and slowly self-destructing. In other words, the bigger girl is an ideal in any culture which possesses the common sense jettisoned by the modern consumer West.

But today's full-figured girl is an exile from another culture, misunderstood, unwanted, the object of scorn for designers such as Calvin Klein whose dictum that any girl over a size 12 should not wear his clothes is small-minded in more ways than one. But Klein is far from alone. His attitude is usually unspoken, but almost always present in the attitudes of the modern fashion industry. To designers, retailers, style gurus, magazine editors and advertising executives, she is an embarrassment.

By any sane standards, she is normal. In our society, she is marginal. The consequences of this are profound and reach deep into everyday life. For many (perhaps most) women in the culture to which most of us belong, eating is viewed as something slightly vulgar or coarse. It might be something to be enjoyed, but never without a twinge of guilt, a count of calories, a guilty hand to the waist. In a strange way, food has become sinful: momentarily pleasurable but ultimately horrible.

Ms Average

The perverse manner in which food and thinness are viewed by today's woman is underlined by the results of a survey in *Cosmopolitan* magazine from early 1993. The survey of 7,000 women questioned about their attitude to food makes for sobering reading. Of those surveyed, none of whom considered they had an eating disorder, two-thirds admitted to thinking about food a lot or all of the time. Seventy-two per cent could remember everything they ate the previous day, one in four was perpetually on a diet, fourteen per cent kept their weight down using laxatives, another fourteen per cent by vomiting. Seven per cent actually bought and used appetite suppressants. Over half confessed that they would lie about what they ate, and a quarter stated that they felt they were 'a better person' if they ate hardly anything on a particular day.

Similarly, research carried in 1994 out by the University of Arizona's anthropology department found that among white girls between the ages of fourteen and seventeen, no less than ninety per cent expressed dissatisfaction with their own bodies, and eighty-three per cent saw dieting as a positive way of exerting control and boosting their self-confidence. Their ideal body shape was 5ft 7in, weighing 100 pounds (seven stone two). As the researchers noted, when scaled down this reproduced exactly the figure of a Barbie doll.

What is frightening about the surveys is the glimpse they give into the normal attitudes of ordinary young women today. The picture is backed up by claims from a British lobby group, Diet Breakers, who claim that ninety per cent of all females diet at some time, and that at any given moment half of all UK women are dieting, including some as young as eight years old. Never mind eating disorders, show us a young woman with an eating *order*. If the surveys are in any way representative, it shows that most women see eating as a problem due to a fear of putting on weight. It shows just how 'normal' it is for a young woman today to be miserable because she is not thin. Since forty-seven per cent of British women are a size 16 or over, that equals an awful lot of misery. Professor Tom Sanders, chair of nutrition at King's College, London, claims that 'In Britain food has replaced sex as the national neurosis.'

And the designers and marketers know it. A top British designer recently developed a range of clothing aimed at women between the ages of thirty and forty, choosing usual size 12 dimensions to be his size 10. Delighted customers would find they could fit a smaller size than usual when buying his outfits, boosting their self-confidence and making them feel younger and more attractive. After all, small is beautiful. Isn't it?

Hence the massive and growing range of diets on offer: in the tabloid and quality press alike, in mass-market, best-selling paperbacks, in tubs, jars and capsules. They come as Cambridge, Grapefruit, Hay, Conley, Rotation, F-Plan, even 'Christian' weight-loss plans (*Slim For Him, Firm Believer, He Must Increase but I Must Decrease, More of Christ and Less of Me* – the titles alone ought to induce a bout of vomiting in even the non-bulimic). Experts tell us the West spends more on slimming aids each year than is needed to feed all of the world's hungry people. In Britain alone, we spend £88 million a year (1994 figure) on the brand leaders in meal replacement products, Slim-Fast and Slender, and the two Boots products: NutraSlim and Shapers. But is it helping us?

We have reached the point where doctors are telling us that our obsession with losing weight is actually harming us. Hardly a month goes by without reports in the Sunday press from doctors criticising specific diets as nutritionally inadequate or unbalanced. Vital internal organs are being weakened due to loss of essential body mass. And young women are being damaged in other ways. Research carried out by Dr Pertti Mustajoki of the University Hospital in Helsinki revealed in 1992 that if women achieved the emaciated body shape of the modern shop-window mannequins, they would never start menstruating and would be infertile. Women need at least seventeen per cent of their body-weight as fat to reach the onset of menstruation, and twenty-two per cent to have a regular cycle. But the Finnish research showed that while the 'fat' on mannequins before the 1950s was mostly in the normal range, since the 50s it has been consistently much less.

Chopping and Changing

For some, the long, drawn-out process of dieting is both too wearying and its results still too dissatisfying. Increasing numbers are turning to the art of the cosmetic surgeon to give them the dream body to carry the latest styles. Indeed, the body itself can be reworked to fit in with these trends. Rock singer and actress Cher is perhaps the best known example of a plastic surgeon's dream. To date, she has not only had her tummy tightened and her thighs reduced, she has had her backside reshaped and her navel reduced, and her breasts have been 'lifted' no less than three times. If she carries on this way, they will soon be round her ears. All at a cost of £24,000.

Nor is surgery limited to the outside of the body in the quest for slimness. The 1980s in the USA saw pioneering work on internal organs to help the would-be skinny achieve her grail. The Jejuno-ileal Bypass aimed to short-circuit the small bowel and thereby prevent absorption of fats into the body. Gastroplasty involved the stomach itself being stapled so that only half of it could be used to digest food. Other fat-conscious consumers had balloons implanted, to use up space which might otherwise be taken up by the dreaded food.

In Britain today, some 40,000 men and women have undergone some form of cosmetic surgery. But why do most of us instinctively feel uneasy about the lengths many go to in order to achieve the perfect Barbie-doll body-shape? I would suggest at least two main reasons.

The first is that the whole process so often involves a defacing of the very image we are trying to enhance. Beauty-related surgery (whether internal or external) has been plagued by doubts about its safety. The pioneering internal work in the

States was accompanied by a range of unpleasant errors, side effects and difficulties, and mistakes made by cosmetic surgeons are increasingly hitting the headlines.

Thirty-eight-year-old Cindy Jackson, Ohio-born founder of the British independent watchdog, the Cosmetic Surgery Network, estimates that of the 200 cosmetic surgeons practising in the UK, only half a dozen are professionally competent. Certainly, research for the *Independent on Sunday* in March 1994 revealed that one in four practitioners had received no specialist training at all in plastic surgery. Ms Jackson says her own £30,000 personal transformation included a series of mistakes, and that she has a bag of letters from other 'victims' of cosmetic surgery, some of whom have ended up looking as if they have been badly burnt, or else have lost all feeling in parts of their body. There are very practical reasons to question the growing trend towards the using the scalpel where the F-Plan has failed.

But a second query about elaborate, drastic diet-plans and cosmetic surgery has to be raised, one of which is even more pressing than the physical dangers posed by both. It is to do with wider issues of a person's self-image.

The whole culture of dieting and chopping is based around two things: personal dissatisfaction and consumer solutions. Both are largely spurious. We are being offered off-the-peg, instant solutions at a price, to problems which most of us never actually had in the first place. We were told what our problem was, we were the misshape in the box of chocolates: unacceptable, ugly and undesirable. Then we are sold the remedy: to reject what we were given for free as a gift of the Creator, in favour of an alternative dictated by the marketers and designers. I know which I prefer, for all its flab and wobbly bits.

Boys' Own Story

Until the late 1980s the issue mostly affected women. However, with the 90s and the aestheticisation of the male torso to an extent not seen since Ancient Greece, it has become a man's problem too.

The slim, trim male body has been eroticised in perfume and ice-cream ads, on Athena posters, in popular film and TV, and in erotic dance troupes such as the Chippendales. And, perhaps more than anywhere else, it has been flaunted in clothing ads. Levi jeans and Calvin Klein undies have done much to idealise the impersonal beefcake with the slim waist. Around half a million men work out regularly in Britain's 50,000 gyms. Body-building is becoming one of the nation's fastest-growing sports. Muscle-inflating steroid drugs are bought in massive quantities by image-conscious males. Tubs of muscle-promoting 'body-fuel' high on protein, low on fat, and packaged like Castrol GTX, are commonplace in the High Street; the beefcake's very own equivalent of the Hip and Thigh Diet.

Males are also taking to plastic surgery. In the late 80s, only ten per cent of clients at the London Hospital of Aesthetic Plastic Surgery were men. By 1993, it was forty per cent, and the number of men with anorexia is rising. Men are finally learning the same insecurities that women have known for centuries, but especially since the mid-60s. The 'Chippendale-syndrome' has led to a culture of self-conscious, insecure men discovering what it means to view themselves primarily as *objets d'art*. Men have finally become sex objects too.

Why? Why do some men go to such extreme lengths of self-punishment to achieve a perfect body? Not surprisingly, it is again a lethal combination of personal factors and social pressures.

Firstly, personal factors. In a 1993 study, Californian sociologist Alan Klein found in a study of body-builders that most had experienced problems in childhood. Particularly prevalent were speech impediments, obesity and dyslexia. According to Klein, body-building has become 'therapeutic narcissism' – a way to feel good about yourself by counteracting a negative self-image retained from childhood. In other words, the stereotype of the swaggering, over-confident hunk, still sweating from his weights-room overdrive, could not be further from the truth. Beneath the iron muscles and pectoral implants lurks a small child, craving love and affirmation.

Secondly, as before, we need to ask: why express this through a desperate urge to beautify the body? And again the emphatic response has to be made: because of the consumer images of impossibly 'perfect' bodies, associated with the fashion and style industries. We all internalise these arbitrary, externally-dictated ideals, and for some (who may already have inner insecurities or lacks from the past) the drive to possess the dream becomes all-consuming.

Creating the Dream

But the reality of the perfect body must remain unattainable, just beyond our grasp. The idea has to persist that if only we dieted and exercised enough, we too would become Twiggy, Kate Moss, a Chippendale or whoever embodies the latest ideal of the body beautiful. The ideal has to remain impossible for the majority of consumers, so that the public will carry on buying the diet books, body-fuel, breast-reshaping bras, girdles and gym subscriptions. Beauty must always be on sale but never quite realised.

Models – Embodying the Dream

How did we get to where we are today, where a slender elite of slender girls set the norm of beauty for the great majority of permanently dissatisfied larger women? The answer in part lies in the changing role of the female model throughout the last hundred years. In the early decades of this century, the model was exclusively based at the premises of a dressmaker, in order to display items to shoppers. She was a real flesh-and-blood woman, giving other real flesh-and-blood women a clearer idea of what a dress would look like when worn.

The pictures in the fashion weeklies were a different matter altogether: they were not photos of real girls, but drawings. They offered stylised illustrations of women with small heads, long slim legs, and faces often painted with minimal strokes of a brush or pen. They were designed to give an artistic impression of new styles, not to give women an idea of what they would actually look like wearing the garment. Almost cartoons, the illustrations were dreamlike absurdities which bore little resemblance to true human dimensions.

To compare the illustrations to the real models or the customers would be like comparing characters in Disney's *Aladdin* to real Arabs. The evil Jafar, with his elongated body and face, and Princess Jasmine, with her absurdly large eyes and painfully tiny waist, are supposed to be taken as fantastic ideals of particular characteristics, not as representational art. So too with fashion illustration in the early part of the 20th century.

By the 1960s and 70s the art of fashion illustration had all but died out, replaced by the arty photograph and a new elite of tall, skinny girls whose main claim to fame was that they actually looked a little like the old fashioned drawings. Unnaturally long and thin, with exaggerated facial features such as full lips, big eyes and prominent cheekbones, the post-Twiggy model embodied an ideal of beauty drawn from the fashion illustration rather than the pretty girl next door. Further evidence of her lineage came from the way the technical advances in photography and graphics were used by the fashion industry.

Far from celebrating the fleshy humanness of the model, with all her natural blemishes, the advertisers developed lighting techniques to 'white out' all facial features other than striking slashes of dark eyes, lips and nostrils, a clear reference back to the facial techniques of the fashion illustrator. Lighting and air-brushes were used to remove pimples, bodily hair or flab, anything approximating to a blemish. The finished picture owed more to the drawing than the dressmaker's on-site employee.

Models – Constructing the Dream

We see in the fashion model some kind of ideal of feminine beauty. Theirs are the images consumed so frequently in the magazines by today's woman that they become an inescapable part of her psyche. But this standard of beauty is in reality the end point of a long process of eliminating most elements of the

'Fashion illustrations . . . dreamlike absurdities which bore little
resemblance to true human dimensions' (p 180)

recognisably 'normal'. It is done by taking a girl and turning her back into a fashion illustration.

A fashion model is not selected according to the usual, every-day criteria of 'prettiness', by which we might weigh up our checkout girl or hairdresser, but what will look appropriately striking in front of the camera or on the catwalk. She is a product. She needs to be tall (at least 5'8" to 5'10"), and thin (usually a size 8 or 10), with the kind of face described above: compare the lip thickness of your average model with that of your average shop assistant. Then, because every photo shoot is aimed at producing a particular image to sell a particular product, the model's face and figure are further selected to fit the ideal to be evoked.

Make-up artists and hair-stylists take around an hour preen-ing the model before any photography takes place, and rearrangements of hair and clothes go on between every shot. The model rehearses her moves, standing in positions to make her legs look longer, turning her waist to make it seem slimmer, pouting her already full lips to add sensuality, sucking in her cheeks to make her cheekbones more prominent. The photog-rapher will shoot several rolls of film, perhaps producing 100 exposures to end up with just two usable pictures. This is not to mention the use of exotic locations and later retouching on the pictures. With the advent of computer graphics, a new era of unreality has dawned. Photos can be doctored, with the result that not only can complete eye, hair and skin colour be changed in seconds, but also legs lengthened, waists tightened, bust enlarged. At the push of a button and the drag of a 'mouse' on a rubber pad, a girl can be created who owes more to tech-nology than nature; a computerised ideal.

Fashion photography at its most idealistic is a heroic attempt to capture a fleeting moment of pure beauty. But it is by defini-tion to do with the unreal, the perfect, the exaggerated, because it is all about creating unattainable dreams.

Perhaps this constant element of the unreal and dreamlike explains the frequent element of Surrealism in fashion photogra-phy. The hallucinogenic, dream-world ideals of the artist André

Breton, Surrealism's main theorist, have triumphed in the fashion photograph more than any other medium. The fashion photographer Cecil Beaton admitted that it was this very quality which drew him to his chosen trade: 'The complete falsehood, the artifice intrigued me.' The whole enterprise is an elaborate game of pure image. And its goal is making you part with your cash.

Real Lives

In writing this, the last thing we want to do is to slight the many good and idealistic people who work in the fashion industry, least of all the models themselves. Of course, these girls and guys *are* extraordinarily attractive, by the standards of our own culture. And they are real people leading real lives – not even a model lives out the ideal dreamscape of the fashion photo in her everyday world. Most of the time she is rushing around, trying to find out where the next assignment will be. She pays the gas bill, phones her parents, reads the paper and mows the lawn like the rest of us. Ask my sister who is a professional, London-based model.

Like fashion design, modelling clothing remains a perfectly valid career option for the Christian. A growing number of models around the world are practising Christians, many converted on the job through contact with other Christian models. In 1984 a successful New York model, Laura Krauss Calenberg, started holding weekly Bible studies for models in her apartment. This has now grown into Models for Christ, a worldwide network of fashion industry professionals that includes designers, stylists and photographers, who meet for Christian fellowship and to discuss professional ethics. The group publishes a quarterly newsletter, *Role Model*, which acts as a forum for news and debate.

MFC works to offer a genuine alternative to much of the egomania rife in the fashion industry. Each year the group places clothing collection boxes at the headquarters of several top New York model agencies, and the garments collected (around two tons a year) are distributed to needy families throughout the city.

If we sound alarm bells about the ethics of fashion marketing and modelling, that makes these areas no different from other controversial areas of work, such as the media or politics. Each of these areas is valid, because it deals in God-given potentialities, designed to be used in God's world: adornment, communication and administration. It is how these potentialities are being used that is the issue.

Modelling is not a no-go area for the believer. The Christian model is called to her trade for three main reasons: firstly, as a celebration of God's gift of clothing, a gift which is dignifying, creative and celebratory. Secondly, as a use of her own God-given attributes. We encourage the Christian academic to use his brain, the Christian accountant to use her head for figures, and the Christian mechanic to use the skill of his hands. So too, we can encourage the Christian model to use the poise, beauty and elegance of her body. To accept one type of profession and not the other would be either a severe case of the bifocals, referred to in Chapter 2, or else plain snobbery.

Thirdly, the Christian model is to do what all believers are to do, which is to act as a channel of God's light into their own sphere of influence. *Model for Christ's* statement of aims concedes that models so often inhabit a world of grime and compromise, and urges fashion professionals who are believers to

> take a stand for their Christian beliefs. . . . If more people would take a personal stand, slowly the darkness of the fashion world would be filled with light. . . . The fashion community has such a powerful influence in the world today and they have to be responsible with this influence. We encourage professionals to use that power for good and to stop adding to the moral decline that has occurred in the fashion world.

The Christian model is subject to the same biblical ethical guidelines as the rest of us. There will be times for drawing the line, when a photo shoot will be refused, even at the risk of losing out on some of the serious money which can be made in the industry. This will be certainly the case in those grey areas where fashion modelling fades into the peddling of pornographic images. Lee Benton, a top Hollywood actress and model, says she has missed out on literally millions of dollars because her Christian faith has led her to turn down jobs involving nudity and partial nudity. But, at the end of the day, she says she has the deeper satisfaction of knowing that she has not compromised her faith. This is no small stand in an industry where some revealing shots are commonplace in most models' work portfolios.

The pressures to compromise at every stage are rife. Christian models reject the sporadic industry practice of angling for career advancement by sleeping with a photographer on a shoot, and frequently refuse jobs promoting products they cannot condone, such as tobacco. The Christian model will experience in herself the jealousy and insecurity endemic in the modelling world, where envy is magnified as beauty is magnified. She lives with the tensions we all experience to some degree, of living in the 'already' but 'not yet' of the kingdom of God. But she stays, called by God himself to be a ray of light in a dark industry.

The particular moral pressures of the fashion industry mean that for the model, accountability is vital. Compromise appears to promise so much in terms of financial reward and climbing the career ladder. Every Christian model must have a supportive fellowship, friends who understand the industry and its particular temptations, friendship with other like-minded people in the industry. And the task of the wider church is not to judge, but to support in love.

Our aim, then, has not been to criticise individuals involved in the fashion world, or even question the existence of fashion itself, both of which are redeemable in Christ. Nor has it been to challenge whether fashion is a valid calling for the Christian. Rather, we have tried to put the spotlight on the present mechanics of the fashion system. We want to alert the consumer to where the ideals she holds of physical beauty may come from, to help us to understand the dreamscape and hence make us all more critical consumers of the images which surround us daily. Because, at the end of the day, only two things are actually on offer to the consumer: dissatisfaction, and the goods on sale at the local fashion store.

Self-Esteem in a World of Images

The model, then, is presented as an unattainable role model, part of the commercial system to keep consumption turning over. This is achieved by feeding our dissatisfaction. We buy items of clothing to purchase the longed-for identity.

At its best, and among its noblest practitioners, fashion photography represents a yearning for the absolute, for a perfection of beauty. In particular, Irving Penn (*Vogue*) and Richard Avedon (*Harper's Bazaar*) transcended the mere 'reporting' of clothes. They shared with other fine artists a feel for artistic composition, for humanity and made insightful pictorial statements about contemporary culture and mores. Penn not only took fashion shots of unsurpassed intensity and cultural insight, he also took striking anthropological shots with his portable studio, on trips to Peru, Morocco and New Guinea. But in a way, Penn's American and European fashion shots were every bit as anthropological as his far-flung ethnic shots. At the end of the day, the capable fashion photographer is just that: an anthropologist. He adopts the stance of a detached observer, feeding back to a culture the images and dreams it has itself produced. He is an artist, yearning to express an absolute beauty, and he is a sociologist, handing over to future historians the raw material of their trade. At its best, fashion photography can express a truly religious quest for the ultimate. So, in a way, can the yearnings evoked in the consumer of the images.

What other than a quest for an absolute can motivate such lofty ideals of beauty, such extremes of asceticism involving self-starvation, pushing oneself to the limits of physical endurance, the giving of one's last penny in the quest for perfection? What else can motivate the attempts to atone for personal inadequacy, the yearning to redeem lost time, the desire to be loved and accepted? What else can explain the way the entire 20th-century fashion project has been about individual consumers casting off their burdensome inherited lot in life, and being born again as each bright, shiny, new identity is purchased off the peg? Anorexic, would-be Chippendale, bulimic, dieter, all are involved in a fundamentally religious quest, even if they do not recognise it.

It appears that cultural priorities have not progressed. In the 5th century, Simeon Stylites spent more than thirty-five years, starving himself, at the top of a pole in Syria – testifying to the power of God. Today's woman spends more than thirty-five years starving herself, in order to look like a pole, testifying to the power of advertising.

However, the religious intensity of the quest for beauty also achieves what all good religion begins by achieving: it highlights the gap between the noble ideal and the mundane reality. It shows up the contrast between the pure vision and the inadequate self. Perfection and fallenness, if you like. It is in the way it proposes to reconcile these two apparently irreconcilable opposites that one can tell good religion from bad. Good religion not only identifies the beauty of the ideal, it offers a solid, coherent path towards it.

Style, like Romanticism, can yearn for beauty, truth, vulnerability. It shares Keats' claim, in his *Ode to a Grecian Urn*, that 'Beauty is truth, truth beauty, that is all/Ye know on earth, and all ye need to know.' Such a quest must never be belittled. It is exhilarating, fun, charming, even heroic. But historic Christianity does more. It whispers that there is a way to grasp hold of these ideals. But first you will need to pass through a narrow gate and tread carefully along a narrow path, which will wind through dark forests, through sunny clearings, over rivers and mountains, slowly and surely, back to the source of beauty himself. The bold, outrageous claim of Christ is that Beauty is knowable, because He is a person. The dreams, the yearnings, the quest of the entire fashion system (whether photographer, model, marketer, dieter or bulimic) can only find their fulfilment in him.

Chapter 10 is the place where we shall look more closely at a radical Christian basis for personal identity. Now we need to look at one more way in which the fashion system as we know it has been playing havoc with our search for identity, the way the fashion system promotes a regular, rapid changing of styles.

CHAPTER 8

GETTING CHANGED

Cyril too looked as if he had taken a lot of trouble with his clothes – much too much, Jack thought. And yet he looked sloppy, though probably he meant to look artistic. His tie was a floppy bow. His shirt was a peculiar colour. He wore sandals!

(Enid Blyton, *Six Cousins at Mistletoe Farm*)

Why Does Fashion Change?

A gripe constantly levelled at fashion, from the letters pages of quality newspapers to the teenager realising that most of last year's achingly-longed for styles are now unwearable, is that it changes. Not only that, it seems to change with alarming rapidity. No sooner do you feel you have caught up with it, than there it goes again, hitching up its skirts and haring off round the next corner, out of view.

But why should fashion change? What is it about the fashion system which demands such constant updating? In this chapter we shall examine the major theories advanced to account for fashion change. We shall reject most of them as inadequate, and then offer a theory which we believe best does justice to the facts of today and offer a preliminary response to it, which will be expanded in the final chapter. But first, we need to define terms.

Small Waves and Big Swells

As we address the issue of why fashion changes, it is as well to be clear what we are actually criticising. Not even the severest critic of fashion change believes we should all still be wearing bearskins, doublet and hose, crinoline petticoats, or chimney-pot hats.

A helpful distinction is made by the fashion critic Colin McDowell, in his book on high fashion *The Designer Scam*. He compares the rhythms of fashion to those of the sea. He observes that the constant, seasonal changes of contemporary fashion are like waves which crash on the seashore. They seem spectacular and violent, and we react to their drama, but we tend to forget that they are simply the product of massive, deeper swells far out to sea. It is the visible 'waves' which grab the headlines and cause us to fume in exasperation, but the real changes are elsewhere: in the vast, slow movement of eras of human history and in the way fashion gradually adapts itself to the swell.

If we can stand aside from the immediacy of the morning paper and the sale rack at Top Shop, and go deeper, we can detect more profound movements which have shaped today's styles. One is a trend towards greater comfort and liberty in dress, especially for women, which began with the dress reformers in the late-19th century. Out went the whalebone, the corsets, the impossibly tight constrictions. In came freedom of movement, health and clothes appropriate for doing rather than merely sitting and being. Of course, the unprecedented rise of trousers for western women since the 1920s is a part of this movement. Trousers were first seen in the 18th century as an exotic, 'Turkish' style of women's dress beloved of the Romantic movement, eventually gaining acceptability as 20s sports wear, and later developing into jeans, leggings, shorts and so on in the late-20th century.

The deep swell of our century is towards informality, men's as well as women's. Consider the elaborate etiquette surrounding hat-wearing in our grandparents' generation: raised when bowing to a lady or when walking with a lady and bowing to another man; raised by young men in deference to older men; always removed completely when shaking hands with a lady in a public place; always removed indoors, in church, on seeing a funeral hearse, etc, as against the etiquette of our own day where the biggest question is should my baseball cap feature Mickey Mouse or the Chicago Bulls?

Contrast the relatively laid-back sartorial codes of today with Lady Troubridge's 1926 *Book of Etiquette*. In it, she specifies different dress for, amongst other events: luncheon and after-noon parties, dinners and theatres, balls and evening parties, weddings and funerals, a weekend visit, church attendance (note: tall hats and tail-coats are now no longer worn for the country church; the church-goer must wear a blue serge suit), country house visiting, the Riviera, continental resorts, shoot-ing and hunting trips, and (that most helpful of categories) 'Where There is Uncertainty'. The answer to this, incidentally, is for men to wear morning-dress, unless in the country, where a lounge-suit and stiff collar is permissible.

Such major swells are intimately related to wide social changes. The rising profile of women in public life this century has shaped their clothing; social upheavals such as the French Revolution (with its reaction against aristocratic excess), and the First and Second World Wars (less fabric available; more women in the workplace so a greater need for practical dress which facilitates movement; shorter hairstyles as women worked at machines), all produced new cultures with new moods and new clothes to fit the times. Few critics worry about the deep swells. It is the waves crashing on the shore which disturb the modern-day Canutes.

Waves of Fashion

We all know from weary experience how certain styles or colours may be 'in' one season and out the next. If you do not like a current trend, or it does not suit you, tough! You may look good in strong, dark colours, but if delicate pastels are in, hard luck. You may like leather-laced, 'boat' shoes, but if the industry has not deemed them acceptable this season, too bad.

I am writing this part of the chapter in the summer of 1994, and the 'in' colour is ecru, a kind of porridge-coloured off-white. The 'in' textures are coarse linens, the cumulative effect looking alarmingly like the biblical sackcloth and ashes. But what if you do not like ecru, if you would rather follow Jesus' injunction to outdo Solomon in his colourful finery? What if the crumpled potato-sack look is just not you? A trip to most fashion stores will prove depressing.

So why do styles change with such regularity? Why do so many 'waves' crash unremittingly into the High Street? Several explanations have been offered.

Conspiracy Theories

Perhaps the most popular theory especially among Christians and their feminist, green and Marxist co-belligerents, is that we are victims of a fashion industry conspiracy.

It stands to reason, runs the argument, that the people who make and sell the clothes are in it for the money. Static styles means lower sales. If you do not have to keep up with Mrs Jones' expanding wardrobe, you buy fewer clothes. Designers and retailers conspire to produce sweeping changes each season to render earlier clothes unwearable by the hapless fashion victim. Clothes are dumped not because they are worn out, but because of some carefully-planned plot to make them outdated, even a year after they were 'in'. Sure enough, it is hard to look from one's wardrobe to the High Street and back again without feeling conspired against.

But is this an accurate portrayal of how the industry works, is this 'top-down' conspiracy theory an adequate account of the mechanism of style? The answer is: to a small extent, yes, but mostly, no. It is true that some co-ordinating bodies exist across the fashion industry, especially in the field of colour forecasting. The British Textile Colour Group (BTCG), its American and European equivalents, and their international counterpart, Intercolour, do meet to plan the future. Such groups are made up of professional fashion and fabric forecasters, designers and big retailers, who decide together two years in advance what the broad palette for a given season will be.

But other evidence makes an industry-wide plot less plausible. Four arguments in particular weaken the case:

a) Conspiracy theories are usually wrong. Christians, especially in North America, seem particularly prone to seeing culture in terms of conspiracies – be it reds, secular humanists, new agers, satanists or liberal Christians. Try reading the enjoyable but rather paranoid novels of Frank Peretti, where practically all of these groups join forces to undermine the true believers. In truth, the fashion industry does not have the highly-coordinated 'mega' networks claimed by its detractors. True, bodies such as the BTCG exist, but only to establish limited areas of cease-fire in the industry's own style-wars.

Design houses and retailers are in competition with each other. They may talk to each other, influence each other, and even agree on a season's shades, but the fact remains that the real enemy is not the consumer, but each other. There is no (and can be no) forum of conspiracy which shouts 'About turn!' and makes the whole industry, in step, simultaneously perform an elegant *volte-face*.

Each retailer longs for her style to catch on and for her competitors' styles to flop. To this end, each major chain-store employs the advisory talents of one of a number of fashion forecasting companies. Organisations such as the UK's Design Intelligence analyse social and industry trends to predict the 'in' colours and styles for future seasons.

It is their job to ask questions such as: What is the emerging political climate, is the pendulum swinging towards honesty, community and the 'natural', or towards individualism, personal power and ostentatious wealth? What films are Hollywood directors making today, which will influence the trends in two or three years' time? What is the cutting edge of today's nightclub chic? Such styles may well be influencing the mainstream fashions of the future. What sports are gaining momentum? What styles of popular music are catching on? The very existence of rival fashion forecasters, each eager to prove their predictive tea-leaves more worthy than their rivals', should alert us to the dangers of simplistic conspiracy theories.

The historical reality is that the days of centrally dictated styles are long gone. Even women's fashion magazines (those windows into the mysteries of style) increasingly offer a 'lifestyle' approach to clothing, helping women find their own look, rather than insisting on homogeneous styles. Conspiracy theories are too narrow to account for the eclecticism of modern style.

b) Changing fashion regularly is high-risk for designers and retailers. Regular fashion change means having to predict two years in advance what will be 'in' or 'out', and to have regular upheavals in production to respond accordingly. What if your forecaster gets it completely wrong? Or even slightly wrong? You stand to lose large quantities of cash and be left with stores full of unsold garments. In that sense, the end-of-season sale is a sign of failure. How much easier for those allegedly conspiring retailers if fashion were entirely predictable.

c) The public can say 'no' to new styles. It is all very well for a marketer to plan his assault on the gullible public. But he has no monopoly; the public can shop elsewhere. Just as critics tend to overestimate the power of particular adverts (eighty per cent of all new food products launched in the UK and backed by advertising campaigns fail to catch on), so too it is easy to overestimate the manipulative skills of image-makers. If a woman knows she looks ludicrous or inappropriate in a particular garment, it is unlikely that she will persist in buying it (and all her friends likewise) just because her magazine says it's essential. At the very least, she will head off to a rival store to find another item which is also within the broadly-defined parameters of that season's look.

Retailers are not brainwashers; they are always bound by what the public will accept. Forecasters too respond to perceived shifts in public mood: the ecru and linen blitz of 1994 was wholly due to forecasters' perceptions (two years previously) of a widespread public return to 'natural', 'simple', 'environment-friendly' values in the political realm. To use their own phrase, they watch out for colours or designs which are 'coming through' over a period of a few years. Even the forecasters primarily respond to the public mood which they see reflected on TV, in the movie houses, on the sports pitches, urban streets and in the nightclubs.

d) The contrast with men's clothes. If the fashion industry is so adept at conspiring to pull the wool (or cotton or linen) over the eyes of the consumer, why has it taken so long to affect men's clothes? From the decline of the 18th-century's nobles and dandies, to as recently as the 1980s, men's dress has been conspicuously static. Styles were homogeneous, and coloured from a remarkably restricted palette. For over a century in the West, the idea of men's 'fashion' has been all but unthinkable. Until the 1990s, men's style magazines, along the lines of the traditional woman's glossy, were notoriously the graveyard of periodical publishing.

Did the retailers then spend two centuries in a despair as black as their waistcoats? Hardly, because designs, colours and production runs were more predictable in the static world of men's clothing than in the fluctuating, less predictable world of women's and profits were often higher. The current rise in male fashions, male fashion glossies and the general aestheticization of the male torso cannot be explained purely as a marketing coup. This had been tried and had failed too many times before.

Rather, it is likely that the current rediscovery of masculine aesthetics is the start of one of the deep sea-swells in fashion history referred to earlier. Something in masculine self-perception has been changing. How else do we explain the shift from a complete absence of men's fashion glossies in Britain to today's tally of no less than six in such a short space of time?

Perhaps this is due to the gradual replacement of the post-18th-century ideals of reason, science and control by the more eclectic, playful dreams of 'postmodernism'; perhaps as feminism has encroached into traditional 'male' terrains, men have felt free to roam across areas previously defined as the 'female'; perhaps due to the greater public visibility of urban gay culture; or the fact that those reared since the cultural and artistic upheaval of the 1960s are less likely to defer to mere convention; who knows?

One thing is for certain: here again, designers and retailers are responding to the changes more than they are creating them.

Dress as Economic Barometer

A common theory is that many aspects of fashion directly reflect the economic climate of their day. Thus, long skirts seem to proliferate in times of recession; short skirts in times of growth and prosperity. Some claim factors other than skirt length to support this theory: the boom-time of the 1980s saw the rise of big, padded power-shoulders in dresses and jackets, which then disappeared in the recession-hit late 80s and early 90s.

It is certainly true that the mood of the times influences what we wear and how we wear it. Trouser flares, tie width, lapel size and sole height all become nostalgic and embarrassing reminders of a different era. The farther reaches of parents' wardrobes provide an unending source of mirth for their offspring. Unquestionably, the economic climate has some bearing, especially during extreme conditions such as wartime. If nothing else, fabric can become more scarce. Yet this hardly amounts to a complete theory of fashion change. Especially since, as the tyranny of centrally-dictated styles crumbles, the fashion industry and media alike are shifting to a more individually-focused 'lifestyle' approach.

So much for the theory when, as at the present time, tight mini-skirts and flowing cheesecloths, flares and drainpipes, power shoulders and flowing silks, GI-style cropped cuts and dippy hippy locks all coexist. The theory is fun, but limited.

Shifting Erogenous Zones

A third theory purporting to explain why fashion changes is altogether more steamy. Based on certain psychoanalytic theories, it claims that the female body is made up of a number of potentially erotic areas: breasts, legs, waist, hips, buttocks and arms. Styles change, so the argument goes, to highlight or reveal a new erogenous zone on the human body. At some times long skirts hide legs, at others mini skirts reveal them. Sometimes loose tops hide breasts, other times tighter tops highlight them. Each season, attention is drawn to a single bodily 'zone', to the exclusion of all the others.

To some the view may sound far-fetched, but it has its eminent adherents, most notably James Laver, author of one of the standard histories of fashion. He, along with some other fashion analysts, consider the shifting erogenous zone theory to be a complete explanation of all fashion change.

But is it? For a start, the rise (or, rather, revival) of men's fashion in the late-20th century seriously challenges the theory. Its advocates have only seriously applied it to women's wear. Indeed, Laver claims fashion change can only apply to women, since he claims that men only have a single 'erogenous zone'. But today we see men's fashion changing alongside women's. Perhaps then we should enlarge the theory for our own day to include men: zones might include chest, pectorals, buttocks, neck, and waist (although few of us would welcome a fashion which drew too much attention to the male waistline).

Does this now become a satisfactory explanation? The fact remains that the theory is not only historically questionable, it is far-fetched and reductionist. Its reductionism lies in its attempt, like the theories of Freud, to reduce complex human motivations to a single cause: namely, sex. From a Christian perspective, this is simply idolatrous. We are complex, multi-faceted creatures, and our sexuality is one strand in our richly diverse make-up. To single out the sexual dimension, elevate it above all the others, and make it the single explanation of all those others, is not only naive, it is demeaning to our humanity.

The shifting erogenous zone theory may partly explain one visible aspect of women's fashion in history, but falls short as an overarching theory of fashion change.

Conspicuous Wealth

This theory has already been touched on in Chapter 5. Following critics such as Veblen, it claims that fashion is all about ostentatious wealth. Quite simply, you change clothes because you can. Fashion shows your triumph over the restrictions of poverty, that you can afford a life of ease. Changing dress implies wastage, so it is by definition for those who can afford to waste. It also follows from this, claims Veblen, that the poorer members of society copy the 'in' styles as an aspirational statement. They emulate the trend-setters to show that they too have status in society.

We have already noted that this theory goes some way to account for the mechanisms of fashion throughout earlier periods of history in eras when only the conspicuously wealthy could afford to change their styles. An amusing quotation from Flora Thompson's classic account of English country life *Lark Rise to Candleford,* illustrates how fashions trickled down from the rich urbanites to the rural poor, leaving the villagers years behind the times. The author describes how 'The hamlet's fashion lag was the salvation of its wardrobes, for a style became "all the go" just as the outer world was discarding it', and how her brother 'had seen the last bustle on earth going round the Rise on a woman with a bucket of pig-wash' (p103–4).

However, this theory of poor emulating rich is less than satisfying as an explanation of the way modern fashion works. Indeed, its reverse is often true. Not only is it economically reductionist (reducing everything to economic causes as Laver reduced everything to sex) but also, Veblen and his allies are wedded to an invariably 'top-down' theory of how style changes, and today this approach misses the mark.

Whilst once (in the days of private dressmakers and tailors, also earlier in the 20th century) clothes were indeed launched to the rich and then copied for the masses, today, ready-to-wear is the order of the day for all levels of society. The working-class girl is as likely (more likely) to be aware of 'current' styles as the gentry. Mass media sees to that. It is no longer the case that styles were chosen by the aristocracy in consultation with their dressmakers. Now they are chosen by designers in consultation with retailers, in consultation with the public mood. True, the Armanis and Kleins still influence the designs of some cheaper styles. There is unquestionably some 'top-down' movement. But it is equally true that the cheeky teen rebellion postures of punk, grunge and hippy styles work from the bottom up.

Once the street waif dreamed of dressing like a duchess. Today, the duchess pays handsomely to dress like a street waif.

The Culture of Adolescence

None of these explanations fully and adequately explains why fashion changes. Many of them give clues as to why styles have changed at various points in history but the single, overarching theory which not only describes why fashion has changed, but can prescribe when and how it will change again, remains elusive. Simplistic and reductionistic theories founder on the complexities of human culture and motivation.

It is our contention that no theory can do justice to fashion change which ignores the vast shifts in culture which have been taking place in the West since the 1960s. Let us abandon the quest for universal laws which will explain all rising hemlines and plunging necklines at a stroke. Instead, let us focus on something rather more practical and immediate by narrowing the question: why are so many westerners at the tail end of the 20th century so obsessed with staying in fashion? We shall argue that it is because they are part of a culture of adolescence, whose values they have absorbed without question.

All Teenagers Now

We have already cited the words of style guru Robert Elms, that nobody is a teenager any more because everybody is. In the words of a recent Canadian book on youth culture, 'The natural instability of youth, once viewed as simply a stage in

'Once the street waif dreamed of dressing like a duchess. Today, the duchess pays handsomely to dress like a street waif' (p 198)

life, is now projected upon much of adult society, presented as a normative attitude toward life. . . . In other words, age no longer denotes personal stability and maturity.' (Schulze et al: *Dancing in the Dark*, p66)

The way our consumer society works encourages people to remain forever in a perpetual adolescent identity crisis, a crisis whose defining characteristics fuel the rapid cycles of fashion change. These defining characteristics include: the search for sensation, the search for novelty, fear of the future, and the search for security. Since the Second World War these have been a particular preserve of the adolescent. By the 1990s, consumer culture has made adolescents of most of us.

1) The Search for Sensation: Boredom has become a possibility on a scale never before imaginable. Most homes in our culture have the kind of amenities which previous eras reserved for kings and emperors. Most of us can take food and shelter for granted. Energies channelled into survival, until as recently as the immediate post-War era, are now channelled into the quest for distraction. It has become a commonplace to speak of our culture as one wrestling to come to terms with unparalleled leisure time. We have space for reflection, self-analysis, purchasing. The two most popular pastimes in our society are watching TV and shopping, the two things which people also spend most of their time doing when on holiday. Fashion is a part of the leisure boom, a response to boredom, the self-stimulation of a lethargic culture of adolescence. We long for sensation, change and fun. Fashion responds to our craving by providing just such constant change, constant stimulation, constant fun. There is something almost magical about the capacity of clothing. As we pull on a new change of clothes for an evening out, we pull on a release from the nine-to-five, we pull on a utopian dream of how we should love the whole of life to be.

Like the adolescent, we also yearn for heroism. But in a consumer society, this yearning is channelled into consumption: the image of myself as great outdoor explorer bought with my

Timberland shoes; the illusion of myself as top athlete bought with my jogging pants; the prospect of myself as environmental radical bought with my unbleached cotton undies. Even spirituality is starting to have less to do with what is spoken down on my knees than what is illustrated down on my T-shirt.

Our major bulwark against boredom is the mass-media which feeds and sustains our self-images. It is now more possible than at any stage in history for me to live in a designer universe of my own choosing, now that sub-cultures are no longer geographical, but universal and media-disseminated.

I can have a TV in my own room, tuned to 'my' channel, from among the vast and growing range on offer; a radio in my car, tuned to 'my' type of station; a personal stereo as I walk down the street; my own collection of videos and recordings at home, not to mention 'my' type of magazines. Each disseminates the images which initiate me into the clothing styles of my chosen subcultures.

The old ideal of 'broadcasting' is out. No longer do I need to choose between just two or three public-service TV channels or radio stations, secure in the knowledge that the Joneses next door are almost certain to be watching or listening to the same output. The order of the day is now 'narrowcasting': the lifestyle personalisation of media from among the bewildering range on offer. It is possible for each of us to 'buy into' our own chosen sub-culture, constantly surrounded by the 'look', image and identity we desire.

Ironically, it is youths from protective homes who are most at risk from such all-encompassing images. By 1994, half of all UK children in the seven to ten age-range had their own TV in their own bedroom. The figure rises to no less than seven in ten for the eleven to fourteen-year-olds. If the home was once deemed a haven of retreat from the corrupting influence of society, now it is its primary dispenser.

We are a culture of bored adolescents, window-shopping our way through our media and malls, fired by dreams of style-based heroism, craving our next fix of identity stimulation. Fashion change gives us a regular high.

2) The Search for Novelty: The desire for novelty is closely linked to the ideals of modernity. Like a sullen adolescent, our culture glibly turns its back on traditional institutions such as church and home (not to mention its increasing questioning of others such as the monarchy, police and parliament). We are embarrassed to be associated with institutions apparently so backward-looking, so conventional (except where their iconography and terminology can be 'sampled' for our own pick-'n'mix lifestyle – the crucifix as fashion accessory). Because fashion is about newness, the love affair between youth and style has been in part an expression of a desire for freedom: freedom from the past, convention, conformity and blandness. Revolt in late-18th century Paris exploded in street violence. Revolt in late-20th century London exploded in street style.

For today's universal adolescent there is something intrinsically good about being abreast of the 'latest' thing, up-to-date, on the cutting edge. Scorn is poured on those considered old-fashioned or out-of-touch. Even to wear a revived style of a previous decade shows that you are aware that that is the latest thing. Even the blatantly unfashionable becomes fashionable if the right people make it out to be. The current trend amongst British soccer fans is for expesnsive, labelled 'classics' of a peculiarly conventional variety, including Jaeger and Burberry. But in the particular subculture of the wearers, such garments are paradoxically considered avant-garde. At play is what Lévi-Strauss (the anthropologist, not the jeans manufacturer) termed *bricolage*: changing the meaning and significance of an object as it is taken away from its original context and reapplied in a new one. Bricolage is a mainspring of subcultural and youth styles, from the teds' mimicking of the cut of aristocratic Edwardian dress, to the punks' appropriation of the safety pin and swastika, and beyond.

The nervous teenager inside many of us loves to feel in touch, even if some other members of the society think we look ridiculous. We know that we are giving off secret signals to other initiates, to others in the know. The opinion of others on the leading edge of culture is all that matters. It confers a Gnostic sense of the self as one of the initiated, the special, the elite. The teenage dance music composer Adamski appeared on UK breakfast TV in the early 90s wearing a strange pink, furry hat which could have been his grandmother's. Throughout the interview the show's presenters sniggered and offered embarrassed asides about the pink hat, confident that they spoke for the greater part of the audience, which they unquestionably did. No matter. Adamski sat, radiating the confident, impassive look of the true initiate. Anybody else truly on the cutting edge would know that it was he, Adamski, who was in the leading carriage of culture, and the presenters who were the reactionary philistines trailing behind. They were the ones displaying their lack of cultural awareness even if they were in the majority. He was content.

Since clothing is perhaps the most crucial visible expression of identity, then to change one's clothes for the new season tells the world: 'Look at me, I'm in! I'm part of the *avant garde* of our society. I'm a leader, not a follower.' To be 'cool' is to appear effortlessly abreast of tomorrow's preoccupations and looks. By a cruel irony, this very desire to be out in front makes the all-age adolescent the most vulnerable to the marketing media. We may want to be out front, but not out there alone. So we buy what we are told will put us on the cutting edge with the other initiates. That in turn raises another component of our culture of adolescence, which we shall examine in point 4, the search for security.

3) Fear of the Future: The post-60s generation has widely accepted the belief, perhaps more than any other generation in human history, that there is no future. The threat of a global nuclear holocaust dominated teenage minds in the 60s and 70s, only to be replaced in the late 80s by the prospect of planet earth's environmental suicide.

Not only has the global picture seemed bleak, so has the personal. Unemployment, particularly amongst youth, has reach unprecedented levels. Large sections of our culture have grown up never knowing the experience of going out to work.

Similarly, the prospects for long-term security in relationships seem barren. By 1994, more UK couples under the age of thirty were cohabiting than were marrying, signalling a clear retreat from making commitments which affect anything other than the present. Sure enough, in 1994, a cohabiting relationship was four times as likely to split up as a marriage.

The utopian dreams of modernism have been shattered. For the first time, opinion surveys in the mid-90s have consistently found that most people expect the future to be worse than the present, both globally, nationally and in their personal lives. In 1994, Voluntary Service Overseas carried out a major international survey to compare the attitudes of 1500 fifteen-year-olds in the UK and in the Third World. Of the teenagers surveyed in twenty-four developing countries, two-thirds agreed with the statement that the world would be a better place by the year 2000. On the other hand, only a third of fifteen-year-olds in the UK agreed with the same statement.

Today's younger adults, from around sixteen to thirty-six, are a paralysed generation, immobilised on two fronts. Firstly, by the failures of the answers of the past. Why should we marry, when it has so clearly failed to invigorate and bring contentment to our parents and grandparents? Why should we believe in religious solutions, when religious people have been hypocrites, grim moralists and persecutors? Why should we turn to politics, when it is a mere talking shop, which has so clearly failed to produce jobs and reduce crime? Little surprise that my generation has rejected the traditional bulwarks of church, marriage, and politics. They have seen their failures all too often in the lives of an earlier generation.

So there is paralysis due to the failings of the past. There is also paralysis due to the absence of the future. If life on earth will be wiped out before I reach retirement age (a very real fear amongst many today), why build for this non-existent future? Gone is the attitude of the great reformer Martin Luther, who said that even if he knew the earth would end tomorrow, he would still go out and plant a tree today. My generation has retreated from a purposeful future into an aimless, perpetual present.

This has consequences in terms of how we spend our time: there are no answers from the past, there is no hope for the future. All that remains is me, today, my desire for personal gratification. And the main way this is expressed is in terms of my body: how it looks, how it feels. Little surprise that we are a culture which finds escape in drugs and raves, with their trance-like, shamanistic flight from reality. We escape into fast-food, trashy videos and an excessive preoccupation with the minutiae of fashion.

This escape from the future has profoundly affected our designers. The 1990s has been the first decade this century not to possess any definable mood or clear sense of direction in its clothing. If the 1920s can be caricatured as the era of skinny, flat-chested 'flappers' in lightweight slips, and the 1980s as the era of power shoulders and impossibly bouffant hairstyles, what of the 90s? Today's designers, rather than creating some fundamentally new vision, are happy to recyle the old, a fabric equivalent of the 'samples' (of earlier recordings, speeches and sermons) on the dance records of our day. By the early 1990s, even the 80s 'power dressing' look was being revived, despite a general tendency to blame all the world's ills on the 'loadsa-money' culture of the previous decade. The quiet despair implicit in the 90s art of fashion-as-quotation is well expressed by the designer John Galliano:

> Why retro? Perhaps because you crave order in such unbalanced and rudderless times. References to the past can be viewed as a desire for a sense of order that is so elusive in our own time. (*Independent*, 2nd December 1994)

Aimless retrospection rules OK.

Merely a temporary *fin-de-siècle* chaos, or the new face of fashion? I strongly suspect that whether this nostalgia trip is just a passing aberration, or will now remain true *ad infinitum* depends less on the artistic sensibilities of designers than whether our culture can regain its lost sense of history, of a purposeful future, of hope itself. Nineties fashion is the perfect metaphor for 90s culture: full of energy, excitement and perpetual change but, ultimately, heading nowhere. Without a vision the people perish.

4) The Search for Security: The all-age adolescent longs for peer-group approval. The post-60s western teenager is characterised by a permanent identity crisis, a fragile grasp on her sense of self. She longs for full acceptance, for worth in the eyes of others which will bolster a tenuous sense of personal identity and the identity supports chosen will always be those offered by the culture she lives in.

In this context, fashion clothing becomes far more than garments. To be without certain iconic items means something far deeper than simply choosing to wear something different. To wear the 'wrong' item communicates that the wearer has failed to be correctly initiated, that she is socially illiterate. The stakes are high, and constantly raised higher by the popular media, especially the style magazines, in which identity is presented solely as a thin line held up by the latest fashionable props.

The Canadian writers quoted above observe: 'As inmates of adolescence, youth are confined to their own special prison – to a realm of leisure, pleasure, dreams and peers.' (Schulze et al, p257). We could go further. The universal adolescent of our culture feels that without the language of fashion she is reduced to silence. To be up with the current trend is to receive the peer approval she so desperately craves. A mirror is held up to her by her peers. Without the reflection, she questions her very existence.

Turn, Turn, Turn

Not all change is to be despised. God created the world with seasons and changes in the weather which help us look with fresh eyes at familiar landscapes. For many of us, our greatest sin is not so much pride as complacency – the failure to perceive that every cell of creation is charged up with the glory of God (see Isaiah 6:3 for a healthy corrective). Most of us are dulled by a grey monotony of routine which fails to be startled by the sheer wonder of existence. We have much to learn from the four-year-old, for whom life is a constant discovery of new realities, new potentials.

In the same way, changing our clothes can be a part of our resensitisation – our becoming sensitive once again to the freshness of the world. It can be one way of building into our lives a sense of permanent surprise, permanent gratitude. However, in an adolescent culture, this grateful celebration of the diversity and wonder of creation is rarely the motive for fashion change. More frequently it is an escape-route from boredom, a craving for novelty, a flight from a fearful future, a prop for an insecure identity. The modern fashion victim is a person with a firm grip on their credit card but a tenuous grip on self.

CHAPTER 9

THE STITCH-UP

'People in Britain should ask about the conditions in the
factories and not support the bad ones'
Ying, worker in a Thai sportswear factory

Do the Right Thing

Previous chapters in Part Two have focused on the negative
ways in which clothing and fashion can affect the individual: in
terms of idolatry, addiction, unattainable ideals and personal
identity. Now our focus changes, we are still concerned with the
ethics of dress, but from the perspective of fashion production.
In other words, where does our clothing come from and who
suffers in the process?

It is an uncomfortable question to raise, partly because what
I wear feels like such a personal issue to me. Clothes shopping
feels like an area where I am most fully making statements
about myself, where I am exercising my own free will. It is
sobering to be reminded that my purchase will directly affect
other people's lifestyle and well-being, either close to home or
in a distant part of the world.

This issue of justice is one which no Christian can avoid. The
Bible may have a high view of clothing *per se*, but it takes an
extremely dim view of clothing in the context of unethical
behaviour, and it praises those who use dress not only creatively

but also with mercy. The Covenant Law of Israel insisted that, no matter how steep his debt, nobody should have to forfeit his coat: 'If you take your neighbour's cloak as a pledge, return it to him by sunset, because his cloak is the only covering he has for his body. What else will he sleep in? When he cries out to me, I will hear, for I am compassionate' (Ex 22:26,27). The same injunction is also applied to needy widows in Deuteronomy 24:17. The underlying principle in both cases is the same humanitarian issue: clothing is about justice as well as dignity, aesthetics and function.

Jesus gives the familiar Old Testament stress on justice a new and radical twist by his statement that, despite the Law's prohibition on confiscating the cloak, his followers should be willing to be deprived even of that too: 'If someone wants to sue you and take your tunic, let him have your cloak as well' (Matt 5:40). He uses clothing as an illustration of how the believer is to have an utterly unselfish attitude to property and rights.

In the writings of the Prophets, fine clothing ceases to represent dignity and honour when the wearer is guilty of either idolatrous worship (Ezek 16), or else oppression of the poor (Is 3:16–26). Isaiah does not condemn high fashion out of some grim asceticism, but purely because it can embody an arrogance which leaves no concern for the underprivileged. The language of Isaiah, as he conveys God's anger at injustice in terms of adornment and style, is satirical, sarcastic and violent:

> The LORD says, 'The women of Zion are haughty, walking along with outstretched necks, flirting with their eyes, tripping along with mincing steps, with ornaments jingling on their ankles.
> Therefore the LORD will bring sores on the heads of the women of Zion; the LORD will make their scalps bald.'

> In that day the Lord will snatch away their finery: the bangles and headbands and crescent necklaces, the ear-rings and bracelets and veils, the head-dresses and anklechains and sashes, the perfume bottles and charms, the signet rings and nose rings, the fine robes and the capes and cloaks, the purses and mirrors, and the linen garments and tiaras and shawls.
> (Is 3:16–23)

The reason for God's anger has been stated in the verse immediately preceding this paragraph: ' "What do you mean by crushing my people and grinding the faces of the poor?" declares the Lord, the LORD almighty.' (Is 3:15)

Jesus implies that our lives will be assessed by God on the basis of the mercy we show to the poor, as evidenced by our readiness to clothe the naked (Matt 25:31–46). When Jesus satirises the rich man 'dressed in purple and fine linen' in the story of the rich man and Lazarus (Lk 16:19–31), there is no suggestion that the man's sin lies in being well-dressed. The sin is his refusal to share the luxury with the poor man lying at his gate in poverty and degradation. He refuses to share with Lazarus the symbol of human dignity, his fine clothes. Instead, he leaves him lying like a dog in the gutter, not as a person in the image of God. Jesus' message is one of dignity, justice and generosity, and a threat that those who in the present order of things are dressed in finery but have not compassion for the poor will one day lose everything.

Dorcas, the seamstress of Joppa (Acts 9:36–43), not only made clothes, she made them for the poor in the community. The widows (in many ways the bottom of the social heap in ancient Israel) showed Peter the clothes Dorcas had made for them. Through her garments, Dorcas had earned herself a reputation as one whose life demonstrated the faith she professed. Later in Acts, in his farewell to the Ephesian elders, Paul uses clothing as an example to them of radical selflessness and freedom from covetousness: 'I have not coveted anyone's silver or gold or clothing' (Acts 20:33). In a culture where clothing was a symbol of status and honour, he is exhorting his hearers to a life content with what God provides.

Many will respond to the biblical challenge to put on only clothing made and bought with clean hands by saying: 'It is not my problem. I only buy from reputable stores, and at realistic prices, not from questionable market stalls or cheap outlets where prices are so low somebody has to have been exploited in the process!' It is true, the great majority of the £17 billion Britons spend annually on clothes (over £300 each for every adult and child in 1991) is spent in a relatively small number of big chains, with reputable names: Marks & Spencer (with around sixteen per cent of the whole market), the Burton Group (including Top Shop, Dorothy Perkins, Principles, Evans, Debenhams), C&A, Storehouse (BHS, Mothercare, Blazer, Richards), Next, Littlewoods, and Sears (Adams, Fosters, Hornes, Miss Selfridge, Wallis, Warehouse).

However, a good name on the label is no guarantee that those who made the garment are also getting a good deal. Sadly, this is far from the case. Much of what we see on the rails at our favourite fashion store has almost certainly been produced under sweatshop conditions, either at home or abroad. This darker side of the fashion industry needs unpacking. We need to know more facts about a garment than its colour, design and texture if our 'free' choices in the stores are to mean anything. We shall begin with UK-produced items, since some sixty-four per cent of Britain's clothes are produced within its own shores (1991 figure). First a little history.

UK Production

Grim images of 19th-century sweatshop labour in Britain's industrial cities have become all too familiar in museums, history textbooks and the popular media. Perhaps the disturbing scenes of past abuse of workers in the fashion industry are particularly poignant because of the implicit contrast between the visible, easy, comfortable glamour of the wearer, and the hidden, sweated exploitation of the maker.

Until the 17th century all fine clothes were handmade by tailors, an era nostalgically recalled in such children's fiction as Beatrix Potter's *Tailor of Gloucester*, set in the 18th century, but evoking an age-old tradition of the tailor as craftsman. By the mid-18th century a gap was growing between tailoring as an elite craft, and the more mundane clothing production of the factories and sweatshops. Dressmakers were packed into sordid premises in the industrial sectors of cities such as Nottingham, Manchester and London, often in dangerous conditions and working each day until they could physically carry on no longer. Exhaustion, illness and bodily pains (even blindness and deformity) were the order of the day, and all for a pittance. Victorian England was prone to periodic moral panics over the moral state of dressmakers, since many were known to supplement their meagre income through prostitution. Even young children were pressed into service, their small fingers a valuable asset in making certain delicate items such as fine Nottingham lacework.

In 1851, as Prince Albert was planning his Great Exhibition at the Crystal Palace, Singer patented his 'new, improved' sewing machine, building on the first US-patented machines from 1846. The invention further heightened the gap between the old-fashioned craftsmen-tailors and the new breed of casual and semi-skilled workers. These workers were mostly women, and drawn heavily from ethnic minority groups with a strong sense of their own identity (such as the Jewish community), a situation which has remained unchanged to the present day.

The Subcontracting Pyramid

Fashion manufacture and retailing is pyramid-shaped. At the top is the High Street chain-store, who buys from a supplier, who in turn subcontracts out to factories, who themselves frequently contract work out to an army of home-workers. At each 'layer' a cut of the final retail price is taken, and the aim of each middleman is to get the maximum work done for a minimum cost. This pyramid has been in place since the early-20th century, using work methods which would have been familiar to the sweat shop dressmakers of the 19th in cities such as Nottingham, London, Manchester, New York and Chicago.

An obvious question at this point is why the clothing industry still uses such apparently antiquated production methods? Most industries with such a massive turnover have long since abandoned the bad old days of employing thousands of workers to carry out physically demanding tasks, in favour of streamlined, efficient new technology. Why not the clothing producers? And, if cheap labour is the desired commodity, why have the clothing companies not relocated all production to the countries of the two-thirds world where female semi-skilled labour is cheap and abundant? Why keep almost two-thirds of all production so close to home? The answer lies in the nature of fashion itself.

Since the 1960s, fashion has been largely about short runs and rapid turnover, and this tends to make the sort of automation which produces uniform car bodies, yogurt pots or paperback books unrealistic for clothing. The fast, flexible methods of sub-contracting via middle-men to local home-workers are still well suited to the needs of the fashion industry. The man in a van who drops off a hundred unsewn dresses to an address in East London and collects them, sewn, the following week, is a much faster operator than the cargo ship which takes 10,000 unsewn training shoe components to Jakarta (Indonesia).

Ironically, the rapid advances in information technology have, if anything, increased the fashion industry's dependence on fast, flexible home-workers. Thanks to developments in EPOS (Electronic Point of Sale equipment), retailers have instant and accurate records of what has been sold. As each item is scanned, its sale is logged in a central computer, giving the company full and up-to-date information on the styles and sizes which are selling at any given time. Such instant information is useful in proportion to the retailer's capacity to respond rapidly to what the market wants. What is the point in knowing today what is selling, if it takes till next year to produce further appropriate garments? And why take the risk of ordering well in advance when the market may have changed again by then?

This, together with the fragmentation of the market-place in styles already referred to, not to mention the added costs of transport and insurance, and the greater difficulties of quality control incurred in shipping items abroad, mean that local producers will always have a built-in advantage when it comes to fashion production. Items with a relatively short run and fast turnover (which includes most fashion garments) tend to be home-produced, whereas the larger runs of more homogeneous, international items (such as training-shoes) are mass-produced by cheap labour in the two-thirds world. Economies of scale make such production worthwhile.

British fashion production, then, relies on a large pool of cheap, flexible labour. It has been estimated that half of all London's clothing production is carried out by home-workers, ninety per cent of whom are women, the majority semi-skilled and from ethnic minority groups.

Why this particular group of people? There is a long precedent for such a state of affairs, both in the UK and US. In the mid-19th century Jewish immigrants into the UK found themselves largely excluded from the mainstream job market due to barriers of racism and language. Consequently, they turned entrepreneur and set up their own companies, among their own people, which did away with the language difficulties and the need to participate directly in the work patterns of the host culture. Often such companies were involved in sub-contracting. At the same time, German and Russian Jews (later, Italians too) emigrated to the States and began to manufacture clothing for the same reasons.

The same is true today, only the ethnic communities in the UK now are more likely to be Asian or Turkish Cypriot. Entrepreneurs carve out a niche as sub-contractors in garment production, and naturally use their own kinship or community networks to get the job done.

There are further reasons why women from minority ethnic communities are a natural workforce. In many such groups, a woman's place is still very much in the home, especially if she is not yet fluent in English, and if she has children. The job is generally defined as gender-specific (clothing is traditionally 'woman's work'); it is low or semi-skilled (sewing skills are traditionally acquired at home, in childhood) and so require no costly training.

On the positive side, this means employment opportunities for tens of thousands of people who might be otherwise excluded from the job market. On the negative side, it means opportunities for exploitation. As we shall see, the structures of the fashion industry, combined with the hands-off, non-interventionist policies of Britain's government since 1979, has allowed the creation of sweatshops comparable to those of Dickensian London, a Third World economy in its very own cities.

Back to Dickens

Wages for workers in fashion production are among the lowest in Britain. A 1993 survey among home-workers, the bottom of the pile in the pyramid of fashion production, found the average pay to be a mere £1.30 an hour, while one in ten actually earned 50p an hour or less. The *Observer* newspaper surveyed home-working in 1988, and found that at the time, even established, reputable companies such as Marks & Spencer, C&A and Richard Shops were using home-workers paid well below the minimum rates laid down in the 1986 Wages Act.

Nor is the situation improving, it is growing worse. In 1993, the UK government abolished the Wages Councils which set minimum wages. This removed the major legal safeguard for the exploited home-workers, opening the way to still greater exploitation. Wages are often kept abysmally (but legally) low, and the workers have no National Insurance paid. Home-workers rarely have proper contracts of employment and are hired and fired at will; they do not have union representation (since unions have historically been based around the workplace); they often have to pay for their own light, heat and rent, and for their own equipment such as a sewing-machine; they are not subject to the usual Health and Safety legislation; excessively long hours are normal; they have no training and no job security.

So why do they continue to put up with all this? The home-worker rarely has any choice. She is isolated and vulnerable: does she want this job or not? If she queries the conditions, the work is taken away completely. Some of the more unscrupulous middlemen will threaten workers with the prospect of having their work declared to the tax man if they kick up a fuss. In fact, many are earning well below the tax threshold anyway.

A particularly depressing sign of our return to Victorian

Britain is the reappearance of child-labour. In early 1994 a trading standards officer found children between eleven and fourteen working in a clothing factory in Preston. Things seem to have changed little since Dickens used the town as the model for Coketown in his novel *Hard Times*. In 1991 a Low Pay Unit survey estimated that three-quarters of all working children were employed illegally, and Dr Michael Lavalette (researcher in child employment at the University of Central Lancashire) puts the figure closer to ninety-five per cent in Strathclyde, Tyneside and the industrial north-west. To date the UK government has doggedly resisted European Union moves to provide greater protection for young people at work.

Two-Thirds World Production

We have already tried to get in perspective the quantity of clothing entering the UK from abroad. Contrary to the popular myth of 'cheap foreign clothes' flooding the UK market, only thirty-six per cent is actually imported, of which only half is from what might very broadly be termed two-thirds world countries (most of the rest is from the EC, especially Germany and Italy).

However, the issues raised by two-thirds world clothing production are serious, not least because of the worldwide scale of the issues at stake. Globally, the two-thirds world accounts for no less than half of all clothing production.

The Global Pyramid

The sub-contracting pyramid is not only to be found in the UK and US: it covers the globe. We might expect that a label stating country of origin guarantees the item is wholly from that country, but, in the words of the Gershwin song, 'it ain't necessarily so'. Some items are made wholly in two-thirds world countries, the manufacturer benefiting from the cheaper labour on large runs. But equally, a garment may have been made and assembled in a number of different countries, as the buyer one stage higher in the pyramid scours the globe, searching for the cheapest place for cutting, adding zips, sewing in buttons, stitching in a label, etc.

Just as a British or American city has its pool of home-workers, taken advantage of by sub-contracting middlemen in search of cheap labour, so too the two-thirds world is being stitched up by clothing production. A few examples will help illustrate the problem.

Indonesia

Around a third of all Reebok trainers, and over a quarter of all Nikes are made in Indonesia, mostly at Jabotabek. Jabotabek is the country's showcase industrial complex where foreign companies take advantage of the cheap local labour to produce not only sports shoes, but a range of other clothing items such as Calvin Klein underwear. Reebok alone produces fifteen million pairs of shoes annually in Indonesia.

But high-profile training shoes can have a grubby underside. Because western companies such as Reebok do not own their own factories in Indonesia, they can play off one sub-contracting factory against another, haggling for the cheapest labour they can find.

The effects such haggling has in forcing down workers' pay ought to be mitigated by the fact that Indonesia has a legal minimum wage. However, there are two problems with this. Firstly, the minimum wage is extremely low just £1.10 per day (in 1994), the second lowest in Asia. Many experts say this falls below the level needed for the basic survival of the worker and family in a country where rent for a two-room hut is around £25–£30 per month. Most families cannot afford fresh fruit, meat or fish. Secondly, a 1992 survey revealed that less than forty per cent of employers actually paid even the minimum wage.

Consequently, the International Labour Organisation esti-mates that no less than eighty-eight per cent of Indonesian women workers (and women make up the majority of clothing industry workers worldwide) are undernourished. In some fac-tories, wages are cut by twenty per cent if an employee goes to the toilet unauthorised, and maternity leave and sick leave are unknown. The average week in many factories is fifty hours, with no overtime pay, and few health and safety measures in force. Workers who complain are often simply dismissed, and attempts to unionise the labour force have been brutally put down, despite Indonesia having signed the International Labour Organisation's Convention 98, on workers' rights to collective action.

Are there signs of hope? The Levi Strauss jeans company has adopted a policy of always checking that producers comply with Levi's own code of practice in Indonesia and its other producer countries. This includes minimum human rights and pay well above the legal minimum. Levi's have been a model of good practice, and deserve the support of consumers.

Similarly, the Nike company employs a team of 125 people who ensure that at least the Indonesian minimum wage laws, and other basic workers' rights, such as health care and holiday allowance, are met in their subcontracting factories. And the company rightly points out that wages in other local jobs, such as farming, earn far less than their shoe workers.

But the fundamental point remains. Indonesia's indebted military government, like so many other governments in the poor countries of the world, is desperate for foreign investment. It offers its workforce at bargain-basement prices, and frequently turns a blind eye to breaches of its already pitiful minimum wage rates and work conditions. Some companies, such as Levi's, unilaterally insist on higher standards. Many of the rest are only too happy to join in the stitch-up.

The Philippines

Like many developing countries, the Philippines has set up special 'Free Trade Zones' to encourage foreign investment. Conditions in such zones are relatively good, and the workforce has the right to belong to trades unions, but firms frequently subcontract out to factories outside. These factories often have lower wages, worse conditions, and fewer rights to join unions and demand improvements. As elsewhere in the two-thirds world, a threat is held over unions that if they become too active, work will simply be subcontracted elsewhere.

A UN study revealed that one garment factory insisted new workers had to undergo a six-month 'apprenticeship', with low wages and no union rights. After this period, workers were frequently laid off. Even if they continued, the wages they received are generally deemed too low to support a family.

Honduras

The bulk of foreign producers making clothing for the UK market are in Asia. A significant and growing sector producing for the US is in its own back yard: Central America. Since 1993, no less than ten Free-Trade Zones have sprung up in Honduras alone. Their aim: to take on young women between the ages of fourteen and twenty to produce clothes for the States (including such big names as Gap) at impossible-to-resist labour costs. They are also offering potential foreign employers cheap rents, exemption from income taxes, and low import duties on raw materials.

Consequently, the early 1990s have seen a dramatic influx of foreign investment into Central America. Asian companies in particular have been wooed by the irresistible terms, and by the prospect of the massive US clothing market on their new doorstep. Particularly enthusiastic have been the Koreans, Taiwanese, and the Hong Kong companies nervous about the planned hand-over of their colony to China in 1997. This third group has been particularly taken with the offer of free Honduran citizenship with every investment of $25,000 or more. Between 1991 and 1993, some 3,000 Hong Kong entrepreneurs became Honduran citizens. At the same time, Korean textiles joined Taiwanese textiles on the Americans' list of import quotas. Relocation outside the Far East would get round such quotas.

However, there is another reason for the shift from Asia to Central America: namely, the rise in the mid-80s of unrest amongst Asian textile workers. As they started to press for improved pay and work conditions, the companies started to look further afield for cheaper, less unionised labour. This they found in the Free Trade Zones of Central America, where the women work from 7.30am to 6pm, with frequent unpaid overtime, for just three dollars a day. Added to this is the insecurity of the new jobs. The workers know they could disappear as quickly as they arrived, as the companies find cheaper labour elsewhere.

It all adds a whole new meaning to the term 'sweat-shirt'.

Buy British?

The answer seems simple. If two-thirds world labour is exploited to such an extent, then surely one should boycott them and buy British or American. Sadly, it is not so straightforward. As we have already seen, home-produced clothes are far from clean. Conditions in the UK and US are sometimes comparable with those in the two-thirds world. Secondly, clothing exports are vital to the poor countries of the globe. In 1991, they stood at $23 billion a year, second only to oil. Such exports create much-needed jobs at a low cost, focusing as they do on local factories and home-workers who need little more than sewing-machines in order to do the job. Clothing is an ideal industry for the developing world. It is environmentally friendly, low-tech, requiring little up-front investment, and uses what the developing world has in abundance: low-cost labour.

And, it has to be said, even low-paid jobs are usually better than no jobs at all. Faced with the alternatives of urban unemployment or rural poverty, two-thirds world workers welcome the relatively steady jobs brought by clothing production. Union leaders in two-thirds world countries, far from encouraging sanctions, want wealthy foreigners to buy their goods. According to Amiral Haque Amin of Bangladesh's National Garment Worker's Federation, higher sales can only strengthen their hand in negotiations with employers: 'We need international support in our struggle to improve the terrible conditions of garment workers. But not buying Bangladeshi shirts isn't going to help us – it'll just take away people's jobs.'

Likewise, far from supporting a boycott, the conclusion of

'Fashion production . . . gives a whole new meaning to the term "sweat-shirt"' (p 220)

the helpful ethical trading handbook, *The Global Consumer*, is that 'Third World clothes are part of the answer, not part of the problem' (p185). Poor people need real jobs, producing goods for a real market-place, not just charity handouts.

The Case of Bangladesh and the MFA

Before we start to draw practical conclusions and suggestions, it is important to look at the ways in which the world's poorest people have been prevented from working their way out of poverty. A major cause has been the rich countries' heavy-handed imposition of import quotas (restrictions).

Western governments champion free trade. It is a hallowed ideal of the consumerist creed: free markets, unfettered trade in a global market-place. Yet the reality is somewhat at odds with the ideal. Trade may be free between rich countries, but not between rich and poor. Trade blocks cost poor countries as much as all Western aid put together, around $50bn US a year.

To understand why, we need to understand the history of the Multi-Fibre Agreement (MFA). In 1974, a 'short-term' international agreement was signed by countries in the industrialised West to limit imports of clothing and textiles from developing countries. This was the birth of the MFA. It was supposed to remain in force until 1978, just four years, to give the rich countries time to restructure their clothing industries to cope with the increased threat of their markets being 'swamped' by cheap imports from the two-thirds world.

By 1993 it was still firmly in place, and delegates at the so-called Uruguay Round of the General Agreement on Tariffs and Trade (GATT), the world trade body responsible for import and export quotas worldwide, voted to keep it in place till 2005. Quite a lifespan for a brief, interim measure! The GATT in 1993 decided to phase out the MFA over a 10–year period, starting in 1995. The idea is that over this decade, different categories of clothing and textile goods will gradually be removed from the terms of the MFA.

However, anti-MFA campaigners such as the World Development Movement (WDM) are wary. They note that the phase-out is far from evenly graduated, the bulk of the exemptions come at the very end of the 10-year period. Under the terms, no less than forty-nine per cent of the 1990 level of quotas will still be in place on the eve of complete phase-out, 31 December 2004. Will the rich countries, they ask, really be prepared to countenance such a massive drop in quotas blocking exports from poor countries, all at one go? The Netherlands and UK governments claim they are are in favour of lifting MFA restrictions, but the southern Europeans and the powerful US textile lobby are resisting any change at all.

What is the problem? Why can we not keep the MFA, and allow the rich countries to keep full import quotas in place, to protect their own markets? The answer is that such stringent quotas have severely damaged the ability of poor countries to work their own way out of poverty. And if Christians are to pay the remotest heed to the constant biblical insistence on God's call for justice and compassion for the poor, this is something which we cannot ignore.

Take the case of Bangladesh, which started producing clothes commercially in 1978. Just eight years later, clothing had become its main export, earning over a fifth of the country's total income. The industry was ideally suited to the resources of Bangladesh, providing vital work opportunities in a land with a large number of unskilled and semi-skilled workers, with little technology, but with a large rural population relying on seasonal employment.

Added to this is the sheer poverty of the place. Two-thirds of the adult population is illiterate (seventy-eight per cent amongst women), and less than half the population has access to health care. This is particularly serious in a country ravaged by malnutrition, diarrhoea and other illnesses of poverty, where one in five children dies before its fifth birthday.

Women in particular are helped by the clothing industry, since they constitute eighty-five per cent of its workers, and while wages are low in the industry (as everywhere), they are frequently higher than in other types of work and much higher than having no work at all and going hungry. An industry which has directly created half a million jobs in Bangladesh (and as many as an estimated five million indirectly dependent on it, such as van drivers and cleaners) has to be a good thing.

Since Bangladesh is the only UN-designated Least Developed Country (ie the poorest of the poor) to be restricted by the MFA, the need to remove it from the terms of the MFA is urgent. We need to be clear how the MFA works: each rich country covered by its terms has a 'right' to impose the stipulated quotas on another country the moment it feels its own industry to be under threat from excessive imports. Many countries, such as the US and Canada, have imposed these quotas against Bangladesh since the mid-1980s. Britain and France imposed their quotas in 1985 (severely damaging the fledgling clothing industry of Bangladesh), but lifted the sanctions the following year, after a public campaign by the WDM. The present situation is that Britain and other nations covered by the MFA retain the right to apply quotas whenever they feel like it.

Jobs: at Home or Abroad?

The response of many, particularly union bosses in southern Europe and the US, is to express sympathy for the plight of Bangladesh, but insist that jobs at home must be protected. The quotas are a safety-net, they argue, to make sure jobs at home are not lost to a new flood of imports. And one has to have sympathy with such a view. Charity abroad looks less appealing if a member of your own family loses a job, apparently as a result of exporting it.

It would be naive to say there could be no impact on UK jobs from taking the simple step of lifting the threat of quotas on Bangladesh. However, the evidence suggests that the impact would be far less than one might at first imagine. Nearly two-thirds of UK clothes are still home-produced (remember that in the area of fashion, home-production has a major built-in advantage), and over half UK imports are from the EU and other industrialised countries, especially Germany, Italy and France. Of the rest, by far the largest quantity is from Hong Kong. Bangladesh scrapes in at 27th place on the table of countries exporting to the UK, with a mere 0.6 per cent of the UK textile and clothing market. The impact of imports from Bangladesh has been tiny.

But there remains the issue of fairness. A 1993 report from UNCTAD, the UN trade body, showed that restrictions such as quotas hit sixty-seven per cent of the clothing and textile imports from the Third World, but only seven per cent of those from rich countries. The real competition is from the other wealthy countries of the EU and Hong Kong. Why, then, do we keep the Sword of Damocles (that weapon of classical legend suspended by no more than a single hair) hanging over Bangladesh? The WDM is right: we must put pressure on the Government and the EU to drop Bangladesh from the EU's list of exporter countries under the MFA, and encourage the US and Canada to do likewise.

Out of the MFA

How will this help, if many EU countries are not even applying their 'right' to quotas against Bangladesh anyway? A glance at recent history shows how. When a number of rich countries applied their quotas against Bangladesh in the mid-1980s, two-thirds of all Bangladeshi clothing factories closed in just three months, and an estimated 150,000 workers were laid off. The industry in Bangladesh was thrown into chaos, making longer term plans for the industry impossible. The threat that quotas could be reimposed at any time induces a fear and uncertainty which is hardly conducive to business planning. A top Bangladeshi manufacturer estimates that if the EU used all its quota 'allowance', over half the clothing factories in his country would close. For the EU to remove the threat of quotas would strengthen the industry and give a lead to the North Americans to do the same.

Cleaner Clothes

To remove Bangladesh from the threat of MFA quotas would be one way to help clean our clothes. But there are other ways in which we could help. The heart of the problem is knowing where and under what conditions the clothes we buy have been produced. Such information is notoriously difficult to obtain, but there are some positive options open to us.

Alternative Trading Organisations

Recently my wife paid around £70 for a dressing-gown sold by Traidcraft, the Gateshead-based Alternative Trading Organisation (ATO). Quite a high price, I initially thought. But then we read about the background to the garment. It had been made by Village Weavers Handicrafts, a small company based at Nong Khai, in North-East Thailand. It is located in the poorest region of the country, an area frequently afflicted by drought and where countless people have massive debts, since so many are landless or do not have enough land to grow enough food to feed their families. With so little work, the pressure is to work in a range of sweatshops or join the thousands of maltreated women in the brothels of Bangkok.

Supervised by Traidcraft, workers at Village Weavers are given a fair wage for their work, in good work conditions. In turn, my wife gets something far more than just another item of clothing. She gets a hand-dyed, hand-woven, hand-made work of art, incorporating local patterns. In a strange way, she also builds a kind of relationship with the Thai woman who made the dressing-gown.

Traidcraft and other ATOs, such as Oxfam Trading, work with a strict ethical trade policy, so the purchaser knows that no sweatshop labour has been involved. True, prices may be more than one would pay in the High Street but when you consider the wider costs of most clothing, we cannot afford not to support such groups as Traidcraft or Oxfam. (The addresses are at the end of the book.)

Shop Creatively

Why settle for bland and convenient styles from the High Street or mall, when a range of other options (more fun and more ethical) are open to us? Many individuals eke out a living from designing and making their own clothes, and most of them do not cost a fortune. Markets such as London's Portobello Road and Covent Garden, and festivals such as Greenbelt (not to mention a range of other, more local events) often feature a range of stalls where people sell home-made waist-coats, hats, shoes and so on.

The Golf Links Estate Mental Health Project in Southall, West London, runs a dressmaking group. This is organised by two volunteers trained in fashion design. Women on low income have produced quality children's and adult's clothes for local people, all at reasonable prices.

Do not forget charity shops (Britain alone has some 5,000), which stock second-hand clothing. Some, especially the larger stores, have some high-quality goods at low prices. Many items have never even been worn previously. They may have been unwanted gifts or goods which were bought on impulse and never subsequently worn. Many high-powered business people and stylish pop personalities regularly scan their local Oxfam shop for nearly-new bargains.

In addition to running its 800 second-hand clothes shops and trading imported, ethically-traded garments from the two-thirds world, Britain's Oxfam has a further creative initiative for clean dressing: NoLogo. Its aim is to recycle fabrics (bin-ends donated free by several top fashion houses) into new clothes, using fashion students and young designers. This minimises waste, gives a springboard for young talent, and also generates funds for projects in the developing world. NoLogo clothes are available from some Oxfam stores in central London.

Making Waves

However, to be realistic, most people in our society will carry on getting most of their clothing in the High Street. Therefore, a further step is vital. Customers must start to make it clear that they insist on clean clothing, and that will mean being more selective in where they shop, and communicating with retailers direct about their sourcing policy.

Why does international pressure not make countries enforce

better pay and conditions? Simply because most of us enjoy the knock-down prices too much. Few voices are raised against the sweated labour which gives our companies bigger profit margins. The big clothing retailers are scrupulous in checking the quality control, colour and delivery dates of the garments they buy from their sources. Yet few check the production sites where the garments are produced. Very few of them demand good pay and work conditions for employees. They leave that to those lower down the pyramid, which effectively means the job is not done.

Two British companies which are a notable exception are Littlewoods and C&A. Littlewoods were the first (and for many years the only) major retailer to establish a code of practice on the ethics of clothes production. This code stipulates that merchandise must be produced in line with UN guidelines on workers' rights and working conditions, and the local laws covering wages and conditions. Also, it insists on human rights and personal freedoms in the workplace. Littlewoods have recently been joined in checking the ethics of their suppliers by C&A.

Pay and Conditions Close to Home

We have repeatedly noted that the majority of the UK's clothes are home-produced, and that an army of home-workers and workers in inner-city sweatshops are at the bottom of the heap. Is such exploitation inevitable? Over recent years, a legal safety net was in place to help prevent such appalling conditions of work: the Wages Councils. However, in 1993 the Conservative Government abolished the Councils and the work they did, claiming that enforced minimum standards destroyed jobs, because employers could not afford to take on so many workers.

The result has been a rise in sweatshop labour, a return to the excesses of Dickensian London. Union leaders are increasingly warning that if sweatshop rates of pay become the norm outside unionised companies, then decent employers too would be forced to compete by cutting pay and conditions. Sure enough, by 1994, the Low Pay Unit found that a fifth of jobs advertised in Job Centres, which would previously have been covered by the Wages Councils (including clothing manufacture) were being paid at below the old minimum rates. There is growing evidence that employers are simply freezing or even reducing pay, without actually taking on any more staff. In other words, exploitation.

There is room to debate the pros and cons of a nationally laid-down minimum wage. But at the very least, a civilised country cannot allow the continued and increased exploitation of its most vulnerable workers. Not only is the British Government, at the time of writing, refusing to reinstate the Wages Councils or some equivalent body, it is also staunchly refusing to sign the Social Chapter of the Maastricht Treaty on European Integration. This too stipulates minimum standards for workers in all member states. The governments of all the other EU nations, whether of the political right or left, have signed up. The only other major European political party which opposes the Social Chapter at the time of writing is the French National Front. The British government claims its opposition to minimum standards is gaining support across Europe, and so it is. Not among conservatives or socialists, but amongst resurgent neo-fascists.

Cleaning Our Clothes

In a consumer society such as ours, the consumer has power. You and I can make a real difference through the ways we purchase. Every time we shop for clothes, we can each use the following clean clothes principles, starting with 1 as the best option, and working down to 8. Simply to set off on a shopping-spree and stuff an already-bulging wardrobe simply is not an option.

1) Buy from the catalogue of an Alternative Trading Organisation such as Traidcraft or Oxfam, which guarantees fair trade for producers.
2) Buy second-hand from a charity store such as Oxfam, so

that profits from your purchase help a worthwhile cause. Especially in larger stores and in smart areas, there are some real gems to be found.

3) Buy from small-scale local producers and designers in your area. Some run their own market stalls or units in craft centres. This will help the producer stay in business, and will also challenge the homogeneity of High Street styles.

   Many make items to order – but expect to pay more for a hand-made, fitted outfit than you would for off-the-peg in the high street or mall. This is especially worthwhile when the producer channels some of the profits into a local charitable cause or social concern.

4) Buy from a supplier with a policy of fair trade. The only UK retailers currently applying such a policy are Littlewoods and C&A. Or buy from craft fairs and arts festivals, where small-scale fair traders often sell their goods.

   If looking for jeans, choose Levi's in preference to other brands, even if they are more pricey. Forget the idea that cheap always means a bargain, and expensive must be mean a rip-off. Levi's have led the way in insisting on good pay and workers' rights in its factories in the two-thirds world, and has even pulled out of some Chinese factories because standards have not been met.

5) Buy in the sales and donate a portion of the cash saved to a body such as the World Development Movement or Amnesty International, who campaign for better conditions in the worldwide fashion industry.

6) Buy at full price in the High Street, but for every new item you buy always donate at least one you no longer wear to a charity second-hand clothing shop. That way, a good cause will always benefit indirectly from every item of clothing you buy.

7) Get out your sewing machine and alter existing clothes in your wardrobe to make them more serviceable. Add patches, embroidery, new buttons . . . be creative.

8) Make your own! Have fun choosing your own patterns, fabric, buttons, zips and so on. You could even have a go at designing your own clothes.

In addition to these eight principles, there are also three general rules of thumb to bear in mind:

a) Buy fewer, better quality items in preference to more, cheaper goods. This has several advantages. You will enjoy your clothes more. They will better reflect the biblical love of fine, quality clothes. They will give you longer wear. There is less of a built-in likelihood that somebody has been exploited in the process of producing them and it will cut down on the vast quantities of clothing thrown away globally (one million tonnes in the UK) every year.

b) Keep weeding out your wardrobe at regular intervals, say, bi-annually. Be realistic and ruthless about what you are actually ever going to wear again. Why let items moulder there, prey to the nibbling of moths, when they could be making money for charity and clothing others with fewer garments than yourself?

There are no hard and fast rules about how many of any given item (shirts, pairs of shoes, jumpers, and so on) is too many. This will vary according to your job, leisure activities, lifestyle and even the area in which you live. But I should have thought that once the figure goes above ten of anything, some serious weeding and a trip to your local second-hand charity shop might be in order.

c) Cultivate the habit of encouraging good practice in the clothes trade and rooting out bad practice. This might include asking store managers for examples of how the good policies of Littlewoods and C&A work in reality. It might involve writing to your MP and MEP (or equivalent politicians in countries outside the UK), to ask for an early end to import restrictions on clothes and textiles from poor countries. It might mean asking store managers and sales assistants where their clothes come from, and whether there is a company policy of visiting and inspecting the premises where they are made.

Be prepared for some blank looks. The values of the kingdom of God will rarely be understood or welcomed by the dapper young gargoyles of the high street.

CHAPTER 10

ROBED IN GLORY

'"But the Emperor has nothing on at all!" cried a little child.'

Hans Christian Andersen: *The Emperor's New Clothes*

The Problem Restated

Let us summarise the central argument of the book so far. Clothing is good. It is a gift from God to humankind, the pinnacle of his creation. Through our clothing, God 'robes' humanity in dignity for our role as his vice-regents, his 'imagers' on the earth. There is a biblical mandate for clothing as creative and celebratory, on the strict condition that it adorns a life lived honouring God and loving one's neighbour, including the poor of the world. Even periodic fashion change can be a part of our obedient response to God, preventing us from becoming indifferent or complacent towards the glory of God in creation. The claim of this book is that the biblical ideal is of a people secure in their identities as children of God, obediently and creatively fulfilling their calling to fill the earth and subdue it, including the ways they dress.

And yet, as we have seen, this ideal has often been misunderstood or ignored. On the one hand, as we saw in Part One, many Christians have retreated from their God-given call to use their physical bodies, and to use the earth's resources with exuberance and style, preferring an other-worldly pietism and a drab functionalism of dress. A saved soul has meant a lost fashion sense.

At the same time, as we found in Part Two, many outside the church have embarked on a panic-stricken but misplaced quest for lost identity and acceptance through their clothing and body shape. The teenager longs for peer-group acceptance through buying the right trainers; the shopaholic hopes to find in her purchases the cure for inner loneliness, boredom or shaky marriage; the anorexic struggles to express herself in a power-less situation; the body-builder, to overcome the rejections of childhood; the dieter, to be acceptable according to society's standards of glamour; the photographer, model and marketing executive are driven by a restless quest for ultimate beauty. To each of these, the consumer society in which we live sells yet greater dissatisfaction. We must remain for ever a culture of nervous adolescents, permanently in search of self, but never quite finding it.

Each off-the-peg item, each slimming or body-building product merely heightens the craving, the sense of inner empti-ness. Why? What is the reason that the very items which God designed to enhance identity, and give dignity, appear to be failing to do so? Why is the modern garment industry largely such a hollow, superficial place, a hall of mirrors for the inse-cure fashion victim? Why are its followers, in the words of George Whiting's 1912 song, all dressed up but with no place to go? For this simple reason: style is a gift for a secure identity, not a substitute for a lost identity. In other words, clothing is good, but we cannot force it to do what it was never meant to do: namely, give us the love and acceptance we crave.

Reductionist world views on offer within the fashion world patently fail to come up with the goods. The reduction of life to sex and shifting erogenous zones (Laver, Freud) leaves us as little more than one-dimensional copulation machines. Economic reductionism (Veblen, Marx) leaves us as insignifi-cant pawns in a game of big finance; whilst the hedonism of mass consumerism leaves us feeling restless, insecure and with a salt-water thirst for more.

The kind of inner security so desperately craved can only come from the ultimate designer: God himself. Many who work inside fashion are beginning to realise that the only truly satisfying answer will be one which addresses the spiritual aspect of our make-up (no pun intended), and which gives metaphysical significance to the self.

However, the chosen spiritual journey of many in the fashion industry over recent years has not been towards Christianity, but Buddhism. The model Cindy Crawford made her way to the mountains of the Himalayas to be initiated, just one among countless top models, designers and retailers who have seen in the path of Enlightenment a solution to their quest for identity. But their choice of Buddhism is supremely ironic, since it is a path which claims the ideal state of being is only to be attained by the denial of the uniqueness of the self. Siddartha Gautama (known as Buddha, the Enlightened One) was born about 2,600 years ago in northern India, and a central plank of his teaching was that the self is an illusion. According to his philosophy, if a real self did exist, it would only be a cause of suffering. Since the self is illusory, the enlightened disciple may escape suffering by his detachment from created things. The material world is of no ultimate value. 'I' am an illusion. Ultimate reality is Nirvana, the negation of all that is temporal and solid. Even the term Nirvana comes from a verb meaning to 'waft away'. Buddhism is the last word in pessimism towards the material world.

What an unlikely world view for those involved in creating and celebrating objects which are material and temporary, garments which are wholly to do with shaping and expressing the identity of the unique self! At their best, Eastern religions such as Buddhism express a valid critique of the silly, inconsequential nature of much fashion and our insecure, clinging attitudes towards material goods. There is, after all, a tremendous relief in finding a world view (any world view) which tells today's fashion-victim that there is more to life than a two-dimensional image.

But what a marked contrast to Christianity, in which God not only creates matter, declares it 'very good', and becomes a physical person; but actually affirms human culture, invents clothing, acts as the first designer and tailor, pours his Spirit for the express purpose of designing and embroidering fine clothes, and fills the Scriptures with so many positive references to dress as ennobling and dignifying.

So what might be a distinctively Christian response be to those in search of security, affirmation and identity, who vainly try to use their dress and body shape as the focus of their quest? The following survey draws together and builds on much of the biblical material scattered through the earlier chapters of this book. The starting point has to be the good creation.

Starting With Creation

Christianity insists that both the world as we see it now, and human nature as we experience it now, have not always been this way. In the beginning the God of the Bible, revealed to the Jewish race by his covenant name of Yahweh (and represented in most English Bibles as 'the LORD', in capitals), fashioned a perfect creation. Matter was made good, because it was declared good by the One who designed it. Not only that, but the created universe was filled with the glory of God. Aspects of the physical world, especially the skies, light, clouds and fire, functioned as the 'clothing' of God, his visible presence in creation.

Into this good creation was placed humankind, male and female, made to be the imagers of the Creator. Theirs was the task of standing uniquely at the head of creation, radiating the reflected glory of God. Not simply another part of creation, but its pinnacle: representing creation to God and God to creation, a job of responsibility and service. Theirs was to take the raw material of the earth and create, just as God had created. They were to develop culture: arts, economics and sciences. And, as sexual beings, they were to populate the earth. Just as God radiates his glory into the natural world, humankind too (his image on earth) radiates a reflected glory. It was a glory shining from every pore of their naked bodies.

What Happened Next

However, the flip side of authority is answerability. The glory radiated by Adam and Eve was not their own: they were reflecting the dazzling glory which surrounded God as a mantle. The fruit on the tree (Gen 3) was nothing special in itself. The prohibition on eating it was simply a test of obedience for humankind: would they continue to see themselves in their true light, as God's deputies on earth, accepting their limitations, content to be clothed in the glory which was properly God's alone? Or would they, as soon as a choice became apparent, choose disobedience? The promise of godlike autonomy was held up to them and they seized it, fired with a vision of themselves robed in the light of their own glory, no longer mere reflectors of the glory of the Creator.

So what changed after that point? Both nothing and everything. Firstly, nothing happened. Adam and Eve were still the image of God on earth. Because their very bodies were the image of their Maker, the image could not be erased without a complete destruction of humanity. Adam's children and descendants continued to be the image of God on earth (Gen 5:3). They still had the cultural mandate of Genesis 1:28–30, to fill the earth, to cultivate it and develop its potential. That is something we all inherit. We each have dignity and value because we image God in our world. We are still stewards of creation. Our work, leisure and relationships all have ultimate value because we carry them out at the explicit design and will of God. We continue to be the pinnacle of God's handiwork, his children whom he loves and cares for.

All this remains unchanged, as is demonstrated by God's continued decision after the Fall to robe them for office. They no longer reflect his radiant glory on earth as they once did. But they still image him on earth; they were designed to be stewards of the earth, and still will be. God's original plan will not be thwarted. So God makes them tunics and (in the same language the Bible uses of robing for kingship, honour and status) he dresses them, just as he had always intended. Not only this, but also (because God is a Trinity) he sends his Spirit to inspire their descendants to design and manufacture fine, aesthetic dress; he sends his Son, who tells his followers to take their dress sense from King Solomon and garlands of spring flowers. Now, despite the loss of their capacity as glory-reflectors, humans will still be clothing-wearers. Their dress is their symbol of authority, and it is still ours. As we dress, we each pull on our God-given dignity.

And yet, at the same time, everything did change when Adam and Eve fell. The tragic irony is that in desiring their own, unreflected glory, they forfeited even the reflected glory they already had. Instead of being robed in their own dazzling glory, they were undressed of God's glory. As they sinned, they exchanged the glory of God for an illusory image of themselves as gods (Rom 1:22), and fell short of even the glory which they had previously reflected (Rom 3:23).

Little surprise, then, that they looked down at their unglorified bodies and were filled with shame. Not just because they were naked. Of course not, the naked, sexual human body was and still is God's supreme handiwork, his image on earth. They had been naked before the Fall, and had sex before the Fall. The shame came from being naked with the reflected glory stripped away. Suddenly they are not glorified flesh, but mortal flesh, and they desperately try to hide this new, unfamiliar kind of nakedness from God, with the only materials to hand: the leaves on the trees.

Glory removed

Since the Fall, our very humanity has been a paradox. We are the image of God himself, still ruling over the earth, still robed with his dignity. But at the same time every part of our being is touched with sin, the state of falling short of the glory we once reflected. Sin is a misused word. We normally use it to refer to particular crimes, such as murder, or particular sexual acts. But the reality of sin is much wider than that. Not, of course, that everything in us and in the world is as bad as it can possibly be (the Calvinist doctrine of 'total depravity' meant only that the totality of the created order is affected in some way, however small, by the reality of sin). It is plainly not the case that we all live in Sodom or Babylon. Rather, sin is about a brokenness deep within ourselves, deep within our relationships and in our societies. This side of the Fall none of us can avoid living in cultures touched by sin's reality.

One of its many manifestations is in playing havoc with our sense of personal identity and self-esteem. The insecurity at the heart of the fashion-victim, dieter, trainer-maniac, body-builder, shopaholic, is directly traceable back to the moment when Adam and Eve disrobed themselves of God's glory. With it fell away their secure sense of self, their identity, their calling. Like the couple in Genesis, countless people in our society know what it is to stand naked and alone, insecure before the watching world. One psychologist estimates the number of those suffering from feelings of inadequacy or inferiority in our culture as high as ninety-five per cent. The glory has gone. We also lose the sensitivity to see and rejoice in the glory of God himself in creation although it is still there. The earth still pulsates with his glory, the skies are still his shimmering robe. It is we who have lost the capacity to see clearly. We are not only insecure in our identity, our eyes have become dimmed too.

So is it any surprise that we latch onto our remaining symbols of honour and dignity, our bodies and our clothing, and hope against hope that they will restore to us the secure sense of self we crave? Paul was eerily prophetic when he observed that the consequence of rejecting the glory of God lay in swapping true glory for mere images (Rom 1:22). It is precisely the image which is so desperately pursued in our culture, the image of the self, beautified, glamourised, stylish and desirable to others. And as long as we look for the answer in the images, the fundamental dilemma goes unaddressed: we remain naked, lacking the one thing our bodies were designed to wear. From then till now, that has been our native state.

When Job protests to God about the sufferings he is undergoing, God replies with a torrent of violent sarcasm, pointing out just how limited in understanding and capacity Job is. One of the most cutting images is when God pointedly asks Job whether he is capable of robing himself in glory. God knows the answer from Job, a descendant of Adam, must be negative:

> Do you have an arm like God's, and can your voice thunder like his?
> Then adorn yourself in glory and splendour,
>   and clothe yourself in honour and majesty. (Job 40:9,10)

Eli's grandson (1 Sam 4:21–22) was named 'Ichabod', meaning 'no glory'. It is a fitting epitaph for our species. The original glory has gone.

Robed in Glory

The glory which was God's had never diminished. It remained visible in creation to all who had eyes to see it. Likewise, this glory became focused in visual form at key points of the history of Israel: the Exodus, during Temple sacrifice, at the commissioning of Isaiah, and so on. But throughout the Old Testament, the reflected glory which should have clothed mankind was absent. It was past history, and a hope for the future (Ezek 39:21), but not a present reality. Then, in first-century Palestine, something decisive happened.

John, the gospel writer who, more than any other, meditates long and hard on the deeper significance of the events he relates, puts it like this. In the person of Jesus of Nazareth, the glory of God becomes visible in human form for the first time since the Fall: 'We have seen his glory, the glory of the One and Only, who came from the Father, full of grace and truth' (Jn 1:14). John tells his readers that when Isaiah had a vision of God's glory in the Temple, what he was actually seeing was a vision of Jesus (Jn 12:41).

A man robed in glory. Here, at last, is the second Adam, a privilege which should have gone to Adam's descendants, but which was foregone through disobedience. Indeed, it is as if Jesus is at pains to distance himself from Adam, the last, ill-fated human wearer of divine glory. He tells his Jewish hearers that unlike Adam, he is content to radiate only the glory which is given to him by the Father; that he will not use his glory to push God aside: 'Jesus replied, "If I glorify myself, my glory means nothing. My Father, whom you claim as your God, is the one who glorifies me."' (John 8:54).

How can this be? How is it that Jesus is the second Adam, the first since the Fall to be robed in glory? The reason is because he alone combines humanity with divinity.

Jesus could walk about on earth because he was fully human. He could embody the glory of God because he was fully divine. Only a man could wear human flesh. And only God could wear God's own glory. The only one who could restore the glory to the human image had to be both, man and God. In Jesus, someone walks the earth that has not walked the earth since Adam and Eve: a human being who is fully human. The flesh and the glory have been reunited, and the imagery of light throughout John's gospel underlines the parallels with the Old Testament visions of God's glory seen as light. So insistent is John on the reality of Jesus as the radiant glory of God that he refers to the terminology of glory no less than forty-one times, and light twenty-three times.

The glory of Christ is revealed most fully on the cross and in his resurrection. On the cross we see a fresh radiating of divine splendour, and John repeatedly refers to the death of Christ as a 'glorification' of Jesus (Jn 7:39; 12:16,23; 13:31). Paul too tells us that Christ's rising from death was accompanied with glory (1 Tim 3:16; Rom 6:4). Before his death and resurrection, Christ had a mortal body which radiated glory. It was a visible sign of God's glory in the world, but this body was still perishable. After the discovery of the empty tomb, Jesus' new, resurrection body is sheer, unadulterated glory (1 Cor 15:42,43; Phil 3:21).

Now comes the most exciting part. Just before he is arrested, Jesus prays to his Father in heaven. In that prayer, he states that the glory he wears has not been kept to himself, but is a hand-me-down for all those who will believe in him in the ages to come: 'I have given them the glory that you gave me.' (Jn 17:22).

Picking up on the same image, Paul describes the start of the

Christian life in terms of clothing. Both conversion and baptism, the two aspects of initiation, are seen as putting on Christ like a garment (Rom 13:14; Gal 3:27). To put on Christ is to clothe ourselves again in the glory which was our brief privilege so long ago. Not only this, but those who put on Christ are 'clothed with power' (Lk 24:49), through the constant presence of his Holy Spirit. We are clothed with the armour which God provides as we struggle with evil forces in the present age (Eph 6:10–18). We are called to clothe ourselves in a virtuous life in keeping with the nobility of our new robes of glory (Col 3:12; 1 Pet 5:5).

This work of reflecting the glory of Christ in the world is no solitary task. We are only counted believers in so far as we are a part of the 'body' of Christ on earth, the church (Eph 4:25; Col 1:24). We cannot be fully human apart from others, since we were created as relational beings. The church is to be the place, more than any other, where our new robes are to be on display: seen in a quality of mutual commitment, support and love. The church is to be a radical, counter-cultural community of glory-wearers and glory-seekers.

Jesus is the prototype of a new humanity. Only he could wear divine glory and human flesh, because only he was God and man. But the message of the gospel is that the followers of Christ can be robed as Christ was robed, in the glory of God. Not that we cease to be human. We are a glorified humanity, a living paradox: we inherit in Adam the mortality of human flesh, but we inherit in Christ the robes of glory: 'For since death came through a man, the resurrection of the dead comes also through a man. For as in Adam all die, so in Christ all will be made alive' (1 Cor 15:21,22). But this glory is a two-stage process. The glory we possess now as Christians is real, but only a foreshadowing or down-payment of the glorious resurrection bodies which will be our eternal clothing: 'The body that is sown is perishable, it is raised imperishable; it is sown in dishonour, it is raised in glory; it is sown in weakness, it is raised in power; it is sown a natural body, it is raised a spiritual body' (1 Cor 15:42,43; Phil 3:20). On that day, our perishable bodies will be 'clothed' with eternity (1 Cor 15:53).

Nor does any of this imply the doing away with our material clothing. Not a bit of it. God robed Adam and Eve in clothes for their task of ruling the earth, and the Spirit is sent to inspire clothing designers. In the biblical metaphor, clothing is in itself dignifying, so even if the couple had never fallen, there is every indication that God would have gone ahead and robed them in clothes, as well as his reflected glory. Christ, the new Adam, was robed in glory, but also in the clothes of a first-century Jew. Not only this, but Jesus appears to have worn at least some fine garb. Most Jewish garments were made of two pieces sewn together, due to the limited size of most weaving looms. The fact that Jesus' undergarment was seamless (John 19:23,24) marks it out as one of rare quality.

Jesus is clothed not only before, but also after his resurrection, and also when he stands as Judge, bringing the present era of human history to a close (Rev 1:13). Even the fully glorified bodies of the faithful in the New Jerusalem will be robed in fine linen (Rev 19:7,8), and all the finery of the nations will be brought into the city (Rev 21:26; Is 60).

Dressing Up

To be sure, the metaphor of clothing is only one biblical image of salvation. It needs to be complemented by other images, especially to emphasise the absolutely central significance of the cross and resurrection. But it stands as a potent and consistent image throughout Scripture, one which could have been tailor-made for a shopaholic, image-obsessed culture such as our own. It is a biblically-grounded metaphor which makes clear the fundamental mistake of all those who seek to use fashion and body shape as the remedy for their insecurities, hurts and addictions. They look for the clothing, but not the One who robes. They wear the badges of stewardship of the earth, without acknowledging the One whose stewards they are.

Humans are the image of God on earth, designed to be clothed both in glory and fine garments. Many Christians have

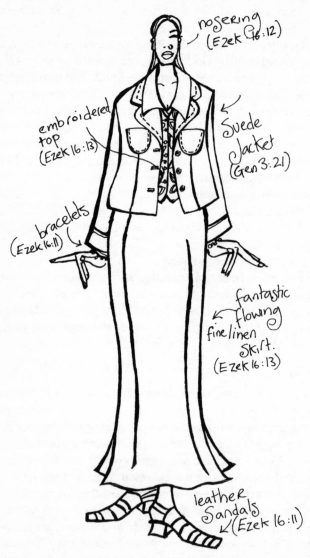

nosering
(Ezek 16:12)

embroidered
top
(Ezek 16:13)

Suede
Jacket
(Gen 3:21)

bracelets
(Ezek 16:11)

fantastic
flowing
fine linen
skirt.
(Ezek 16:13)

leather
sandals
(Ezek 16:11)

'The resurgence in fundamentalism had led to some clergy and church wardens only letting in parishioners dressed in biblically-sanctioned garb such as nose-rings (Ezekiel 16:12), suede jackets (Genesis 3:21), and pure linen shirts (Rev 19:8)' (p 249) had the former without the latter. Most people in our culture have the latter without the former. Some, such as the Puritans, had both.

Our robing in glory is God's answer to the brokenness of our world, the ripple-effects of human disobedience in ourselves, in our culture, in creation. It puts life back into its true perspective: we acknowledge our creaturehood, and the possibility of forgiveness and healing for the broken years becomes a reality. The way is open again to experience the intimate parenthood of God, the one who walks and talks with us in the garden. As Jesus said, just after his words on the splendour which clothes the wild flowers, if we seek first God's kingdom and his righteousness, all these things – our material needs – will be given us as well (Lk 12:31). But as we vainly chase the trappings of honour, wielding our credit cards as we go, we are doomed to permanent frustration.

Clothing which is not accompanied by glory is an archetypal image in the Bible of transience and futility: 'The earth will wear out like a garment . . . Do not fear the reproach of men or be terrified by their insults. For the moth will eat them up like a garment' (Is 51:6,7,8). By contrast, the very next chapter of Isaiah's prophecy exhorts the people to clothe themselves in true glory: 'Awake, awake, O Zion, clothe yourself with strength. Put on your garments of splendour' (Is 52:1). The verb which the NIV translates alternately as 'clothe yourself', and 'put on' is the same verb in the original Hebrew, repeated. As always in Scripture, this double image of putting on clothing is all about revealing the authentic character and status of the one being clothed. It is not an exercise in disguise or donning some alien garb which Israel has no right to wear. In chapter 51, Isaiah addresses God, calling on him to show his true colours: 'Awake, awake! Clothe yourself with strength, O arm of the LORD' (Is 51:9). The exhortation to Israel in chapter 52 stands in direct parallel to this. Through Isaiah, God is saying to Israel, 'Be what you are! Show the world what you are really like!'

We who live in contemporary western culture are looking to clothes to provide something they alone cannot provide: peace with ourselves. That can only come as a free gift of God himself. All we have to do is ask, and any of us can be robed in the glory of Christ. This is no insurance policy against suffering or difficulties in life, as the biblical writers and many of the great Christians of the past have found. But it is the only path to our full, integrated humanity.

Of course, Christians are not immune from a continued idolising of personal image. Paul reminds Timothy (his young colleague who had become a friend and travelling companion) that if we possess good clothes and wealth, there is a greatly increased likelihood that we too will focus on the material gift and not on the Giver (1 Tim 6:6–10).

Nevertheless, here is the heart of the gospel to the fashion industry, its followers, and those who yearn after the ideals of beauty it embodies: God loves you. You are already his image on earth. You create fine clothes and dress up in them because you are his creative stewards of the earth, and because the Spirit of God inspires your task. All this is good in God's eyes. But you will never discover your own full humanity and inner peace, nor understand the true dignity of your work unless you are also robed in Christ.

Style and Shalom

The Hebrew word 'shalom' has a range of meanings, which include peace, integrity, justice, wholeness, wellbeing, even salvation. It is about a quality and wholeness of relationships: with God, with our neighbour, within ourselves. Too often clothing has been used as an embodiment of the very opposite of shalom. It has been worn by humans indifferent to God, or in active rebellion against him, its symbol of dignity abused to boast of human self-sufficiency. The production and sale of clothing has been an act of sustained, legitimated violence against our neighbour, especially the poor in the world and in our own cities. And it has been worn as a desperate attempt to bolster a lost sense of self-esteem and personal worth.

Little surprise that clothing has had a bad name, particularly amongst those whose lives have been gripped by a vision of God's kingdom: of living under his rule in a state of shalom, now and in the New Jerusalem.

But the claim of this book has been that it does not have to be this way. Style and shalom can embrace. Used as the designer intended, our wearing of material clothing and our robing in Christ's glory can together embody the reality of shalom. We can experience shalom in a right relationship with God, and peace in ourselves, as we wear on our God-imaging bodies the symbol of our dignity, and as we allow ourselves to be robed again in the reflected glory which once dignified Adam and Eve. We can build shalom with our neighbour through an insistence on the ethical manufacture and purchase of clothing, starting today, with our own buying habits.

One day, when we have been changed from our present degree of glory into another, such utter and complete shalom will be our destiny. For now, we live in the 'already but not yet': robed in style, robed in Christ, but looking forward to the day when we (with the whole creation) are robed for the bright, jubilant carnival of the renewed earth.

POSTSCRIPT

The Bishop of Bath and Wells flicked back the mane of green hair out of his eyes, so that he could read the letter. It was headed with the crest of the Pontifical Institute of Textile and Design in Rome. He read on:

Dear Bishop Carlton,

We are writing to you in your capacity as Chair of the Archbishop's Commission on Urban Street Style (ACUSS) and primary instigator of the worldwide Anglican communion's Decade of Design.

Every year we invite a theologian of note to deliver the Pontifical Institute's lecture on Spirituality and Style. This year we are inviting yourself and Professor Spearing, Chair of Sartorial Theology at King's, London, to address the Institute jointly. Our theme for 2008 is to be 'The Plump Puritan: Lessons in 17th-Century Chic'.

The Institute has heard of your involvement with the great West of England Revival, following which we hear the wearing of grey suits, anoraks, the colour beige and sandals with socks were almost totally eradicated. I hope the drastic fall in the sales of dieting products since the Revival has not left too many out of work.

We feel that we in Rome have much to learn from the Anglican Church's readiness to give a biblical lead in the field

of bodily aesthetics. I do hope you and Professor Spearing
feel able to deliver our 2008 lectures.
Sincere Regards,
Cardinal A Armani

The Bishop smiled. It was good to have a bit of good news.
Recently things had been getting rather out of hand in the
Diocese. The resurgence in fundamentalism had led to some
clergy and church wardens only letting in parishioners dressed
in biblically-sanctioned garb such as nose-rings (Ezek 16:12),
suede jackets (Gen 3:21), and pure linen shirts (Rev 19:8). And
the local Elim Pentecostals were starting to insist that a sudden
urge to design fashion accessories was the only sure sign of
baptism in the Spirit (Ex 35:30–35).

A trip to Rome would be a good break. It was becoming an
interesting place, especially since the statements from the Third
Vatican Council encouraging the wearing of radical street style
amongst clergy and their wives. And the Benedictines were certainly looking snappier since their restyle by Benetton.

He rubbed his hands in glee. He had been looking for an
excuse to buy a new outfit. On his next visit to Lambeth Palace
to see Archbishop Joy, he'd have to spend some time browsing
in the new Traidcraft Megastore in Oxford Street.

TAKING IT FURTHER

Alternative Trading Organizations selling fair-trade clothes:

Traidcraft plc
Kingsway
Gateshead NE11 ONE
England
(Ask for the 'Alternatives' clothing catalogue)

Oxfam Trading
PO Box 72
Bicester
Oxfordshire OX6 7LT
England
(Ask for the Oxfam Trading catalogue)

Campaigning for better conditions for garment workers worldwide:

World Development Movement
25 Beehive Place
London SW9 7QR
England

Amnesty International (British Section)
99–119 Roseberry Avenue
London EC1R 4RE
England

Consumer advice on ethical purchasing:

New Consumer
52 Elswick Rd
Newcastle upon Tyne
NE4 5BR
England

Support for Christian fashion industry professionals:

Role Model magazine
PO Box 895
Lake Arrowhead
CA. 92052
USA